One of the RAF's most successful fighter pilots, Tom Neil is credited with the destruction of more than 17 enemy aircraft besides 'a handful of trains, tanks, lorries and other bits of the enemy lying about'. After being heavily involved in the Battle of Britain and in the action over Malta, he flew Spitfires over the Channel and elsewhere throughout 1943. Attached to the American 9th Air Force in 1944, he took part in the invasion of Normandy and remained with the USAAF until the border of Germany was reached. Later, he briefly saw action in Burma. After the war, he spent four years as Service Test Pilot and has flown more than 100 types of aircraft. Serving for some years in the British Embassy in Washington, he returned to America as a businessman before retiring to Norfolk where he now lives, writing and lecturing. Married, he has three sons, two of whom were in the Services and who still fly.

D1322168

Onward to Malta

Memoirs of a Hurricane pilot in Malta – 1941

Wing Commander T. F. Neil
DFC*, AFC, AE, RAF Ret'd

CORGI BOOKS
Published in conjunction with
Miller Distributors Ltd, Malta

ONWARD TO MALTA

A CORGI BOOK : 0 552 14142 9

Originally published in Great Britain in 1992
by Airlife Publishing Ltd

PRINTING HISTORY
Corgi edition published 1994

Set in 10pt Linotype Times by
Phoenix Typesetting, Ilkley, West Yorkshire.

Corgi Books are published by Transworld Publishers Ltd,
61–63 Uxbridge Road, Ealing, London W5 5SA,
in Australia by Transworld Publishers (Australia) Pty Ltd,
15–25 Helles Avenue, Moorebank, NSW 2170,
and in New Zealand by Transworld Publishers (NZ) Ltd,
3 William Pickering Drive, Albany, Auckland.

Printed and bound in Great Britain by
Cox & Wyman Ltd, Reading, Berks.

Contents

Foreword

In *Gun-button to 'FIRE'*, I described my experiences before and during the Battle of Britain, when, as a youth of nineteen and a member of the RAF Volunteer Reserve, I had been called up at the outbreak of war and afterwards posted to 249 (Fighter) Squadron, in process of forming at Church Fenton in the late spring of 1940. Eight months later, I had survived the Luftwaffe's pre-invasion onslaught with little more than a painful leg and having enjoyed a modicum of success and outlasted others of my colleagues who were perhaps more suitable in terms of age and seniority, I had been promoted to Flight Lieutenant in the December. Thus it was that January 1941 saw me in charge of 'B' Flight, 249 Squadron, stationed at RAF North Weald in Essex.

With six months of hard fighting behind me, I was at the time a fairly self-satisfied young man, possessing confidence, ability, and a powerful instinct for self-preservation in about equal measure. Arrogance? Possibly so, but with some justification; in fact, I doubt that there was a single member of the twenty-odd fighter squadrons deployed around London who did not share my belief that we were the best. After all, were we not Fighter Command? – the Brylcreem boys, in popular parlance – and had we not clobbered the Hun and scuppered his plans for invasion? And now, in the new offensive phase about to commence, we'd jolly well show them!

But, as events were to prove, success in the air depends not only on morale, ability and conviction, but is also conditioned by the performance of one's aircraft, and those of us who flew the Hurricane Mark 1, initially, and the Mark 2, later, had already reached the stage when we were unable to engage the Luftwaffe's fighters on equal terms, an unhappy situation which was to deteriorate with time.

In writing this account, I have used as my principal source of information the contents of more than 600 letters written to my parents throughout five years of war and only discovered in 1977. This has been supplemented by details from my flying log-book, personal recollections – depressingly unreliable at times – and data from other sources, including extracts from 249 Squadron's Operational Record Book (ORB).

About ORBs in general, a word of caution. These documents are invariably regarded as being complete and irreproachable. In fact, they are usually neither as they often contain errors – principally of omission – and do little more than sketch an outline of a squadron's activities at any given time. Moreover, as much of their contents formed the basis of other records produced by higher formations, their inaccuracies tended to be reproduced.

In most fighter squadrons, the ORB was written by the squadron adjutant or intelligence officer, each of whom, as a non-flying member of the unit, was dependent on accounts, excitedly verbal or sketchily scribbled, of what actually took place in the air. Occasionally, too, some junior officer who had transgressed was given the task of writing the ORB as a minor punishment, in which case it tended to become more a subjective description of events, even though his words subsequently appeared under the signature of his squadron commander. Moreover, circumstances were occasionally such that the ORB was only completed as something of an afterthought. For example, the squadron history of 249 squadron from May 1941 to January 1942 consists almost entirely of seven one-line entries written retrospectively and amounting to little more than, 'Nothing to report'. And this at a time when the unit was in Malta and the island heavily under siege! If, therefore, our own records are unreliable, so too, presumably, are the records of the enemy; indeed, research and experience suggest that this is so.

Although throughout 1941 I served in only a single unit, this account of my activities is in no way a squadron history but is primarily intended to fill in the gaps by providing a human-interest description of places and events where, and in which, I was involved. Campaigns, wars even, are often decided less by the gun or the bayonet than by circumstances regarded as peripheral – sickness among the fighting men, loss of morale caused by deplorable living conditions, indifference at home or by Government, poor equipment and serviceability, and the personal idiosyncracies and professional ability of a few in command.

In 1941, Britain, virtually without allies, was having a difficult time; immediate defeat had been warded off, but victory was not even a pious hope. In the Mediterranean, the Navy was desperately short of ships, our citizen Army in the Western Desert[1] was still untrained and did not have a home-produced tank worthy of the name, and the RAF, though in good heart in Britain, was so stretched and ill-equipped overseas that in May of that year it fought a minor war in Iraq with Hawker Audax biplanes!

At squadron level, except in a general sense, we knew very little about the enemy, who precisely were our day-to-day adversaries, what were their capabilities and resources, even how things were going. Up-to-date intelligence, though no doubt available, seldom percolated down to pilot level and even had it done so, I doubt very much that we would have paid much attention to it. Those of us at the sharp end, so to speak, tended – to use a rugger analogy – to have eyes only for the ball and the few members of the opposing side who were likely to bring us down with something more vicious than a tackle. Moreover, contrary to the *Boys Own Paper* version of war, the better man did not always win, as, more often than not, success depended on the speed of his aircraft and the size of his gun. Furthermore, except in the most obvious way, the immediate causes of success or failure were not

[1] Egypt and Libya.

usually the subject of much debate; one simply accepted things as they were and got on with the fighting. It is only when time affords the luxury of analysis and hindsight that the 'reasons why' are more clearly seen and understood.

Such, then, is the background to events described in these pages. It remains only for me to add: 'Now read on!'

1 Offensive Action

Friday, 10 January 1941 – bitterly cold but bright, south-east England frozen into petrified silence and enrobed in a mantle of white. In the distance, yellow smoke rising from a tall chimney leaned towards the heavens as though congealed into a drunken pillar.

We had climbed into our cockpits to buckle on parachutes and straps with fingers clumsy with cold, our breath steaming in the frigid air, our minds soothed by the calming ritual of preparation. After which we had taken off from North Weald a few minutes before noon, curving away to the south in an untidy gaggle, to climb up shallowly over Essex in the direction of Southend.

There were 36 of us, all Hurricanes – 56 Squadron ahead, then 242, with Douglas Bader in front, and finally 249. As flight commander of 'B' Flight, 249, I was leading the final section of four at the rear with Victor Beamish directly ahead of me – in the box, to use the accepted term. Victor, restless warrior that he was, always followed, never led, being able then to come and go as he pleased, which only he as Station Commander and a lesser God was entitled to do.

As we flew south, the routine of piloting and station-keeping loosened the fetters of tension; there was little hurry, no frantic climb. We had barely 7,000 feet to make as we were to act as escort to the first bomber formation to attempt a daylight raid on a target in France since the so-called Battle of Britain. So-called, as that then-familiar phrase related to a national crisis which for us had been merely part of a sustained period of activity against the Luftwaffe, a tidy but emotive expression for a tidy fourteen-week event,

11

conveniently terminating on 31 October 1940. As though the war for us had started in July and ended in October, which it most definitely had not! And now, here we were, on the offensive. For the first time. Six Bristol Blenheim bombers and nine squadrons of fighters – 108 Spitfires and Hurricanes. About to commence a campaign to achieve what the Germans had manifestly failed to accomplish four months earlier – air supremacy. Today, the six Blenheims were the bait and I, and 107 others, were there to knock down the 109s like ninepins; I, in a Hurricane Mark 1, whose hope of catching a 109, other than by accident or freak of circumstance, was unlikely, to put expectation at its highest. Whatever next? Were we not about to repeat exactly the policy and tactical errors the Hun had made the previous summer?

We were over the Thames and in the area of Gravesend when the Blenheims appeared; one moment nothing, then, suddenly, there they were, six camouflaged twin-engined shapes, huddled together, tilting, turning. We curved in their direction, 56 forming up alongside, 242 and 249 in a slow meander left, right, and behind. Then, all together, we slanted ponderously towards the Channel, knowing that aloft, six more squadrons, Spits from Hornchurch and Hurricanes from Northolt and elsewhere, would eventually be stepped up behind us to more than 20,000 feet.

As we flew in the direction of Deal, I looked down on the silent white undulations of Kent with a new affection. For more than four months, I had fought over the area almost daily, so that Canterbury, Maidstone, Gravesend and Dover were names indelibly etched on my heart and mind. But, would this be the last time? Would I ever again surge over its hills and woodlands in pursuit of some crippled and streaming enemy? Because nothing was more certain than that our future battlefield would be the broad acres of France, deceptively docile to the eye yet bristling with flak, whose malicious threat already loomed larger than life in our imaginations. Hun fighters were one thing, impersonal, faceless flak, which thrust upwards at us with sly, lethal digs, was definitely another. And, of course, in between France and Kent – or Sussex – there were from twenty to ninety miles of cold, inhospitable water. Despite being brought up in a major port, as an airman the sea had very little charm for me; just one stray bullet in my Hurricane's coolant system or any other of its vital parts, and *in* I would be, floundering about in its freezing embrace. To survive in winter for what – twenty minutes? Our adversaries, the Hun fighter pilots, were reported as having personal dinghies, but no such luxuries for us! In fact, even my old and familiar Mae West was suspect; one of the original type without an inflating CO_2 bottle. If the time came, would I have the puff to blow it up?

All these and other thoughts passed morbidly through my mind. Then, with Dover off to my right with its attendant halo of balloons, I was out over the water and heading for France. After which, speculation was firmly put aside and reality advanced with a grim face . . .

Our target that day was an ammunition dump in the Forêt de Guines, some ten miles inland from Cap Gris Nez. The bombers would go in at around 7,000 feet and 242 and 249 were there to protect the Blenheims from Huns climbing into them from below. For this reason, our 24 aircraft were to fly at around 5,000 feet. Five thousand feet! Over a part of enemy territory bristling with guns – an unpleasant enough prospect in all conscience.

We had discussed tactics at the AOC's conference at Hornchurch on Christmas Day, when, to my dry-mouthed concern, I had heard an expert affirm that 7,000 feet was the best height at which to fly over enemy territory, being too high for the low flak and too low for the high stuff. Seven thousand feet! Was he absolutely sure? If the Huns had done that in September, we would have thought them mad. I would have liked to have questioned the man, a penguin[1] needless to say, but juniority had shackled my tongue. So, here we were, at 5,000 feet. Simply asking for trouble.

[1] Penguin – derisory term for non-flying ground officer.

As we approached the enemy coast, I scanned my cockpit with a professional eye. Seat the right height; straps tight and locked; oil pressure 70 lbs; oil temperature 50-plus degrees; coolant 85 degrees, or thereabouts; gunsight 'ON', brightness just right and the range-bar set at 40 feet (for a 109, naturally); gun-button to 'FIRE'. Everything set. I then leaned forward to 'pull the plug', which cut out the governor controlling the engine boost, increased my revs to 2,850, and wriggled my bum firmly into my parachute cushion. All set and ready to go.

The Blenheims crossed in over Gravellines, as briefed – less flak there, we had been told – at which point I found myself well to the right of the formation and gazing down almost dispassionately on the Hun fighter airfield at Calais Marck. From slightly less than 5,000 feet too! My whole body tense and expectant. Waiting.

But nothing came; no red balls, no tracer, no angry crimson-centred puffs of black, nothing. Northern France, a wilderness of snow lined with thin tracings of hedgerow, rail and road, was as still as a tomb. Nothing stirred. The old Hun was asleep, by George! Surely he must have known we were coming. Didn't he have RDF[1], too, or something similar?

Then the Blenheims were tilting to starboard and the Hurricanes in front accelerating. Weaving about. And going lower. Lower, for God's sake! Were there 109s about? On edge but full of resolve, I cast anxiously around but could see nothing. The Blenheims level now and running in – huddled, determined, unflinching, splendidly brave. Aiming straight for the dark mass that was the Forêt de Guines. At which point the first ack-ack appeared.

It was quite innocuous at first, dark puffs, pecking away in front, not far from the bombers and moving with them so that it was behind and below them but slightly above my own height. Then closer, until I was flying through residual traces of smoke that flicked disconcertingly past my cockpit hood.

[1]RDF Radio Direction Finding – early name for Radar.

Nothing really nasty though, nor dangerous. And no tracer or clusters of those glowing things either. Yet!

The Blenheims dropped their bombs. Watching with half an eye, I did not see them fall but picked out pin-pricks of red at the centre of several explosions whose violent circles of blast flattened the trees. Then the bombers were turning and I, with others, was on the far side of them. Racing. Dropping down further and turning. Following the others. What in heaven's name was Douglas Bader doing? – we shouldn't be down at this height, damn it! More brown flak-bursts but above me now and some way off. Hurricanes everywhere and the Blenheims high and in the distance. Huns? I couldn't see any. Down to 2,000 feet now and going north like mad. Bouncing about in someone's slipstream with 280 on the clock. Fields, roads and isolated buildings streaming beneath. A water-tower. Lower still and following others in a shallow dive. What the hell were we supposed to be doing now? Then, in the distance, the coastline. And water.

I was at about 800 feet when I crossed the coast and had a fleeting glimpse of yellow and white sand-dunes and marram grass. And flak!

It started coming in the shape of white streaks and red balls, the latter rising obliquely in clutches of five or six, curving quickly towards me then whipping past. On my right mostly, where there were other Hurricanes in an untidy gaggle. In a moment of naked fear, I pulled back and climbed steeply – then wished I hadn't. As my speed fell away, I had the sensation of being suspended in space, hanging! Meanwhile, the balls kept coming, overtaking me with vicious intent and curving away into oblivion. Steeper still now with my speed right down to 140. An aircraft just ahead of me and to my right, the fiery projectiles flashing between us. Then, in a brief moment of shock and horror, the chap in front was hit. Amidships. The aircraft staggered as though struck by a club and fell away downwards, turning over and dropping like a crippled bird. To disappear from what? – little more than 1,000 feet? A goner for sure! More fluorescent things streaming past. Me, cringing, waiting for the lethal bang and jolt. Pulling, turning, but climbing still, my engine raging with all the boost I could muster. Then . . . my nose dropping . . . levelling out. Sea, in every direction, with its cold, grey sneer. But safety, thank God! Safety . . . more or less!

Some three miles out, I turned and took stock. There were Hurricanes everywhere, flying northwards close to the sea and forming up. No bombers, though, nor any sign of 56 Squadron. Several small boats were lying like matchsticks a little to the north of Calais and the flak had stopped. There were one or two other aircraft, moving urgently but not in my direction, which may have been Huns but were too far away to identify. Completing my turn, I flew towards far-off Dover and the welcoming white cliffs, crossing eventually into snowbound Kent. Immediately, my engine sounded much more cheerful; no damage there it seemed. I formed up on several other Hurricanes and set course for North Weald with a light heart. Thank God! What a glorious relief to be flying over dear old Kent again. Terribly sad about the chap who had just been hit, though. One of 249 almost certainly, but who?

I landed, with others, a little before half past one, having been airborne one hour and 35 minutes.

In the dispersal hut there was relieved laughter and excitement mingled with annoyance. What had possessed Douglas Bader to go down like that? Vulnerable enough at 5,000 feet, at less than 2,000, we were sitting ducks. 'Hopalong' Cassidy was in full voice, having been hit in the tail by flak, and 'Tommy' Thompson had lost a piece of his airscrew. Bloody silly business! Had I been hit? No, I didn't think so, just frightened. But, as it turned out, I had. Only a minor hole, though. Straight through my elevator, which, because it was fabric, could be repaired in minutes. Trivial, hardly worth mentioning or worrying about. All the same, I tried hard to persuade myself that the damage had been caused by a stone. But a stone wouldn't go through top *and* bottom surfaces, would it?

16

Victor Beamish had fired at the boats, apparently, and had also shot down a 109 which was attacking a Hurricane over the Channel. And there was the chap I had seen hit amidships by flak, wasn't there? Who was he? Concerned, we all looked round, counting. Two – McConnell and Maciejowski – were missing. Anyone see them? 'Shirley' Woolmer, the Intelligence Officer, was looking from face to face, being ignored by everyone and appearing totally bewildered by all the chatter. I repeated my story of the Hurricane being hit by flak and he wrote something down, his brows gathered, his pencil tripping over the words in his excitement. Was I sure it was one of ours? Of course it was! – me, tersely abrupt; it couldn't have been a Hun, could it? Not within 30 yards of me! He agreed, grudgingly, then pushed his way through the crowd, eager for other reports.

Gradually, a picture emerged. McConnell had been shot up by a 109, which, in turn, had been attacked and shot down by Victor Beamish. Wounded, and his aircraft streaming glycol, Mac had limped back across the Channel and had baled out when crossing the Kent coast, his Hurricane crashing into the cliffs at Dover. But it was only some time later that Sergeant 'Micky' Maciejowski landed and clumped into dispersal. His story, delivered in fractured English and accompanied by a wealth of Polish hand-signals, was different – it always was! He had shot at half-a-dozen Henschel 126s on the small airfield at Guines and had then run into two 109s at low level. Following a brief fight, one of the German fighters had apparently crashed into a wood but, in the course of the engagement, Micky's throttle had jammed in the fully-open position so that he was obliged to roar around France at full bore before high-tailing it for England, finally putting down at Hornchurch, short of fuel. We all shook our heads in amused despair. Everything happened to Micky!

I retold my story about the flak and its victim, adding hotly that it was nonsense to suggest that it hadn't happened. Woolmer kept saying he was sorry but McConnell was our only casualty and there it was. Perplexed and not a little irritated, I had occasion to telephone Group some time later and brought up the subject. There *had* to be at least one more casualty, I persisted. One of the other squadrons, perhaps? But there wasn't, it seemed, the voice at the other end snidely hinting that I must have been seeing things, which did nothing to soothe my ire. Silly blighters! I knew exactly what I had *seen*; I wasn't blind! On the other hand, I hadn't seen the 109s, had I? Or the Henschels. Or very much else, apart from those loathsome red balls coming at me from all directions.

Everyone was agreeing that although useful in terms of experience, it had been a pretty pointless exercise. Six bombers, 108 fighters. McConnell's aircraft lost and the poor chap wounded and in hospital, all for what? A few twigs off some trees in the Forêt de Guines and very little else, unless one counted the 109s, of course. And I had not even seen a Hun! Strange, that. Nothing was more confusing than air combat.

The following day, a little to our surprise, we received a signal from C-in-C Fighter Command, passing on a message of congratulation from the Prime Minister, Mr Churchill, and adding that, he, too, thought we were all splendid fellows. Splendid? Nothing I had done was particularly splendid. In fact, the whole show, in our view, was a bit of a non-event. We were quite willing to go over to France and fight, but no more of those low-level escort dos, thank you very much!

2 The Start of the Year

I had returned from leave on Tuesday, 7 January. By train, and at night, needless to say!

The journey from Manchester to London normally took four hours. However, with Britain blacked out completely and being bombed almost incessantly, anything less than six was a bonus and an interminable journey of seven or eight not unknown. Those periods of hanging about in trains, usually at such unstimulating places as Watford Junction or Willesden, were sheer purgatory, the compartments and corridors jam-packed with reeking humanity, the glimmering five-watt bulbs – even in the first-class sections – making reading impossible, and the windows, plastered with curtaining material to reduce the effect of bomb blast, running with smoke-rich condensation which collected maliciously in pools on the mahogany surrounds before seeping into elbows and thighs. Sleep, if it came, was never more than fitful.

On that occasion, however, I was lucky as the train was only an hour late into Euston. Even so, it was approaching midnight, bitterly cold outside and the pavements ankle-deep in slush, when I found a taxi and began my nocturnal hunt for accommodation. An hour later I was back at Euston having tried no less than six hotels and found them full. So, the railway hotel it had to be.

The night was hideous, full of clanks and thumps as I shivered in a bedroom that was seedily damp, ghoulishly Victorian, and almost the size of an aircraft hangar. The following morning, I sat down to a breakfast curling at the edges and served by a minion wearing an undertaker's outfit of black tie and tails, after which I left, having been charged an extortionate sixteen shillings and sixpence (about 80 pence) for a night of memorable discomfort.

But my misfortune was not to end there. Deciding to take the Green Line bus to Epping and having enquired of a passing inspector where it started from, I stood in Portman Square for more than an hour, stamping my feet and freezing to death, learning only then that the route had been changed and that I should have been standing in Cavendish Square. Two hours later, I arrived at North Weald, miserable, my nose streaming with a head-cold, and in a savage frame of mind, to find my hutted room like an ice-box, my stove unlit, and my batman missing. Outside, the fog was thickening to a pea-souper. Bloody hell! What a war! What a country! And what a homecoming!

And it was whilst I was indulging in this bitter soliloquy, that a Hun bomber droned across the top of the mess, very low indeed but invisible in the murk. I went out, hunched and shivering, to listen to the unfamiliar beat of its engines, and to observe. But nothing happened. Silly blighter! Probably lost, and serve him right!

During the night it snowed again and I awoke the following morning to a silent wonderland of white. Driving down to dispersal, I learned that things had been very quiet since my departure ten days earlier. The most excellent Sergeant Beard had been commissioned and 'Butch' Barton and Dicky Wynn had carried out a low-level 'mosquito'[1] raid in France some days before, running into flak south of Boulogne and attacking a petrol-bowser on St Anglevert airfield. A whole petrol-bowser! That would shorten the war!

Later, just to reacquaint myself with flying, I took off in GN-V and acted as target for someone doing cine-gun. Nice and simple, nothing strenuous. Despite the weather, it was good to get into the air again and, landing comfortably on

---

[1] 'Mosquito' – original term for low-level attacks on enemy targets by a pair of fighters.

the snow a little later, I was reminded of FTS[1] at Montrose a year earlier. However, the weather clamped completely in the afternoon enabling a number of us to be given a Cook's tour of the Bofors-gun emplacements around the airfield. What a life! Who'd be a gunner, standing about all day in a woolly Balaclava hat, bored to death and being called into action once every Preston Guild?

The following day, 9 January, being much better with a clear sky, I took my flight for a formation exercise, our first since the previous August, in fact. Very morale-raising, though not in my own aircraft unfortunately, GN-W being on inspection. I had a hollow feeling that if the fine weather continued, the bombing attack we had planned on Christmas Day would almost certainly take place. And how right I was! Later on, I was told that 'Der Tag' was to be 10 January. The next day. Wow!

With a few others that evening, I went to the cinema in Epping, outwardly unconcerned but with an unpleasant niggle in my mind that it might be my last visit to this or any cinema!

After which, to bed. My hutted room temporarily warm and cosy in the cherry-red glow of the stove, I knew that in the morning there would only be dead ashes in the grate, my breath a fog of condensation and the windows opaque with ice. Brrr! What a life! I snuggled down. But, expecting to have the drone of bombers and the thump of guns in my ears all night, I was pleasantly surprised. Nothing at all. The Huns must be having the day off!

249 Squadron had been at North Weald since 1 September 1940 and now shared the airfield with 56. We flew Mark 1 Hurricanes, as did the various squadrons operating in turn from Stapleford Tawney, our satellite aerodrome situated a few miles to the south. Apart from 249, which was to remain at North Weald for almost a year, a number of

---

[1] FTS – Flying Training School.

other squadrons had come and gone as casualties occurred – 151, 25, 46, 257 and of course 56 – all of them joining us for a few weeks, or months, at a time. In terms of losses, having suffered eight fatalities and around a dozen wounded and injured during the Battle of Britain and after, 249 had fared better than most, and as many of the lesser damaged pilots had since returned, the squadron retained much of its early identity and character.

At the commencement of 1941, Squadron Leader R. A. Barton – 'Butch' to us all – commanded 249, John Grandy, the original CO, having moved on after an injury sustained in September when he had baled out. Keith Lofts, late of 615 Squadron, was now the flight commander of 'A' Flight and I commanded 'B' Flight, longevity, good fortune and a modicum of success resulting in my promotion in December to Flight Lieutenant – acting, needless to say! During our six months of fighting, we believed we had become the second highest scoring squadron in 11 Group and with one Victoria Cross and eight or nine DFCs and a DFM to our credit, among the most highly decorated. All in all, we were pretty pleased with ourselves, justifiably so in our view, and smugly aware of our prowess as fighter pilots. One fly only was there in our ointment; we were equipped with an aircraft which, whilst it had been adequate during the Battle of Britain, could not now engage enemy fighters on even terms. Not surprisingly, therefore, we constantly, and often belligerently, discussed the late delivery of our Mark 2 Hurricanes which we had been promised for months past. Most of the Spit squadrons had been re-equipped with the Mark 2 Spitfire the previous autumn and there was even talk of them getting something called a Mark 5, with cannons and all sorts of things! What about us? What was going on, for heaven's sake?

After a summer and autumn of frenzied activity, December's winter weather had brought with it a period of relaxation which showed every sign of continuing throughout January and beyond. For the first time since June, 1940, we had time to examine tactics, polish up our formation flying, and check up on our marksmanship using our cine-guns in mock combat and our eight Brownings against ground targets at Dengie Flats, a firing range off the Essex coast. At the same time, we still had our operational duties to perform, principally the protection of convoys in the Thames estuary and up the east coast, the interception of lone raiders by day and night, and the occasional foray into France both in strength and in harassing sections of two. These last named excursions were left to volunteers and were not exactly popular; considered in terms of profit and loss, the odds were heavily weighted in favour of loss, as, at low level, the chances of being damaged by flak were considerable, and the likelihood of inflicting any worthwhile hurt to the enemy pretty remote. However, these 'mosquitos', so called, were encouraged by both Command and Group as a means of fostering the offensive spirit. Offensive spirit! Although only 20 years of age, I had already made more than 150 flights against the enemy, so that I did not consider it necessary to demonstrate my offensive spirit by taking part in any such unprofitable exercises; with eight machine guns we could not inflict much lasting damage on a water-tower or even a railway engine and the French farmers were not likely to thank us for killing their livestock, destroying their farm vehicles and buildings and generally putting the fear of God into their workers. In fact, the only enemy installations worth attacking were airfields, gun positions, military transport and trains, together with shipping, and it was a very short-sighted Hurricane pilot indeed who took on any of those targets without a good deal of careful thought and planning. Germans, in the main, shot back and could not be relied on to miss; moreover, we were flying an aircraft which was at least 30 miles per hour slower than the Me 109[1] in level flight, so that, if intercepted, we had a fight on our hands whether we liked it or not.

[1] The Me 109 is now referred to as the Bf 109. We never knew it as such during the entire period of the war.

It was against this background and because it was 249's allotted day, that I prepared for my first 'mosquito' on the morning of 12 January, having selected Sergeant Davidson to accompany me. 'Appy 'Arry Davidson was one of 249's stalwarts and had been in the squadron almost from the outset. A long-time acquaintance of mine, having been with me at No. 17 Elementary and Reserve Flying Training School in Manchester before the war, Harry Davidson and I knew each other well and I had the greatest respect for his courage and ability. Moreover, besides having a northern accent that would shatter glass, he had a grand sense of humour and his laughter – positively infectious – was one of the squadron's greatest assets. Together we pored over a map and made our plan.

We would go in over Gravellines, I proposed; they hadn't shot at us there last time and there was at least a chance that they would not do so again. Davidson nodded – all right so far! After which, we would go round the back of Calais, cross the main railway line running from Calais to St Omer and Arras, then continue round the rear of Boulogne to come out a little north of Le Touquet. With luck we might catch some military vehicles on the roads or an unsuspecting train; on the other hand, if luck was against us, we could well run into some of the 109s based at St Omer. How did he feel? Davidson approved, but not with any enthusiasm. What did we do if we bumped into any of those little yellow buggers? – Davidson's frequently used term for 109s. My reply was succinct: nip into cloud as quick as a flash and head for home; two Hurricanes taking on the whole German Air Force over one of its own bases was simply asking for trouble. My partner agreed – none of this hero stuff for him, if I didn't mind. Then, after discussing emergencies and other tactics, we separated for lunch, a meal I ate with far less than my usual relish.

We took off at 2.45 p.m. There was complete cloud cover at little more than 1,000 feet and a good deal of thick mist. Splendid! Just the conditions we needed. Maintaining RT silence, we flew south over Essex and Kent, feeling our way forward in the fringes of the cloud, and eventually crossed the coast north of Deal. At which point, the mist thinned out, the clouds broke up and the sun shone through. Still heading south and now about twenty feet above the waves, my heart sank. However, as arranged, I maintained a tight-lipped silence and pressed on.

By the time we were approaching the French coast, there was hardly a cloud in sight. Davidson, on my right, was looking at me stoically but with a mute and pleading stare that suggested he was willing me to turn back. I couldn't, though, could I? Not until we'd had a proper look.

With the flat coastline at Gravellines racing towards us, my mind was in a whirl. Did I press on as a hero, or make the common-sense decision and turn round; 'mosquitos' were never intended to be carried out in clear weather, *the* essential ingredient was cloud cover, and of that we had none. Were we not inviting trouble? But, too late; the water's edge slid obliquely beneath us and France lay ahead, white with snow, blue sky above, and visibility more than tolerable. Perfect, in fact – for the Huns!

Feeling a responsibility for Davidson's skin as well as my own, I broke RT silence. 'Red two. How d'you feel? Do you want to go on?'

My partner's response was prompt and to the point. 'No!'

Without another syllable being uttered, we flung our aircraft into rate-four turns and beat a hasty retreat. No heroes, we!

As a postscript to this incident, shortly after, two others of 249 were engaged on a similar exercise. Following roughly the same course, they let down from the fringes of the cloud, expecting to find the French coast immediately ahead. It was. But so was a flock of 109s. Horrified, they barged their way through the enemy before turning to escape. Which they succeeded in doing, but not with much to spare.

Landing back at North Weald limp with emotion, they immediately contacted Sector and Group demanding to know the reason for the quite unusual Hun activity, soon to be informed that aircraft of 242 Squadron had apparently been abroad since early morning, stirring up the enemy on what was *not* their allotted day.

The solemn prayer that rose from our dispersal hut on that occasion invited God to *bless* Douglas Bader and 242 Squadron – and to reward them, richly!

January dragged on with fog, and snow, and cold. Our Hurricanes, silent mist-draped spectres, stood chocked and tarpaulined on their hardstandings – dripping. In fact, everything dripped. Then froze. Then dripped again.

Several times, we attempted to clear snow from the main runway using garden shovels, becoming painfully aware of its vast dimensions. Victor Beamish joined us, exhorting us to greater efforts in his Irish brogue – 'Come on, Ginger! You can do better than that!' And Ginger, exhausted and with his feet and fingers frozen to stone, grinned back and wished he were miles away; in a desert somewhere, anywhere but North Weald at that particular moment. Someone observed that not only did we have to fight for our lives, we were 'Works and Bricks' as well; we'd be painting the ruddy aircraft next! But our grinning protests were made in the best of spirit; anything we did, Victor did. A fine man, whose watchword was example; example, *the* fundamental of successful leadership.

No sooner had we dug the runway clear, however, than the snow came in a blizzard and nullified all our effort and sweat. And with it on the 15th, the unsmiling Sholto Douglas[1] with heartening news of our Hurricane 2s and an outline of plans for the better spring weather ahead. Our new aircraft were on the way, he assured us – within two months, anyway – some with twelve guns and others with four 20mm cannons. As for the future, we were going to have a busy time; lots more

[1] Air Marshal Sir William Sholto Douglas, appointed C-in-C Fighter Command, November 1940.

bombers to escort, many more fighter-sweeps to take part in, masses of everything, in fact. We listened in silence, on the whole uplifted but with reservations. Seeing was believing as far as our new aircraft were concerned; we had heard those promises before. Moreover, no-one at North Weald had yet flown a Mark 2 so that we knew nothing of its capabilities; we just hoped it had the performance, particularly above 20,000 feet, that would enable us to fight with some expectation of success. The sweeps over France, two and three squadrons strong, seemed promising enough but playing nurse-maid to bombers raised doubts in our minds. The Blenheims always insisted on staying low and didn't go fast enough for our liking; moreover, we in Hurricanes seemed always to be stuck with the unenviable task of providing close-escort. Why didn't the Spits take their turn? Instead of waltzing about at height, away from all the flak and having that cushy speed advantage that height always afforded?

The following day, Leigh-Mallory[1], the AOC 11 Group, turned up and repeated Sholto Douglas's message, more or less. However, I was not there to hear him, Victor Beamish and four others of us in 249 being summoned to Duxford that day. To an investiture. To meet the King.

I travelled up to Duxford muffled to the ears and exhaling a fog of vapour in the back of Victor's ice-box of a staff car. The countryside crisply white and in the iron grip of winter, we hardly saw either a vehicle or another living person during the 25-mile journey. Strangely, I had never been to Duxford despite it being so near; Duxford to me was 12 Group, up north, and as foreign and remote as Tibet. At North Weald, we always looked south towards the enemy and flew in that direction.

We arrived a little before lunch and assembled in the ante-room of the officers' mess. Shortly after, the King and Queen joined us and were introduced to a number of the more

[1] Air Vice Marshal Trafford Leigh-Mallory – AOC No. 11 Group since November 1940.

senior among us. Victor Beamish was called forward and immediately went into shock, remaining frozen at attention and almost speechless as the royal couple attempted, not with much success, to converse with him. I was surprised and amused, secretly that is; Victor, a lion in the air, totally abashed in the presence of his Monarch.

The occasion was stiffly formal at first but within minutes the ice was broken when the royal couple was invited to play shove-ha'penny. An inexpert game followed in which the King used his left hand and he and his spouse exchanged a flow of light-hearted banter, the Queen making loud and uncomplimentary asides about her husband's lack of expertise. And all the time, he responded without a trace of the stammer we knew so well, a profound relief to all of us who, over the years, had listened to him labouring through his Christmas Day broadcasts to homeland and Empire. As honoured guests of the mess and in the presence of their loyal officers, Their Majesties were relaxed, charming, and utterly normal, personifying for me in a quite remarkable and emotional way, the spirit and steadfastness of the nation. The King's moving broadcast message that first Christmas of the war remained fresh in my mind: 'And I said to the man who stood at the gate of the year, Give me a light that I may tread safely into the unknown—' and so on. An inspiring expression of faith from a sensitive man who so genuinely and obviously cared.

After lunching together, we walked across to one of the hangars where, because of the weather, the investiture had been arranged. As we were being marshalled and briefed, one of the resident squadrons circled the airfield as a precaution against attack.

There were about 25 of us to be decorated. When my name was called, with a degree of composure that surprised even myself, I made my approach, saluted, then stepped forward. I was conscious of the King very much below me, quite a small man really, very brown with blue eyes, his face drawn and finely chiselled. The Queen alongside, her head cocked and a half-smile on her lips. The decoration was attached, His Majesty frowning in concentration. Then a few murmured words of congratulation, and a hand-shake – merely a touch of the fingers. After which I was turning and marching away, wondering what on earth I did next. Not to worry, though, my medal was spirited away and boxed, after which I was led off, all very quietly, smoothly and expertly done. No fuss. I hadn't tripped or bumped into the furniture! The investiture was over.

Minutes later I was with Victor Beamish and part of a small group around which members of the press were circling like vultures. Victor, embarrassed, was protesting and waving them away. The men with the cameras were insistent, though, following us about at a run. Victor had his way, however, and they gradually fell back. We didn't want all this publicity, did we Ginger? Ginger, not sharing his reticence, lacked the courage to say so. With the result, I was led away like a lamb, looking sorrowfully over my shoulder at our pursuers who were trailing behind and losing ground.

Back at North Weald the following day, I was one of only two who took to the air a little after dark. Bogeys[1] expected off the east coast, was the urgent message. As I climbed away eastwards and into the blackness to wander about miles out to sea off Clacton at 12,000 feet, the ritual and ceremony of the previous day seemed as remote and as distant as a dream. Would the royal couple – sitting down to meat and two veg., no doubt – be aware that their 'trusty and well-beloved' Flight Lieutenant Neil was protecting the nation pretty well single-handed? Freezing to death, too, by George, and trying hard not to think about what would happen if the Merlin engine, roaring and flaring in front of him, suddenly conked out.

Days later, in all the daily papers, there were photographs of the Monarch decorating some of his gallant 'Few'. But none of Victor Beamish nor of me. My parents were surprised

[1] Unidentified aircraft, probably enemy.

and disappointed. I did go to the investiture, didn't I? In which case, what had happened to the pictures of *their* son?

For the last ten days of the month it was English weather at its most vile – snow, low cloud, and fog. Most of the squadron went into hibernation, yarned and read around the huge coal-fire in the anteroom, played endless games of shove-ha'penny and snooker, or went to the cinema and the pubs in Epping. Even toiled all the way into the seamier corners of London.

One morning, in order to ginger ourselves up, a football game was arranged between 56 Squadron and 249 and held at 56's dispersal. Victor Beamish took part and trotted on to the pitch all togged out as though for Twickenham.

It was a game notable for its enthusiasm rather than its expertise, although there were several among us who were more than competent. After an hour of racing about, shouting and kicking, fatigue took its toll and it was clear that 56, who were winning, were rather the better side. Victor, who was playing with 249 and had very little skill at soccer, even to the point of trying to stand on the ball, kept roaring us on, his face set with determination, calling us a 'clapped out set of bloody ducks'. Alas, his insults and exhortations had very little effect, as, bent double with laughter as much as tiredness, we were quite unable to respond, which, of course, infuriated him even more. No, Victor Beamish was not one of nature's losers, not even in a game he knew so little about.

And it was on 17 January that I learned I was to be sent north on an unusual duty. A telephone message from Air Ministry explained that I had been selected to take part in a month-long Cotton Industry War Exhibition in Lancashire and that I would be expected to give a number of speeches to various official bodies and tour a group of mills in the area. Meanwhile, as a preliminary, I was to call upon Wing Commander Lord Willoughby de Broke at Air Ministry, to be briefed.

The briefing was harmless enough. I was taken to lunch by the Wing Commander – a charming man who had commanded one of the Auxiliary Squadrons before the war – who explained that as I came from Lancashire and knew all about mills and cotton and that sort of thing, I was the natural choice. I replied that although I came from Lancashire I knew absolutely nothing about mills and cotton, except that the raw material – very smelly – came into Liverpool and Manchester in big ships. Not to worry, said the Wing Commander comfortably, any speeches I would be required to make would be produced for me by experts. And, of course, I could expect to be warmly entertained by officials of the Cotton Board, if I saw what he meant – he gave a conspirator's wink. He would be sending details of who I was and what I had accomplished over the past six months, so that there was no question of my not having a good time. Which he did, causing me endless embarrassment, as his letter was sent to my home where it was opened in my absence by my parents, who, among other incidents I had never thought fit to mention, learned for the first time that I had recently had a mid-air collision and been forced to bale out. But, unaware of the frowns and rod-in-pickle that awaited me, I was happy to be given the opportunity of spending an unscheduled week at home, and travelled north to Manchester by train.

The crowded week that followed, during which I was given a fascinating insight into the life-style of the Lancashire cotton-worker, broadened my education no end. Although I had grown up within a few miles of some of the largest mills in the county, I had only occasionally rubbed shoulders with the male element of the cotton-mill community when watching Rugby League football at Swinton or soccer at Old Trafford. And, as I was soon to learn, they were astonishingly different – and not just the men!

The exhibition opened in Oldham, where, in company with a Flight Lieutenant Stanton of Bomber Command, I was called upon to address an impressive gathering of local MPs, Mayors, mill managers, cotton VIPs and union officials, all of them sombrely and noddingly attentive in dark, shiny suits and gold chains of office. And my speeches, mostly high-flown compliments and mild exaggerations, were formulated without a single word of guidance from the so-called 'experts'. After which there was the first of an endless series of pub lunches, the menu unvarying – wafer-thin slices of almost inedible topside beef, rubber circles of Yorkshire pudding, and mounds of wet cabbage, followed by trifle or sticky pudding topped with inches of custard the consistency of yellow glue. All of which, I shudder to admit, I fell upon with the zest and appetite of youth.

But it was the visits to the mills that really opened my eyes.

The Lancashire cotton-mills played a vital part in the war effort making the basic fabrics for a wide variety of articles, including the parachute harness I strapped to my behind and the Sidcot flying suit I seldom wore. The spinning and weaving mills themselves were enormous, vast five- and six-storey buildings crammed with clattering machinery producing a cacophony of sound that beggared description. The mill workers – thousands of them – were mostly lip-reading women, old and young and of all shapes and sizes, most of them wearing clogs and all with a peasant earthiness about them in matters of dress, manner and speech. Even the most spectral of Lowry's paintings of the industrial north fail to convey to me now the starkly primitive atmosphere of the cotton industry in war-time Lancashire. And these were the people of my audiences!

Problem number one was to make myself heard. As the machinery could never be switched off, I was usually obliged to make up to twelve speeches in each mill, one at each end of the six floors and all at the top of my voice. After which there was always one extra performance for management, followed by a 'jug o' summat roun' t' corner'. Twelve speeches each mill! Five mills each day! And two or three 'bevvys' to follow. My week was anything but tame.

Most off-putting, however, were the female operatives. To them, I was fair game. Twenty years old, clad in my best

blue uniform with wings, decorations and gloves, pinkly
naïve and having a posh accent, I must have seemed like
someone from outer space. Throughout, I was referred to as
'luv' or 'chuck', invited to sign everything from autograph
books to pieces of lavatory paper, given buns and 'toffees'
as though I were a Belle Vue chimpanzee, and touched,
pinched, kissed, generally explored and made the recipient
of some pretty earthy proposals. All of which I bore with
manful aplomb, my cheeks a permanent scarlet. In fact, a
remark made before one of my earlier addresses will long be
remembered. I was standing on a box, looking down rather
uncertainly on a crowd of about thirty girls, all of whom were
eyeing me with every emotion from amusement to downright
lust. As I opened my mouth to utter my first sentence, a voice
cut through with crystal clarity:

'Ayee! Wot about one night o' luv in bed wi' 'im?'

That was the sense of the remark anyway; the words
employed were more colourfully farmyard!

I drove back to North Weald on 7 February to find that
little had happened in my absence. There was still a lot of
snow about and the threat of more to come. The squadron
had made two uneventful sweeps over France in conjunction
with 56 and 611, the latter flying Spits from Hornchurch, and
there had been sporadic activity by individual Hun bombers
in our area, resulting in one or two interceptions. 'Butch'
Barton, with Palliser and Thompson, had caught an Me 110
off Clacton and forced it into the sea and had then shot up a
second which was later seen to crash off the Kentish Knock
lightship. C-in-C Nore had been greatly bucked and had sent
fulsome congratulations to the squadron; the average matelot,
poor chap, was always tremendously uplifted by the sight of
Huns crashing into the sea. On the debit side, however, the
newly promoted John Beard, who had been detached temporarily to ferry some aircraft around the country, had crashed
a Spitfire and was back again in hospital at Melksham. Poor
old Beard; misfortune really dogged his steps.

On the 8th, I took up GN-T and did a few loops to get my hand in, being pleased and not a little surprised when one of them turned out to be straight so that I thumped through my own slipstream. It struck me at the time that I had never really done any aerobatics since leaving FTS, flying in combat not requiring any such artistic irrelevancies. 56 Squadron was terribly good at the showbiz stuff, someone always seeming to be turning his aircraft inside-out over our dispersal. Strangely, 249 was not an 'aerobatic' squadron; I never saw any of our fellows put on a show, although we appeared to be the more successful operationally. 56 was full of good chaps, even so – Gracie, Wicks, Brooker, Higginson, Constable-Maxwell and others, and a little later their new commanding officer, Norman Ryder, whom I had met when he was with 41 Squadron. In all, a grand crowd.

February the tenth, and action – action I was to remember mainly for its consequences.

We had been instructed to escort six Blenheims of 114 Squadron, who were to bomb the docks at Dunkirk. Clinging to the old formula, the Blenheims had decided to attack from 7,000 to 8,000 feet, and 56 were to act as close escort. 17 Squadron, with whom we had not worked before, were to fly on the right flank at 14,000 feet, with 249 to the rear, acting as top cover, 1,000 feet higher. I was fairly light-hearted about the whole event. I would be well above the low flak, which had frightened me half to death in January, and, high up, we would have complete freedom of action to move around as we pleased.

Making up the state board, I decided to lead the rearmost section and chose Crossey, Lewis and Davis to make up my four. In my opinion, I could not have had a more worthy bunch; Lewis, who had about eighteen Huns to his credit, Crossey, who had fought alongside me since August, and the charming Sergeant Davis, who reminded me so much of P. G. Wodehouse's Bertie Wooster. For Davis it was a red-letter occasion. He had heard only the day before that he had been commissioned, but being unable to provide himself with a pilot officer's uniform, had turned up at dispersal in the only uniform he possessed, that of an NCO. We all congratulated him, laughing meanwhile and speculating as to what would happen if he were shot down; he would never be able to convince the Huns that he was an officer and would probably spend the rest of the war digging lavatories.

We took off at 11.50, with the weather fine and clear. I was feeling bright and alert, eager to see something and to have a go.

After meeting the bombers over Kent, we climbed up in the direction of Calais, having decided to cross into France at Gravellines and to fly inland before turning left towards Dunkirk. Around Calais, the first ack-ack began to pockmark the sky with its silent puff-balls of venom, not too accurate though and no threat to me or my section. At around 15,000 feet, I led my three companions in a wide meander at the rear of the main formation, the bombers a long way below, the rest of 249 and other Hurricanes, dots of varying size, moving en masse to the south and east. This was it! If we were going to be jumped, this was the place it would happen.

Just short of Dunkirk, there was an urgent jabber of RT; the enemy somewhere, but where? Eyes darting, I tucked down my nose to work up a little speed, my cockpit already prepared for an emergency. Thereafter, events moved quickly before degenerating into confusion.

At about 14,000 feet, I was tidily leading my section of four in a streaming turn. On the *qui vive* for 109s, I saw a twin-engined aircraft far below – plainly not a Blenheim and therefore a Hun – and deciding that there was nothing much doing at height, tumbled down in pursuit, the thrill of the chase an ecstatic, bubbling surge.

A little inland now and going very fast. Far below, the Hun was flying parallel to the coast but veering south, no doubt alarmed by all the commotion above. Then, more ack-ack to my left, rather high this time, and something distinctly red, a signal flare, possibly. For the 109s? I had no idea. My

Hurricane now tight and shivering with speed. Where were the others? I looked about but could see no-one. Damn it, why had they left me? Very fast now, at about 40 degrees, fairly racing down and absolutely committed. Some aircraft away to my left but not identifiable. Bomb bursts in the water off a town I assumed to be Dunkirk. And smoke, rising – they'd hit something, anyway. But, having taken my eye off the Hun bomber, it had disappeared, as had everyone else! Where *was* everybody, for God's sake? I pulled out, everything bending and draining, and turned left. Then, climbing hard, crossed the coast without interference. Feeling very naked, I looked urgently for 109s; but there weren't any, or none that I could see. Masses of flak, though, and Hurricanes in the distance, turning away. What was happening? I flew towards them. More urgent chatter on the RT. I was not much more than 5,000 feet, on edge and unhappy, clearly missing something, but what? Then, in the distance and at about the same height, the Blenheims, going home, with more aircraft which I hoped were Hurricanes. I climbed in their direction and found myself flying north-west. Masses of cold-looking sea. Lord, what a mess! Still, I was in one piece, wasn't I? Feeling more secure, I maintained a careful watch on my tail even so, until, after a long time, the coast of Kent approached to within gliding distance. At which point there were Hurricanes everywhere. All going home. Unconcerned.

When later I taxied on to my hardstanding to stop, I saw Gerald Lewis's Hurricane just ahead of me. He was still in the cockpit as I dropped to the ground and I saw him waving his arms in my direction. When I walked towards him, I could see why. There was massive damage to the left-hand side of his cockpit, as though some demon axe-man had been hard at work. No wonder he was upset; it was a miracle he had not been killed or wounded badly. His voice, when I approached, was shrill with outrage.

'Look at this bloody lot, for God's sake!'

As I looked up, surveying the damage, Crossey approached. We had been heavily attacked, it appeared.

Attacked! By whom? I had seen nothing.

They were 109s apparently, Hun fighters seen by both of them, but not by me.

We discussed and commiserated together excitedly, the aftermath of battle quickening our speech. Where was Davis? We looked about – counting. No Davis! We looked again. No sign of Davis or of his aircraft. Not a goner, surely? Poor old chap! So cheerful and happy a mere 90 minutes ago.

Full of suppressed annoyance, more from my own lack of involvement than anything else, I walked off in the direction of dispersal, fell into step with Victor Beamish, who was also returning, and let fly. What on earth was the use of trying to take on the Huns in Mark 1s? We couldn't catch anything, we couldn't even run. And now Davis looked as if he had been shot down, with Lewis, as near as dammit, another casualty. I would rather be anywhere than this, I lamented, the Western Desert, anywhere. At least in the desert the weather was decent and, if clobbered, a chap could always force-lob and walk home. If only we had some decent aircraft!

Victor listened sympathetically, more than mildly inter-ested, I sensed. Was I really serious about going abroad? The adrenalin surging, I rashly confirmed that nothing would suit me better. The squadron, too, for that matter.

In the dispersal hut, things were being sorted out: the Blenheims, with 56 and 17, had returned unharmed, only 249 had been engaged. Our two Polish NCOs, Maciejowski and Bjeski, were each claiming a 109 destroyed and the little man Palliser was describing how the pilot of the 109 he had shot at had apparently been killed, his aircraft continuing to fly dead straight and level. He thought, too, that he had seen Lewis being attacked by a 109 and that Davis had most certainly gone, shot down into the sea, probably.

Talk and more talk, queries, laughter, explanations. The emotion ebbed away. Slowly. Poor old Davis. Such a nice chap, who had fought so gallantly for months on end. To be lost on the day he was commissioned, too. Most strange that I had not seen those 109s, though. How could it possibly have happened? No, on the whole *not* a good day, in spite of the several Huns to our credit. And so confusing.

Nothing happened the following morning, but in the afternoon we were back on the treadmill of scramble, climb and patrol. Ten of us swarmed up above North Foreland then turned south to beat a path between Manston and Dungeness for more than an hour, a wilderness of cloud beneath us with glimpses of Kent still white from the ravages of winter. We froze, our hands and feet leaden with cold, and were monumentally bored. As there didn't seem to be any Huns around, why all this patrolling, we wondered? The enemy knew perfectly well we were now on the offensive, and as their invasion plans had plainly been shelved and with their own fighter attacks on England only of nuisance value, surely their best course of action was to sit tight and wait for us to turn up over France, escorting our slow-motion bombers and doing all the damn silly things they had done six months earlier. So what were we doing up here, freezing to death?

Then, a day or so after, there started an endless series of convoy patrols in the estuary and up the east coast, a chore which was happily denied me as Air Ministry telephoned and instructed me to go north again to make more speeches and visit more cotton mills.

In the event, it was the mixture as before, except that this time I was better prepared to cope with the more tiresome and embarrassing aspects of the visit. And the pub lunches with the wet cabbage!

My penance completed, I returned to North Weald on 16 February. It was good to be home again.

3   A Time of Change

The early months of 1941 saw 249 Squadron in the midst of change. Those of us who had been with the squadron since the previous summer had each completed around 200 hours of operational flying, many being shot down, burned, wounded or having suffered some other traumatic experience. Inevitably, therefore, the first weeks of the year saw a gradual drifting away of some of our longer-serving members, a period of sadness and nostalgia for those who remained, despite there being a lively flicker of rejuvenation as new faces began to appear.

At the outset, 249 was largely made up of Volunteer Reservists, stiffened by a nucleus of regular officers who provided Service if not combat experience, our average age being 22. The vast majority of squadron members in Fighter Command were from the United Kingdom, although in 249 there was a significant overseas element, principally from South Africa. There were, in fact, quite a few South Africans in the Royal Air Force at the outbreak of war, as were there New Zealanders, Canadians, Australians and others from the Dominions, all forming a gallant and highly successful fighting element in our midst, if indistinguishable from the rest of us in terms of language and uniform. But of French, Polish, Belgian, Czechs and others, in 249 there were none – none, that is, until the last few days of September, 1940, when several suddenly appeared on the doorstep of our dispersal hut. Such was their contribution to 249's success and their sometimes unique flair for the unusual, that not to mention them would be to distort history.

When France fell in the summer of 1940, a substantial

number of trained airmen from the recently subjugated countries moved across to Britain where plans were made to form them into national squadrons within the RAF. By the spring of 1941, these plans were well advanced but, in the meantime, a number of the more experienced had been farmed out to most fighter units, 249 being host and guardian to five or six over a period of seven months.

Not unexpectedly, there was a language difficulty, which was less of a problem on the ground than in the air, where the exchange of vital information could not only be a trial – and a yawning bore to everyone else who happened to be on the same radio frequency! – but sometimes, too, a wildly hilarious exercise in non-comprehension. Getting our allies to the scene of the action proved easy enough, they simply followed the rest of us and piled in on arrival; getting them home, however, was another matter entirely, particularly in bad weather and at a time when Air Traffic Control, as we now know it, did not exist and the means of identifying and 'fixing' aircraft involved radar and triangulation procedures carried out at Sector, often miles away from the parent airfield.

249's first group of 'foreigners' included a Polish officer, 'George' Solak, who not only spoke good English but was soon to emerge as the squadron philosopher and Job's comforter, and four NCOs, two Polish and two French. The two Polish airmen were delightful – but silent! One in particular, Sergeant Maciejowski, soon to be christened 'Micky' because of his unpronounceable name, quickly resolved the problem of returning after combat by landing on the first convenient spot he could find, if not an aerodrome, a field – any field! – a solution which occasionally resulted in situations degenerating into pure farce. On one occasion, having landed in a pasture near the south coast and being unable to make himself understood, he was marched off by the police and locked up on suspicion of being a fifth-columnist, only being released when one none-too-pleased member of the squadron had been obliged to travel

40

more than 100 miles in order to identify him.

Operationally, the five more than played their part during the late-autumn battles. Within days of arriving at North Weald, 'Micky', later to be awarded a much deserved DFM, had a spirited encounter with one of our own Hampdens and, at about the same time, Sergeant Bjeski stunned us all one day by announcing that he had engaged a four-engined Focke-Wulf Condor off Cherbourg. Focke-Wulf Condor! Off Cherbourg! We could scarcely believe our ears.

The Frenchmen, too, Perrin and Bouquillard, threw themselves into combat with true Gallic flair and panache. Within days of arriving, Bouquillard had run out of fuel and crashed his aircraft and both managed to sustain battle damage at times when it was difficult to understand why, Perrin, in particular, not exactly endearing himself to me when he baled out of GN-F[1], my own beloved Hurricane, when I was away on leave. Even so, they were liked and admired by everyone so that we greatly regretted their departure towards the end of the year, at which time they were replaced by two French officers, François de Labouchere and Emile Fayolle. At about the same time, two additional Polish pilots were posted in, Flying Officer Skalski and Sergeant Popec, and later still, another French officer, Capitaine de Scitevaux.

Having watched their homelands crumble to defeat and been shattered by personal misfortune, it is hardly surprising that the newcomers were, in the main, survivors. Despite being in England only a matter of months, each of them had a knowledge of the less salubrious parts of London that had the rest of us wide-eyed with respect, and to witness the two French officers, in a perfumed fog of talc and pomade, preparing themselves for a night of *divertissement* in the big city, was something of an education – for me, anyway. Labouchere, who was devastatingly handsome and looked and sounded more like Charles Boyer (with hair) than the

---

[1] As I write, the remains of this aircraft (V7313) are in process of being dug up in the area of Canterbury.

man himself, had captured the heart of Cecilia College, the then world ice-skating champion, a ravishing young lady in whose direction I was only too happy to make sheep's eyes myself when the opportunity arose. Even George Solak, who exhibited few signs of being a ladies' man, was in a class of his own when it came to knowing not only the 'dives' but also the more respectable establishments, including one on Euston Road which dispensed a three-course meal to rival that served in Claridges for a mere half-a-crown (12½ pence).

Even the more mature Skalski was awash with talents. In one of my letters home during the latter part of January I described how I, and others, had borrowed 'Butch' Barton's venerable Opel in order to spend a night in town – always a risky venture this as 'Butch's' cars seldom had a street value of more than £5! A little beyond Epping on our way in, smoke began to emerge from beneath the dashboard and there was a powerful smell of burning car, eventually diagnosed as no water in the engine. After filling the radiator several times, we eventually arrived in London and separated, agreeing to meet later that night for the return journey.

It was approaching midnight and pitch black when we set off and we were still well within city limits when all the electrics failed – no engine, no lights, nothing! In Stygian darkness we collected around the bonnet, looking miserable. Who knew anything about Opels and their innards? No-one, it seemed. At which point Skalski stepped forward, eased us aside, then burying his head in the hot blackness of the engine, by feel alone conjured up a galaxy of sparks and had everything working in minutes. Except that the light switch operated the trafficators and everything else worked through twisted connections that could only be guessed at.

And Skalski possessed other talents, too.

As bad weather had ruled out all but essential flying since December, neither he nor the two new Frenchmen had done much in the way of aviation. To rectify this,

Skalski was sent off one afternoon on a low-level sector reconnaissance, disappearing with a wave of his hand and a glittering gold-toothed smile.

An hour or so later, just as it was growing dusk, much of eastern Essex suddenly found itself without electricity; our intrepid Pole had flown through the main power cables near Colchester.

Later that night, he arrived back at North Weald by car with his face looking like a well-wrapped parcel. He explained that, unsure of his position (not lost, mind you), he had been consulting his map, when – pouff! – lights! At which point his Hurricane had hit the ground and his face had connected violently with the gunsight. When we enquired at what height he had been flying, our continental colleague admitted with engaging frankness – twenty feet! As though twenty feet was *the* only height at which to consult a three-foot-square map in the gathering gloom and in the confined space of a Hurricane cockpit.

Some time later and mindful of Skalski's potential for disaster, I carefully briefed him and two of the Frenchmen, Labouchere and de Scitevaux, for a simple formation-flying exercise. Various formations were to be attempted and each member was to take a spell at leading on an agreed signal, details of which we then discussed. Everything clear? A trio of heads nodded agreement and all three of them took off and disappeared into the eastern sky.

After a silence of twenty minutes or so, there came a spine-chilling wail. Tumbling out of dispersal to investigate, we observed a Hurricane limp slowly and painfully into the circuit before dropping to the grass like a shot grouse. Tottering to a standstill, it remained there – leaning – smoking – spent. Skalski had returned!

We raced across the airfield to where the aircraft stood and as we approached, the cause of the din became apparent. The Hurricane's Rotol airscrew was less than half its usual diameter of eleven feet, the oil tank in the port wing root had been torn out, and there was considerable damage to the bottom of the fuselage, most of which was coated with a thick layer of black goo.

At first, Skalski was not in a fit state to say anything, after which the horrible truth was revealed. Apparently, the first fifteen minutes of the exercise had gone swimmingly, after which Skalski as leader had made a sign which had been misinterpreted by both Frenchmen, each of whom had decided to take over the lead simultaneously, the whole event culminating in a wild and clamorous explosion of wings, airscrews, and bits of fuselage.

Skalski, the least affected, had been able to toil back home, his engine over-revving almost to melting point. The others, crippled, had fallen away earthwards from a very low altitude, de Scitevaux managing by some French miracle to round out sufficiently to strike the ground at a comparatively shallow angle, after which his Hurricane had made a brisk excursion through several fields, hedges and ditches, shedding pieces as it went, before rearing to a standstill – wrecked. Meanwhile, Labouchere, unable to control his aircraft, had jumped out at around 800 feet and by the greatest of good fortune had hit the ground on the first swing of his parachute. Later, the two of them returned to North Weald grinning like gargoyles and not in the least abashed, having with the aid of Skalski destroyed three perfectly good Hurricanes in the space of twenty minutes, something the Luftwaffe had failed to achieve since Christmas. That night, in our apology for a bar – bars were still officially frowned upon in officers' messes – there was loud laughter and hilarious descriptions of the event, in the course of which someone was heard to mutter in a rueful aside that we might do worse than persuade all three of them to fight on the other side!

Such a draconian solution was unnecessary, however, as within weeks, all our foreigners, Poles and French alike, had departed, to fade anonymously into the mists of distance and time. And little more than a year later, Bouquillard, Fayolle, and the handsome Labouchere were all dead, leaving with us only the memory of their deeds, their laughter, and their comradeship.

For most of 249, the final two weeks of February were remarkable for a single event, our new aircraft were delivered on the 15th. Up north at the time, I returned to find dispersal a mass of Hurricanes, eighteen of our old Mark 1s and fifteen Mark 2s, some with eight guns, some with twelve, and several with four cannons. The squadron was delighted. Like children with new toys.

Four days later, I flew the one I had selected – GN-W (Z2638) – and was excitedly impressed. Like my first Hurricane nine months earlier, it was tight and bouncy, the engine silk-smooth, and there was the heady, intoxicating aroma of new paint. Super! I could hardly wait to go to war in it.

In fact, and on reflection, there was very little difference between the two marks of aircraft. The Mark 2 had a Merlin 20 engine which produced around 250 more horsepower, the principal advantage being that it had a manually controlled two-speed supercharger which, when engaged, came in with a disconcerting thud but increased the performance above 20,000 feet very substantially; whereas in a Mark 1 I was never too optimistic when going into combat above 25,000 feet, the Mark 2 was still pretty active at something over 30,000. Moreover, in addition to allowing us more boost to play with low down, the makers had stuck a rudder-bias control on one of the cross members of the cockpit, the fuel tanks were self-sealing, and there were wing-root blanking plates installed to reduce the powerful draughts from wings to fuselage and therefore the risk of fire in the cockpit. These, plus a few other minor refinements, all added up to an aircraft some 20 miles per hour faster than the original, more spritely at height, and a little more comfortable in which to fly. One thing they had not done, however, was provide us with any creature comforts; we were going to operate at altitudes where the ambient temperature was around minus 60 degrees centigrade, without a vestige of heat. I was in despair.

Why, oh, why? Surely they could have done *something*!

In the days following, Pat Wells, who had just returned to the squadron having been shot down and wounded twice in three months, took his Mark 2 to 38,500 feet. I took my own to just under 37,000, at which height I was so cold, so lacking in breath and so bored, that I gave up. Our oxygen system in the Hurricane remained fairly primitive as we still wore the old, ill-fitting fabric masks into which oxygen blew in the general direction of nose and mouth in a constant and wasteful stream. Moreover, I had never properly appreciated that towards 40,000 feet, due to the rarified atmosphere, the voice disappeared almost completely, and that one's sinuses had to be in pretty good condition, too!

The introduction of our new Hurricanes, however, altered our activities not one jot, except that between bouts of sleet, rain and fog, our patrols over Manston, Dungeness, Boulogne and Calais, were at 30,000 instead of 20,000 feet. Patrols! Endless patrols, high and low, and as the days dragged by, increasingly over convoys moving in slow motion up and down the east coast. But ne'er a Hun did we see. Well . . . almost none.

On the night of 25 February, I spent well over an hour high over Harwich and succeeded in intercepting one enemy aircraft which melted into the blackness before I could get in more than a fleeting burst. Lots of excitement, though, as my de Wilde ammunition produced a brief firework display in the darkness and, for one moment, I really thought I might have shot down my first Hun at night. I then intercepted two of our own Wellingtons in quick succession, after which, with the adrenalin surging, I found myself in the midst of an intense ack-ack barrage which had me screaming abuse at the trigger-happy fools below.

It was about that time, too, that we heard that Davis, who had been lost over Dunkirk on the 10th, was a prisoner-of-war. The news bucked me up no end. Some chaps who had gone missing in the past hadn't concerned me particularly, but for Davis, who had been a member of my section at the time, I felt a special responsibility. Good old Davis! And having been identified as an officer, it seemed he wouldn't be digging lavatories after all.

We also had information that most of our Polish colleagues were to join 306 and 317 Squadrons immediately – Solak, Maciejowski, and the quiet and smiling Bjeski. Sad, sad news. And, at about the same time, an Air Commodore turned up to talk about the air-sea-rescue organization, bringing with him one of the new seat-type dinghies, which he demonstrated. We were all to get them, apparently. Soon, too, enabling those of us who fell into the winter waters of the Channel to die of exposure by degrees instead of freezing to death quickly and painlessly. Yes, things were looking up all right.

Making up my logbook for the month, I saw that I had only flown twelve hours in February. Still I had been away for almost a fortnight, hadn't I?

Being in a fighter squadron just north of London in the early months of 1941, was, however, not all convoy patrols, flak, and sweeps over France. Since Christmas, and because of duff flying weather, we had been blessed with more than enough time off. Also, the publicity merchants were about in strength arranging photographic sessions and visits by foreign potentates – mostly American, coming to see whether or not we were going to lose the war (and their money) as predicted by their toothy Ambassador, Kennedy – and war artists, the latter commissioned to record Battle of Britain scenes and personalities. In December, with a number of my companions, I had sat for two of this small and prestigious group of war artists, Cuthbert Orde and Eric Kennington, on each occasion perched on a chair in the Ladies' Room of the mess, trying to look solemn whilst they sketched my face for posterity. Orde did me in charcoal and was really quite chatty; Kennington drew me in pastel and hardly uttered a syllable. Orde's drawing, in my opinion, was indifferent, Kennington's very good, although I did not think so at the time. He was a very tall, rather lugubrious-looking man

47

who had been a close friend of Lawrence of Arabia and had illustrated Lawrence's famous book, 'Seven Pillars of Wisdom'. Throughout the sitting he produced not even a smile and when he had finished, I asked if I might examine his work.[1] When he agreed, with characteristic lack of tact, I damned it with faint praise, remarking that I thought it was 'all right' but that he had drawn my mouth incorrectly. Kennington, of international fame and who clearly had never before had his artistic accomplishments criticized in such a manner, was quite taken aback. That was the way he saw me, was his quietly contemptuous remark, and if I didn't like it, I had only myself to blame. And, of course, he was right, it was an excellent likeness, mirroring all my youthful moodiness and impetuosity. Sadly, as the man is long since dead, I shall never be able to apologize and tell him how wrong I was.

And with the war artists and other visitors, there were the photographers, chief among whom was Cecil Beaton, who arrived at dispersal looking like an advertisement for Sandeman's Sherry. Most of us, including our Intelligence Officer, Woolmer, who, unbeknown to us, was a friend of his, were in the dispersal hut when he arrived and the several seconds that followed were nothing short of memorable.

Crossing the threshold, his face alight with recognition, Beaton cried out: 'Shirley!'

And Woolmer responded joyously, 'Cecil!'

After that, the rest of the day was never quite the same.

But no-one could fault his photography. After taking a score or more photographs of the squadron in groups, I was invited to pose singly, which I did, then with one or two others, plus Wilfred the duck,[2] most of the pictures appearing in the glossy magazines a few weeks later and in exhibitions and book-form for the next forty years! One

[1] This portrait can now be seen at the RAF Museum, Hendon.
[2] 249 Squadron then had a small menagerie of dog, kittens and ducks plus, from time to time, a broody hen to hatch the duck eggs – produced by 'Wilfred'!

early series was printed in the American periodical *Vogue* and went around the world, the photographs superb but the accompanying text quite nauseating – gross exaggerations and untruths which had me, and others, curling up with embarrassment. Were future generations to learn about the war reading this sort of nonsense?

And on our days off, I occasionally went into London, mostly with Crossey and the others, but now and then on my own. One such visit was rather different.

Throughout the winter, the Huns had bombed London constantly, the East End in particular being reduced to a shambles and even the West End shattered and torn in places. Rarely a night passed without our hearing the discordant drone of enemy aircraft, en route to somewhere if not London, accompanied by the whistle and thump of bombs and the rapid 'tonk-tonk-tonk-tonk' of our own ack-ack. Eventually raids became so commonplace that the citizens of the capital city hardly reacted, continuing to go about their daily affairs with a quite extraordinary attitude of indifference.

I had gone into London to meet an old school acquaintance of mine. Some three or four years older than me, he had been at university reading chemistry when war had broken out and now, in a reserved occupation, had taken up an appointment in London. After spending the afternoon together we had dinner in the West End, after which he insisted on taking me back to his digs which were in Kensington.

As darkness fell, the bombers began one of their nightly visitations and towards midnight the raid became so heavy, with some pretty violent thumps in our vicinity, that it was deemed prudent to go down into the basement.

Having by this time been persuaded to stay the night, I found myself below ground and in the company of a dozen other people of varying age who shared the same four-storey house, mostly professional men and women, some dressed, others in night-wear and slippers, all of them with pillows, torches, candles and flasks. There was no fuss or excitement; they had obviously done this many times before and either conversed quietly, read books, or tried to sleep. After all, it was business as usual tomorrow, wasn't it?

I was sitting on the floor, dozing, with my back to a wall and the head of some strange young woman, who was asleep, on my shoulder. It was about 2 a.m. Suddenly there was a single crash which shook the whole building and brought down bits of the ceiling. Everyone awoke with a jerk but after a minute or two of relieved laughter and conversation, peace was restored and nothing more was heard for the rest of the night. An hour or two later, the all-clear sounded, although I did not hear it at the time.

With everyone else, I was up early the next morning and ready to leave shortly after seven. Very much aware that I was in uniform but unshaven – there was neither water nor electricity – I went out into the street intending to get back to North Weald as quickly as possible. Further down the road, about 50 yards away, there was a mountain of rubble crawling with men of the fire, ambulance and rescue services, obviously the source of the big bang we had heard in the night. As I approached then stopped to watch, stretcher bearers were carrying out bodies, alive and dead. I looked on, silently shocked by the sight of so much tragedy. There was no dignity in some of the sprawling forms, night-clothes filthy, ripped and torn, waxen figures with bloodied and naked limbs splayed out, private parts modestly covered, even on the dead. At one point I stepped forward to lend a hand as two dust-encrusted men in tin hats stumbled and almost fell with one of their lolling, stretchered burdens. One of them looked up and taking in my uniform and rank, motioned me away with a jerk of his head.

'Mind yer back, guv. You'll only get yourself dirty.'

I fell back. Dirty! Get myself dirty! I, who had been fighting almost every day for more than eight months! I felt a sharp pang of rejection, hurt and shame. Dirty, for God's sake!

And my school chum? I never saw him again. His quietly envious glances at my uniform, wings and decorations during our all too brief time together had disclosed feelings of

50

deep unease. Shortly after, he talked his way out of his reserved occupation and volunteered for aircrew. More than a year later, and a trainee navigator in an Anson, his pilot flew him into a Welsh mountain and he was killed. A sad, sad loss. He never saw combat, never even reached a squadron; one of three fine brothers who were to die in action or on active service. Some families seemed fated to suffer so much, and so unfairly.

March. Wind, rain and low cloud. And convoy patrols.

Convoy patrols! The memory of them remains. Two aircraft at a time. Take-off, but keep below the fringes of the cloud. Zero-nine-zero degrees on the compass, set the DI.[1] The Blackwater – always the same mirror-smooth inlet with its stationary sailing ship at the top end, probably a wreck but it looked whole enough from the air. Then Clacton, or somewhere, and the sea. The sea! – my Hurricane's single engine suddenly much less smooth. Grey, endless, chilly water and in the distance, ships lying like matchsticks end-to-end in a gutter. Over the mast-tops now, a quick wag of the wings for recognition purposes, then up and down at 1,000 feet; up and down, up and down. Endlessly. Further north now, the balloons at Harwich off to the left, glowering at us from the fringes of the cloud. Balloons! Avoid those blighters at all costs! Backwards and forwards, huddled and bored. Anything doing? 'Lumba's'[2] reply: nothing to report. Counting the minutes, 30, 45, then 60, occasionally longer. Now and then as far north as Southwold. Southwold! God, we'd be in Scotland next! Eventually turning wearily for home. First the coast and the balloons again, then the familiar, dead-straight railway line from Colchester to Chelmsford, racing a train below pluming a long trail of smoke and steam. At Chelmsford, right-turn on to 270 degrees to fly for three long-drawn-out minutes. Then, if greenhouses suddenly appeared beneath,

---

[1] Direction indicator.

[2] Call sign for RAF North Weald Sector Control.

turn round and go back because we had overshot. Eyes straining for the faint lines of the North Weald masts through all the mist and cloud. Bloody weather! Thank God for the masts!

In our new Mark 2s, we flew on nothing other than convoy patrols for the first twelve days of March, stopping only for bad weather, of which there was plenty. No Huns. Nothing. Only the cold grey sea, and ships, and boredom.

Then, on the 13th, with 56 Squadron and 303 from Northolt, we took six Blenheims to bomb a target near Dunkirk. Poor old 56 were alongside the bombers yet again, with 249 stepped up to 20,000 feet. And above us the Poles of 303, not exactly to our liking as we were well aware that if our gallant allies became fed up – which was more than likely – they were not above dropping down on those beneath and giving a quick squirt, apologizing afterwards with the excuse that they thought they were shooting at 109s!

I did not see the bombs explode, nor did I see any Huns. And the flak when it came plopping silently in our direction was pretty feeble. The whole show very uncomplicated, probably because we were much more confident now in our Mark 2s, fairly romping around at 20,000 feet. Back on the ground someone said he had seen a Hun destroyer off Dunkirk, but I hadn't, probably because I was rather too high and looking for 109s.

There was lots of to-ing and fro-ing within the squadron throughout the month; besides the departure of most of our Poles and others, Keith Lofts, who commanded 'A' Flight, had already left and many new faces were beginning to appear – Matthews, Munro, Marshall, Welman, Davis – another Davis! – and Cooper. Every doorway seemed to frame a new officer or NCO pilot. The old order changeth! A great pity, even though there were at least fourteen of us remaining from the previous summer.

And a further surprise: we heard that 'Boozy' Kellett, formerly a flight commander of 249 and more recently the commanding officer of 303, was being posted in to become our newly established Wing Commander Flying – 'Whisper

King', so called. The incomparable Boozy! With his old Rolls Royce, I wondered? It would be nice seeing him again.

The month dragged on: more convoy patrols, miserable weather, the occasional sweep high up over the Channel coasts, and night operations.

The Hurricane was an easy aircraft to fly at night, much easier than the Spit, which had a longer nose and an indifferent view from the cockpit besides being waywardly frisky on the ground. However, because our aircraft were not normally fitted with exhaust-blanking plates, the flare from the engine effectively ruined our night vision. Also, as so few of 249 were regarded as fully night operational, it fell to only several of us to do the night flying.

In the North Weald sector, in the event of a threatened attack at dusk or in the early hours of darkness, the routine, referred to as 'forward layers', was to place single fighters at heights varying from 10,000 to 20,000 feet out to sea off Clacton. Why Clacton, particularly, and why 20 to 40 miles out to sea, was a mystery, appearing to be a knee-jerk reaction among controllers: what's that, a possible night attack? – send the Hurricanes 40 miles out to sea off Clacton! Dead easy, they didn't have to do it; sitting up there in the blackness, freezing to death with the hood open, and knowing full well that if anything stopped, we were in the water and goners. I never much cared for the 'forward layer' arrangement; we so seldom saw anything and when we did, the bogeys were usually our own Wellingtons. I did several of these in March and on at least two other occasions was kept at 'Readiness' the entire night but not called upon. The working day of a day-and-night fighter pilot at that stage of the war could be of anything up to 24 hours' duration.

On the 19th, we were patrolling Dungeness at 33,000 feet when we saw a sizeable formation at about our own level. Eureka! Huns! We swung towards them full of venom and expectation and piled in, only to find they were Spitfires. For a full minute thereafter, we circled each other like packs of stiff-legged dogs before separating. I was terribly disappointed; my first sight of a likely target for ages. Ah, well; at least we had shown ourselves *capable* of fighting at altitude, although during those turns at 33,000 feet, I found it almost impossible to maintain height.

The following day, being called upon to visit Hendon, I took Pat Wells and one other along with me. We landed and I recalled that it was my first visit since sitting in one of the nearby fields as a fifteen-year-old, watching the 1936 Hendon Air Display.

After we had conducted our business, we killed time in the old Auxiliary Squadron mess, an elegant place which had more the air of the Athenaeum or Reform about it than anything connected with the Air Force. We found ourselves sipping our after-lunch coffee and whispering in its hallowed surroundings, fearful lest we should disturb the dozen or so elderly officers who were reading, or, with papers over their heads, sleeping off their midday meal. We darkly discussed the situation; the war against tyranny raging in Britain, Europe, the Middle East and beyond, here were these chaps really roughing it, living in abject squalor and having to put up merely with five-course lunches and *all* the daily newspapers and glossy magazines to keep in touch; in short, fighting as heroically and as hard as they knew how. They needed a morale-raiser, by George!

Shortly after, we took off and, climbing to several thousand feet, aimed ourselves at the mess. In close formation, the three of us swept to within twenty feet of the roof and blasted across the top at more than 300 miles an hour before climbing away rapidly to make ourselves scarce. Lovely! That had shifted the blighters; we only wished we could have seen their faces. At the time, the feud between old and young in the Air Force, between those we perceived to be the doers and the deadbeats, was sometimes bitter and always more than just a game.

It was in March, too, that several of us sat down and gave some thought to designing a crest for our new squadron, the general view being that as we were associated with the Gold Coast, we should have an elephant, or tusks, or a couple of coconuts even, as the centre-piece. Settling on the elephant, I sketched one which I copied from a picture of the Gold Coast coat-of-arms in my Children's Encyclopaedia. After which came the motto. With much hilarity, we went through a score of possibilities but found all the good, pithy ones, such as 'Seek and Destroy', already used. Finally, we settled on 'We Shall not Fail', which I thought a bit overly Churchillian, being further put off by some wag who kept muttering, 'Not all the time, anyway'. In due course, this was the version submitted to Air Ministry, and subsequently rejected. Much later, a revised version appeared using the original elephant but having a motto which only Latin scholars could translate.[1]

The month drew to a close. We heard that Percy Burton had been awarded a 'Mention in Dispatches', Percy, who had been killed on 27 September, when, mortally wounded, he had rammed an Me 110, bringing them all crashing to earth. So long ago now but still so vividly in my mind. Just a 'Mention', though; we all thought he deserved something more than that – some people appeared to receive 'Mentions' for just polishing the aircraft!

The following day, we were airborne with 56 and several other squadrons, whom I did not even see, for the purpose of taking six Blenheims to bomb two ships in the Cap Gris Nez area. The weather clear and fine, I found myself barely on edge as we flew southwards towards Maidstone to pick up the bombers. Pretty run-of-the-mill stuff these days and so rarely any Huns about. Where did they all get to?

With 56 again acting as close escort, 249 were spread out in sections at around 5,000 feet. As we crossed the English coast and headed for France, I found myself almost eager to witness some really effective precision bombing; the Blenheims were going in at 2,000 feet this time and couldn't possibly miss from that height, surely.

As we approached the French coast, the ships lay dead ahead, silent, motionless victims, defenceless targets in an

[1] Pugnis Et Calcibus – 'With Fists and Heels'.

attack they could do nothing about. I felt almost sorry for them.

Then, flak; a dozen or so bursts from around Calais, not too close to me though and no real threat. The bombers running in. My own section wheeling in a fast curve within a mile or so of the French shore. Anxiously watching for 109s, I kept more than half an eye on the bombers, even so. Any minute now.

The bombs fell, innocuous curving specks. Fascinated, I followed their descent – and was vastly disappointed. Not one of them on target; all instead plummeting harmlessly into the sea, producing slow-motion eruptions of grey-brown water and smoke which collapsed gently into pale green discs. They had missed! All of them! Missed! What a damn silly business. Six Blenheims, twenty-odd bombs, and heaven knows how many fighters, for what? Nothing! I raced on in a wide curve, looking inland into France before turning towards the north. What a dreary waste of effort.

It was around this time, too, that an incident occurred which was an example of the occasional pig-headedness and insensitivity displayed by some in control of our affairs.

With a heavy cold, one of several I was plagued with throughout the winter, I had flown at height for longer than was good for me and on letting down, was so badly afflicted by sinus pains that I had to break formation and climb up again in order to relieve the discomfort. Finally, when running short of fuel, I was forced to land with dagger-thrusts above my eyes and my head about to explode. Still in misery and completely deaf in one ear, I had crept off to sick-quarters to spend an hour there inhaling menthol steam with a towel draped over my head. After which, feeling utterly wretched, I had returned to the mess, missed my dinner, then retired to bed around 7 p.m., intending to sleep the clock around.

But, what a hope! Several hours later, I was dragged from the deepest pit of unconsciousness by my batman who was shaking my shoulder and telling me in a quite unnecessary stage-whisper that a heavy raid was in progress over London and that the squadron had been ordered to put as many aircraft as possible into the air. Without delay! Now, in fact!

It took more than a minute for my sleep-befuddled brain to grasp what was being said to me. What was that? Fly? Now? What on earth was he talking about? What time was it, for God's sake? On being told, I could scarcely believe my ears. The middle of the night! What was going on? Then, clutching at a straw; someone was pulling his leg, one of my *dear* brother officers telephoning from the Coconut Grove or some such place in London, having a lark. But the youth, who was growing steadily more apprehensive as the bad news brought me to life, assured me that someone wasn't. As many pilots as possible, the man had said, although there seemed to be only several of 249 in the mess. Perhaps he could get me a cup of tea?

I rose as though from a grave and, sleep-walking to the window, removed the blackout frame. Outside it was unrelieved darkness tinged with the grey opaqueness of mist bordering on fog. Fly? Now? Sector must be out of their collective mind! Anyway, the squadron had been released hours ago; most of the chaps were in London and I was ill, wasn't I? No, the whole thing was a ridiculous mistake! I'd have a word with the controller.

But in spite of the word I subsequently had and the flood of savage and mutinous thoughts that cascaded through my mind, within half an hour and feeling like death, I was down at dispersal in company with 'Butch' Barton and Pat Wells, whilst out in the dark beyond, a handful of NCOs and men, hastily mustered from the various messes, were struggling with tarpaulins and making ready a few of our aircraft. Everyone numbed by resignation, we were puzzled and affronted by the injustice of it all. Why us? for God's sake.

Then 'Butch' was on the telephone to the controller, querying the instruction and, in his most forthright Canadian voice, pointing out that the weather was totally unsuitable for flying and that the whole exercise seemed ridiculous. After speaking for several minutes, he finally confronted us with a grim face. We would have to go, it seemed; orders from above, the controller's hands were tied. The weather was a bit better to the north, apparently, and if we could manage to get off, they would probably bring us back to Debden, Duxford, or somewhere even further afield if conditions didn't improve. Probably! I didn't like the sound of that. But, that seeming to be the end of it, we began to make ready.

The three of us grim-faced and silent, I had a private vision of some very senior gentleman sipping his after-dinner port and casually ordering the North Weald Hurricanes into the air with a flip of his hand. What a stupid and pointless business. Outside in the blackness, the thin drone of enemy aircraft filtered down to us through a wilderness of seemingly impenetrable cloud and fog.

'Butch' was the first to leave, his boots clumping out of the dispersal hut and into the darkness, followed by Pat Wells. My head still bursting and feeling utterly miserable, I trailed in their wake, humping my parachute, helmet and other equipment.

My aircraft on its usual hardstanding just beyond Victor Beamish's blast-pen, I had about 100 yards to walk, a simple enough chore in normal circumstances but rather more of a problem on a pitch-black night, in a heavy mist, and without a torch. As I moved forward, I heard the muffled noise of 'Butch's' engine as he taxied away into the fog and saw in the far distance a nodding pin-prick of light which I took to be the shaded torch-beam of one of my crew. Stepping cautiously but blindly in that direction, I was about halfway there when I trod on something – which I later discovered to be a wheel-chock – and, staggering sideways, fell heavily into a group of parked starter trollies, the sharp edge of one of them catching me on my right shin just below the knee.

For a few brief seconds, the world stood still. In the most excruciating pain, I found myself draped across the flat top of a heavy battery-cart, having dropped everything I was holding in the mud. And it was then that something *snapped*. That was *it*! Not one step further would I go! Almost in tears of hurt, anger and frustration, I gathered my equipment and mutinous self together and limped back towards the dispersal hut, mouthing my opinion of those who didn't fly themselves and who didn't give a damn about those of us who had to.

Within seconds I was on to Sector and speaking to the controller in language that can only be described as vehement. Did he *really* understand what he was asking us to do? The weather was unfit for flying; not only did I doubt that we could get ourselves airborne but, thus far, I hadn't even managed to *find* my aircraft, which was true, but not for the reason I was hinting at. And even if we did get into the air, our chances of an interception were nil – *as well he knew*! So, what was the point of all this? Perhaps he could tell me, because the logic of it escaped me! On and on, my bursting head and aching shin spurring me on to new heights of eloquence.

Rather to my surprise, as I was expecting a blast in return, the man listened in silence before responding calmly. I was invited to hang on for a moment, which I did, quaking with anger meanwhile but half-regretting my outburst and wondering if I had already overstepped the mark. Then, the voice again, as nice as pie. All right, if conditions were as bad as I had described, of course we could stand down. Had anyone taken off yet? Trying to find the end of the runway, were they? In that case, perhaps I could stop them.[1] Unbelieving but vastly thankful, I jerked my head in the direction of the airman-of-the-watch, who almost fell out of the door into the night before sending a red Very light curving into the darkness. All over! Thank heaven for that! The others would be relieved.

Some ten minutes later, 'Butch' stamped into the dispersal hut having taken an age to taxi back from the far side of the airfield. Looking as white and as angry as ever I had seen him, he snatched up the telephone and demanded

[1] In 1941 there was no Air Traffic Control, as we now know it.

to speak to the controller. What the hell was going on? First we had been ordered into the air, against our better judgement, let it be said, then, because his flight commander had had the *guts* to make a fuss, the whole thing had been called off. Was it essential or wasn't it? Because if it wasn't, what the hell were we doing down at dispersal in the middle of the night? Whoever was issuing these orders should *make up his mind*! And so on, the exchange was quite lengthy but that was the gist of it.

In the next room, Pat Wells and I listened to the tirade. Guts! It had nothing to do with guts. I was hopping wild because I had been dragged out of bed feeling like death; because I had walked into that damned starter-trolley and well-nigh broken my leg; and because the insensitivity, the injustice, and the time-wasting nonsense of the whole affair had rankled. No thought of *us*! Our lives and aircraft were being jeopardized when everybody knew that nothing, but nothing, would be achieved. Moreover, it seemed that no-one cared or understood. Wasn't it simply a case of someone wishing to cover himself in the event of questions being asked later? As we talked about it, Pat confided to me half-seriously that he had even thought of taxying into a blast-pen and knocking a bit off his propeller – only a little bit, mind! And after a time, we were all able to laugh a little – just a little! All the same, and because we were normally on very good terms with the controllers at Sector, it was an unpleasant incident which ruffled our feathers. Whoever *was* responsible was being more than just silly, his decision had bordered on the criminal.

It was well after midnight before I was back in bed, still simmering with resentment. Strangely, though, my head seemed much better. Probably the shock of it all!

April: for the first six days of the month, an endless succession of convoy patrols; ten miles out to sea off Clacton, then Barrow Deep, after which Clacton again, followed by Harwich and all the way up to Southwold. On one occasion, huddled in a goonskin[1] and bored to distraction, I actually fell asleep in the cockpit. My last recollection was of turning at the southern end of the convoy and flying north; then, after a time, looking down to find the convoy not there. Gone! Missing! Good God! I turned about in shocked concern and found it several miles astern. How on earth had I got up here if I hadn't nodded off? Later, when my No. 2 remarked rather pointedly that he wondered what I had been up to, I explained, not too convincingly, that I thought I had seen something. Asleep! My oath, what next?

Then, on the 7th – tragedy!

We had started off with more convoy patrols, eight sections of two aircraft throughout the morning, after which there was a wing-show over the same convoy – 56, 249 and 242 squadrons, in all 36 aircraft. It was, of course, to boost morale and no doubt the sailors gazing skywards from below were suitably heartened by the sight of us; it was a trying life for them, constantly on the *qui vive* and being bombed from time to time without the means to defend themselves adequately. But for us, it was merely a diversion; 36 aircraft at little more than 1,000 feet, wheeling about uncomfortably for almost an hour. What if a Hun popped out of a cloud now, to come face to face with this armada? Frighten the blighter to death, probably, and serve him right!

Then in the early evening, a further six aircraft of 249 were returning from the same convoy when Dicky Wynn, who was in the middle of the formation, for no apparent reason, broke away at low level and dived straight into the ground. Within several minutes flying time of North Weald, too, and with everyone preparing to land. We were shattered. No warning. Neither sign nor word from him. Just a straightforward plunge into oblivion. What a tragedy! The smiling, level-headed, experienced Dicky, who had been with the squadron almost from the start and who had fought bravely for more than six months, being shot down, wounded nastily in the neck, and

[1] Goonskin – leather, sheepskin-lined coat (and trousers).

crashing more than once through engine failure. To die not as a victim in battle, but as a casualty in an inexplicable and seemingly needless accident. Had he, too, fallen asleep? Surely not, not within two minutes of landing and in the middle of a formation. What a way to go! We were all sobered by the thought of his passing.

The following day on an air-test, I flew over the crash-site, a field close to the village of Ongar, and circled several times the brown scar in the earth and the few remaining fragments of his Hurricane. A sad and silent trace of a gallant colleague.

That night, I was airborne for almost two hours on a 'forward layer'. Alone in the cold, blue-black solitude of space and a long way out to sea with only the magenta flare from my exhausts to claim my attention, my thoughts were with him more than once. How grossly unfair that someone as talented, as mature and as companionable as Dicky Wynn should have died so casually and to such little effect. A terrible waste. The endless expanse of frigid, starlit blackness was a quiet companion and fitting venue for my poignant musings.

April the 10th; the day fine, bright and cold.

I led an offensive formation of six – Wells, Crossey, Palliser, Mills and 'Boozy' Kellett – on a high altitude sweep to Le Touquet and beyond, then northwards to Boulogne and Calais. Looking for 109s.

It was the first time that 'Boozy' – 'Whisper King' – had flown with us and I was quietly and smugly amused that only nine months earlier, he had been my flight commander and instructor during my first, very amateurish circuits and bumps in that new-fangled, low-wing monoplane, the Miles Master. Deciding that he would act as weaver, he tagged on to our rear and said not a word throughout.

We took off at noon and full of consideration for my five companions, I climbed up at a very gentlemanly rate towards the south. At 19,000 feet over Kent, I bent forward and pulled the small handle that moved my two-speed supercharger into

FS. There was a mild 'clump' up front and the boost needle shot an extra five pounds around the dial as my Hurricane gave a comforting surge. Mmmm! Very nice, too! We climbed on steadily and in mid-Channel were at 33,000 feet and on the alert for Huns.

Some fifteen minutes later, by which time we were well into France and flying north-east, my enthusiasm for combat had died the death. It was *unbelievably* cold! My feet and hands like stone and my body beginning to crystallize, I lowered my seat to the bottom of its travel and, with my right hand, fished about for the hot pipe that ran between engine and radiator. I could touch it – just – but with only the tips of my fingers and to little effect. I sat there, straining – and suffering. Through the frost-caked metal frame of my hood, some 30 yards away I could see only the top of the helmet of my nearest companion, who was no doubt equally cold and doing much the same as myself. Why, oh why, couldn't they put some heat into these *bloody* aircraft?

Meanwhile, 'Boozy', at least ten years older than any of us and 1,000 feet higher, was fairly zipping around above our heads. I sat there, watching his white-trailed manoeuvres in frozen awe, my mind congealed into a stupor. Wasn't he, too, feeling the cold? And why did his aircraft always appear to be so much faster than my own?

Then, away to the south, four distant, slow-moving pencil-lines of white. Huns! Not in the least concerned by their presence, what did disturb me was that they were a good 1,500 feet higher – 34,000 at least. What *did* we have to do to get above these blighters?

There was little point in attempting to climb up and fight, even had we possessed the performance to do so; we had already been airborne for more than an hour and were wallowing about as it was. They approached. Then stood off. And looked. Watching them carefully as they kept to a respectable distance, when roughly over Calais we turned away slowly to the north and began to let down. Frozen to the tripes! Thank God for warmer altitudes!

A little to my surprise, 'Boozy' did not turn up at our dispersal to discuss the flight and we later learned that he, too, had been greatly affected by the arctic conditions. Later still, we heard that he had gone to sick-quarters, or was it hospital? Wherever it was and for whatever reason, we did not see him again at North Weald. Ever! Poor old 'Boozy'. What the Huns couldn't do in months, the frost and his Hurricane had achieved in a single flight – unaided.

Dicky Wynn was buried in North Weald churchyard on the 11th and the following day I did some air-to-ground firing on Dengie Flats. Our new 12-gun Hurricanes performed excellently but the four 20 mm cannons in the several aircraft equipped with them gave a lot of trouble. The cannon Hurricanes were noticeably heavier than the machine-gun variety and, when fired, the guns did so at a much slower rate than the Brownings and with violent thumps which shook the wings and airframe unpleasantly. Invariably, one or more cannons would stop after a few rounds, causing the aircraft to slew sideways, depending on where the offending weapons were situated. The 20 mm rounds of ammunition were huge by comparison with the .303 bullet, the ball and armour-piercing heavy chunks of metal which pulverized anything they struck. I would have hated to have been hit by anything fired by our new Hispanos; the Huns mostly used ammunition which exploded on contact so that only the small armoured nose ploughed on, a characteristic for which many in 249 had been profoundly thankful during the autumn battles. I didn't much care for our cannon Hurricanes and only flew them when I had to; I liked guns that fired *all* the time and not just when they felt inclined.

Later in the month, leading most of my flight, I took off for Sutton Bridge to use the ground targets there, only to be overtaken immediately by bad weather which forced us all to make an emergency landing at Bassingbourn.

Fretting with the unexpected turn of events and being obliged to kill time in the officers' mess for the rest of the day, with my back to the fire in the ante-room, I found myself in conversation with a pleasant-faced little fellow wearing a DFC and Bar, who told me that he had started off on fighters but had now moved on to the bigger stuff. I pulled a face and said he was welcome to heavy boilers, thank you very much; I didn't have the sort of courage needed just to sit still and be shot at. He shrugged, implying that it wasn't that bad. I remember him smiling a lot and having twinkling eyes. Before we parted, he introduced himself as Gibson – Flight Lieutenant Guy Gibson.[1]

April drifted by – more convoy patrols, uneventful sweeps over France, some practice flying now and then, and more than sufficient days off. The Frenchman, Fayolle, in one of his last flights with the squadron, ran into an Me 110 over a convoy and claimed it as a 'probable'; otherwise we barely saw a Hun, except from a distance. Anywhere!

Since the heady and violent days of the previous summer, autumn and early winter, the war for us had changed dramatically. Here we were, all ready and willing in our new Hurricane 2s, doing a fair amount of flying but encountering nothing to shoot at. Where had all the Huns got to?

Things were also changing on the ground, new faces each day in dispersal and, to our great sorrow, even Victor Beamish was said to be 'on his way'. Victor! So splendid a man and so gallant a leader; it was like mourning a parent. Without him, North Weald – the war even – would never be quite the same.

But, a little before his departure, it was he who came into dispersal one morning just before noon and shattered us with a single sentence. I remember every word, where I was in the hut at the time, and its effect on those around me.

'You chaps are going overseas!' I recall the grin on his face. And the silence that followed.

- *   *   *

[1] Later, Wing Commander Guy Gibson, VC, DSO, etc., of 617 Squadron and Dambuster fame.

When we all heard of the squadron's posting, I was standing in the middle of the hut, just beyond the stove. Harry Davidson, soon to be commissioned, was on my left and I turned to him, excited by Victor's statement but privately concerned that it might have been my outburst some weeks before that had prompted him to bring up the subject at Air Ministry, where he was a frequent visitor, and somehow start the whole business in train. Whatever the truth of the matter, when I looked at Davidson, his face, normally so cheerful, was condemning.

'I don't bluddy-well want to go overseas.' Then, with a look of frozen hostility I had never seen before: 'That was *you*, wasn't it?'

His words were like knife-thrusts and, in the event, our posting proved to be a turning point in his life as he was soon to join the newly forming Merchant Ship Fighter Unit and be killed in tragic circumstances. Poor unfortunate Harry! The most willing of fighter pilots, a great morale-raiser and a good friend whom I had known since we started training together in the summer of '38. Was I really responsible, even remotely, for his untimely end? I like to think not but the doubts have remained.

And it was in line with Air Ministry policy which decreed that married officers should, whenever possible, remain in the United Kingdom, that Gerald Lewis and others were soon to go their separate ways. But, at that point, we had no idea where we were going, not even that we were off to the Middle East.

With the war at stalemate in Western Europe and the Navy beginning to cope with the magnetic mine and, to a lesser extent, the U-boat, the focal point of conflict had undoubtedly shifted to the Middle East. Wavell[1] had captured literally armies of Italians in the Western Desert, compelling the Germans, now less than happy with their lame-duck ally, to reinforce Libya, having for months past been heavily

[1] General Sir Archibald Wavell, G.O.C. Middle East.

committed in southern Europe and in Greece. For them, one route to victory led through the Suez Canal to the oil-rich deserts beyond and the soft underbelly of Russia.

But although there was something of a lull in and around Britain, the Hun bombers were overhead almost every night, if not to attack London then other major cities of the realm. In fact, nightly bombing raids were so commonplace, we were beginning to regard them much as we did the cloud and the rain – part of the national scene. Bombing, blackout, and the endless, hollow 'tonk-tonk-tonking' of the guns – that was the sound and picture of England. Plus the five-bob meals and food rationing, the fire-watching, ARP, and new Home Guard. And the shattered buildings, the sandbags and tin-hats, the tawdriness, and the general lack of paint. No, I wouldn't mind going overseas, and not only for the better weather. But where? At the outset, none of us knew.

On the 17th, though, we did – almost! The official warning order arrived and, soon after, a small group of officers appeared from somewhere-or-other to answer questions and build upon the bare bones of the initial instruction. All very secret, of course.

We would be going abroad by aircraft-carrier and flying off. Flying off! Wow! Precisely where, though, would remain a secret until we were seaborne. Our troops would not be accompanying us, however, but would go separately, to join us at our destination. Frowns, objections, and dismay! The squadron split up? *Why*, for heaven's sake? The voice was continuing: we would cease operational flying at North Weald on 1 May and would be granted a week's embarkation leave. Meanwhile, additional pilots would be posted in and others would leave. There would be inoculations – groans! – and kitting out, and each of us would be allowed 30 lbs of accompanied luggage, the rest of our baggage to go separately 'by other means'. 'Other means' – what were we to understand by that? And two Hurricanes with long-range tanks would be attached temporarily to the squadron to enable us to familiarize ourselves with our new mounts. They would be the tropicalized version (more than a pointer, that) and would all be brand new. Brand new Mark 1s.

We were all struck dumb. Mark 1s! Oh, *no*! Not again! We were back again on the old, out-distanced, out-performed, out-everythinged Mark 1, and this time the tropicalized version, which was even slower and less combat-worthy than those we had flown in the Battle of Britain. *Anything,* it appeared, was good enough for the overseas units. A remark made to me months before by my father came to mind: 'Take my word for it, when you are in the Services, the further you are from London, the worse off you are likely to be in terms of equipment – and consideration!' If that were correct, we were surely bound for the Far East!

Both elated and sobered by the news, we went about our business; another major sweep over France, a long night's vigil at Debden waiting for a scramble that didn't come, and convoy patrols. Endless convoy patrols! My last operational flight from North Weald was on 29 April; a convoy patrol of more than one and a half hour's duration. After almost a year of strenuous combat flying, it seemed that we were to go out with merely a whimper.

Meanwhile, so many new faces were appearing in our midst that I gave up trying to keep track of who was in my flight. As I was the only flight commander at the time, a new officer arrived, a Flight Lieutenant F. V. 'Tony' Morello, who looked very much like his name, dark and Italian, though very English-sounding and pleasant.

And the two tropicalized Hurricanes appeared, each with 44-gallon underwing drop-tanks and a bulky Vokes filter disfiguring the nose. With all the built-in headwinds, I thought they looked dreadful and climbed aboard one of them with a heavy heart. Same old Hurricane 1! Then some expert appeared to tell us that, used economically, it would fly 1,020 miles, or for six hours and twenty minutes. I remember thinking sourly, not with me in it it wouldn't! Hurricane 1s, for heaven's sake!

After which, I went on leave for a week, my left arm stiff with jabs and laden with pith helmets and masses of heavy woollen khaki stockings and unwearable shorts and shirts. Who on earth designed this stuff, and when? I thought of General Gordon's army going down the Nile to Khartoum fifty years before in temperatures of more than 100 degrees, wearing thick, flannel spine pads! Well, we didn't have spine pads, but we seemed to have everything else!

The arrangement was that we should all meet on Euston station on 8 May before journeying up to Liverpool by train. Liverpool! My birthplace and where I had spent much of my childhood. What an odd coincidence.

4   Journey to the Middle East

I arrived on Euston station shortly before 8 a.m. The train was already at the platform and most of the squadron were in our reserved compartments, looking decidedly jaded. Some of the tales I was greeted with were harrowing. The South Africans, Rhodesians and others without an English base, had indulged in a final orgy of good-fellowship in the Coconut Grove and other places of doubtful reputation, and were barely able to tell the time. Having returned to North Weald from one of these exhausting forays, one officer had dozed off when low-flying in one of the new long-range Hurricanes and had only come to when his aircraft was in the act of ploughing through the topmost branches of a tree. Surfacing with a jerk and recognizing catastrophe a mere second away, by a miracle of reaction he had snatched the aircraft from disaster and was counting himself lucky to be accompanying us. Had the Commander-in-Chief, Middle East been treated to the sight of one of his reinforcing squadrons, he would probably have retired that night in no easy frame of mind.

We arrived at Lime Street, Liverpool, in the early afternoon. There was a heavy overcast and it was foggy. But the air of desolation within the station was only a foretaste of what lay beyond.

The city had endured seven nights of almost continuous bombing, the previous night being the most recent. The main square, on to which the station faced, together with John Brown Street and the area around St George's Hall, was deserted – and this at 1.30 p.m.! The streets were patterned with hoses and blocked with fire-engines and ambulances whilst on all sides, columns of smoke arose from unseen fires

70

before spreading out like a dark stain in every direction. The stench was abominable. This was Liverpool! My Liverpool! The city I had grown up in! I was stunned into silence.

It is a testimony to the resilience of youth and the rapidity with which one becomes accustomed to catastrophe in war that, after the first shock of being confronted by such chaos, we surveyed the devastation more with interest than concern. Clutching our belongings, we piled into three-tonners and set off for the Gladstone Dock at the Seaforth end of the city. Then, as we proceeded at snail's pace along the dock road – an unhappy choice in all conscience – bumping and wallowing between the craters and the paraphernalia of fire-fighting and rescue work, we were treated to the depressing spectacle of twenty or more ships in the basins and docks, in varying postures of defeat – listing, lying or simply upturned – many smoking and on fire, some upright but twisted and shattered by high explosive.

To our right, huge warehouses which I had explored as a child when bulging with sugar, cotton and the produce of a dozen nations – all redolent with nostalgic aromas – burned and crumbled, cascading showers of sparks into the smoke and mist. And all around, tired men in soiled uniforms hurried about like worker-ants, picking their way across ground criss-crossed and littered with the appliances of rescue. A weird and terrible sight, hell reconstituted!

After a stop-go journey of more than half an hour, we turned to the left and there, much smaller than I had expected, a flat-topped silhouette in the heavy mist – dark, grey, war-stained and silent. HMS *Furious*! Motionless in a green-black cesspool of jetsam-strewn water, with gulls wheeling and crying overhead, her spectral outline suggested a breaker's yard rather than a major ship of war. We halted and dropped stiffly to the ground. A voice, thick with awe and foreboding, breathed in my ear: 'Cripes! Are we going to war in *that*?'

Preconceived notions are often far from the mark. My *Boys Own Paper* image of the Royal Navy, with which I had enjoyed little contact prior to 1941, was of ships pristine in appearance, of jolly Jack Tars in bare feet, knuckling their forelocks and holystoning the decks until they shone, and of officers with jutting jaws and white-topped hats set at rakish angles, crying 'Close the enemy!' or 'Keel-haul the dogs!' Alas, HMS *Furious* was a great disappointment. As we approached with our bags like a group of itinerant salesmen and gazed up at its steep rusting side, concern was reflected in every face. Was this the right ship? Surely the Navy could do better than this!

Our arrival was greeted with total indifference. Laden with luggage, we stumbled up the gangway and, as carefully briefed at North Weald, solemnly saluted the quarter-deck, although few of us would have recognized that area of the ship had it been introduced with a fanfare of trumpets. Then, we were pushing and shoving our way below through the crowded, clanging, banging, steel-sided corridors towards our quarters. En route, I suddenly became aware of a Royal Marine standing properly-at-ease with rifle and bayonet. As I squeezed past, the man eyed me so sourly that I had the uncomfortable feeling that were I to decide at that late stage that a voyage to the Middle East was not exactly what I had in mind, I would have had trouble convincing him and no doubt a few others on board.

Being a flight commander, I rated a cabin of my own – all of six feet square! There was a high-sided, rock-solid bunk, some heavy mahogany drawers, an electric fire, and tubes, channels, holes and pipes seemingly by the dozen, each of which appeared to hiss, suck, blow, howl, or in some other way contribute to the cacophony of sound that appeared to be part and parcel of every cabin, corridor, corner and area of that ship. The reason for the Navy's unparalleled record of defiance in the face of overwhelming odds was plain to see: the order to surrender never percolated down to the crew through all the din!

Later, in search of a little tranquillity, I found my way to the flight deck. Crossey and several others were already there, still reeling from the news that they would be sleeping in hammocks. Like redundant grave-diggers, we stood around, hands in pockets, and watched as a continuous stream of ant-like figures threaded its way to and from the dockside carrying boxes, bags, crated stores, 20 mm cannons, ammunition, and every shape and size of commodity capable of being transported by hand. Above us, cranes clanked and whirred as netted stores and tarpaulined mysteries came swinging dangerously in our direction. A dozen times, we shifted hastily to the roars of, 'Mind yer backs!' and other instructions more crudely expressed and in no way considerate of our rank and status. Clearly, this was not a naval crew, these were pirates! There was not a uniform in sight, no white hats at rakish angles, no forelocks being knuckled, nothing. Not even an aircraft. This was certainly not the Navy I had read about!

Word then filtered through that the ship had received a direct hit during the night, a 500 lb bomb, apparently, striking the back end. Deciding to examine the damage, we wandered astern but, after poking our noses into several places and nearly being asphyxiated by hot and pungent fumes rising mysteriously through grilles at the rear of the flight deck, we found neither bomb nor hole and concluded facetiously that either it was lying unexploded in the basement or that it had gone right through, in which case the ship was probably not floating at all but sitting on the bottom! Such was our nervous and childish mood and the nature of the remarks we exchanged.

Within the hour, it was announced that we would be moving out of Liverpool with all haste; the Royal Navy at that time – indeed, at *all* times – had a phobia about air attacks and those in charge were plainly in no mood to face another night in a prime target area. By late afternoon, tugs had appeared, the ship began to tremble and produce froth at one end and, sliding gently astern, we manoeuvred backwards into the Mersey. After which, enveloped still in a thick mist so that no land was visible in any direction, we forged slowly towards the bar and into the Irish Sea, finally working up to twenty knots and heading blindly towards the north. Soon after came dusk then bone-chilling darkness, at which point we all retreated to the warmth and comfort of the wardroom and later to our sleeping quarters.

By no stretch of the imagination could it be said that I had a restful night as my cabin appeared to be the focal point of every sound that was manufactured within the hull. It was patently obvious that I was travelling in an enormous steel-sided sounding box so that every blow and bang reverberated with deafening intensity. Somewhere, I concluded, a sailor had been specially briefed to drop one of the anchors at 30-minute intervals throughout the night so that a shattering crash resembling the noise from a thousand cymbals would ricochet from a hundred steel walls within the ship until, satisfied no doubt that everything built of flesh and blood had been reduced to a quivering jelly, it would filter out through a hundred nooks and crannies to disappear into the blackness beyond. I woke twenty times, on each occasion to whistles, hisses, suckings and bangs, my only consolation being that a torpedo strike in the next cabin was likely to pass entirely unnoticed.

I was awakened finally by silence and an almost eerie atmosphere of suspense. I sat bolt upright in my high-sided bunk and decided that we had reached wherever it was we were going and, dressing hurriedly, threaded my way aloft. Up on the flight-deck in the pale, clear light of a cool early morning, I saw that we were in a bay surrounded by hills, the whole scene tinted delicately in the palest of yellows, greens, blues and purples – a most moving experience. It was Scotland – Scotland at its loveliest. We were anchored off Greenock.

Around the *Furious,* there seemed to be 1,000 ships, motionless in a wide expanse of water, although, in reality, there were probably no more than forty. Next to us, about 100 yards away, the lip of the funnel and the top of the mast and superstructure of what was obviously a destroyer peeped almost mischievously out of the water, the ship itself appearing to be firmly planted on the bottom. It turned out to be a destroyer of the French Navy which had decided to join the Allied cause and which, with typical Gallic flair, had apparently sunk itself, the word going around that its crew had somehow contrived to launch one of their own torpedoes which, after careering around the bay like an intoxicated dolphin, had returned most inconveniently to sink its erstwhile owner. I remember laughing and pulling a face at what was so obviously a tall story and one which had clearly been embellished in the telling. But, whatever the truth of the matter, the destroyer was on the bottom right enough and presumably didn't get there on its own. In any case, we were prepared to believe almost anything of the French; they were decidedly unpopular at the time, Marshal Pétain having recently gone across to the enemy, and it was just the sort of damn silly thing that they were likely to do. Poetic justice, in fact.

Later that day – it was Friday, 9 May – we went ashore in order to bid a final farewell to Britain, home and beauty. If we had heard about the air attacks on Clydeside, which presumably we had, I, for one, was not fully aware that Greenock had been heavily bombed on the nights of the 5th and 6th. Nor was I prepared for the melancholy sights I was shortly to witness.

We were first confronted with the results of the Luftwaffe's handiwork when, on stepping off the liberty boat, we encountered a compound in which there were a dozen or more Catalina flying boats piled one upon the other in total chaos – mutilated, crushed, destroyed. Then, in the town proper, we were confronted by a funeral procession half-a-mile long as a score or more hearses proceeded at snail's pace to the place of burial. If our morale was in the doldrums before, it reached an all-time low as we stood and surveyed the lines of grieving faces, standing as we did among the onlookers three-deep on the pavements. Then, as the crowds drifted away, we became aware that the whole town was closed, all, that is, other than one rather seedy-looking bookshop, whose front door had been left furtively ajar. There, I purchased two small books[1] published by the pretentiously named 'Thinker's Library', one being the classic 'The Life of Jesus' by the renegade priest Ernest Renan, which I carried off probably with the subconscious thought that it might prove a useful crib were I suddenly to turn up unexpectedly at the Pearly Gates.

Back on board, we found the ship had been tidied up and the flight deck cleared. We knew that our aircraft were down below in the hangar but the word was that, as chaos reigned there, it was an area best left alone. Instead, we tried to familiarize ourselves with naval routine, to find the wardroom without doing a tour of the entire ship, and to keep in touch with other members of the squadron in different parts of the vessel.

As the day drew to a close, it was fairly obvious that we were about to move off again and, with most of us squadron pilots lined up on the flight deck, the engines began to tremble and the *Furious* nosed its way towards the sea. Left, right, and in the distance, other ships kept pace with us – six or eight destroyers, a biggish looking ship later identified as the eight-inch gun cruiser HMS *London,* and a massive but squat creation on the horizon which looked as if it might be a battleship.

I found myself alongside an elderly, weather-beaten naval man who nodded in its direction.

'See that thing over there which looks like the *Kay-Gee-Five*?'[2] I nodded – cautiously. 'Well, it isn't!' My informant was almost smacking his lips. 'It's the old *Centurion,* which we've used as a target ship for donkey's years. All the guns and upperworks are made of wood and, as it's only carrying a skeleton crew and won't do more than twelve knots, we've got a long trip ahead of us.'

Reduced to silence by this chilling piece of intelligence, my mind grappled with the prospect of our taking on a brace

[1] I still have them, as I write.
[2] The new battleship, HMS *King George V.*

of German pocket-battleships with our principal means of defence a twelve-knot, First World War hulk with wooden guns!

Reading my thoughts, the man gave a twisted smile. 'You needn't worry, old son, the *London* there is capable of taking on anything we're likely to come across.'

I looked at the venerable square lines of the *London* which was trotting beside us like an Old English sheepdog, and was not entirely reassured.

Soon after, when daylight began to fade, we all went below. Later, and alone, I climbed up to the flight deck again and, with a chill night wind plucking fiercely at my hair and clothes, stared blindly into the velvety blackness, uncomfortably aware that we were in the centre of a dozen or so hidden ships. As a tiny precaution, I offered a silent prayer that the chaps doing the steering be given a little Divine guidance so that they wouldn't either run into each other or trip over an island they had somehow overlooked on their charts.

When I awoke the following morning, we were well and truly into the Atlantic. The sea heaved and tumbled with a terrible slow intensity and the *Furious* creaked, trembled and groaned like a 16th-century galleon. Up on the flight deck the wind tore us to pieces, but I noted with satisfaction that our escorts, spread out from horizon to horizon, were more or less where I expected them to be, the nearest being the *London* which sat comfortably on our starboard side, some 400 yards away, a formidable moustache of white creaming from the plunging knife of its bow. Above, the clouds were dark and low enough to touch and it was clear that the weather was determined to be as beastly as it possibly could.

In the days that followed, it deteriorated to such an extent that the destroyers were frequently lost to sight in the huge troughs between the mountainous, wind-snatched waves. Heaving, soaring and butting their way forward, they seemed to spend most of their time below water and, magnificent spectacle though it was, my heart went out to their occupants for whom life must have been intolerable.

Conditions eventually became so bad that plaintive winks were received from them, asking that the speed be even further reduced so that, for a time, we were forced to proceed at a fast walking pace until the wind and sea had abated.

By the time we had reached mid-Atlantic, we had established something of a routine and could find our way about. With three RAF squadrons on board, the ship was vastly overcrowded and there was a clockwise one-way traffic system. As the Navy seemed to do everything at a thumping double, to attempt to go against the tide invited not only the coarsest of comment but physical abuse as well. The Navy, I decided, was a brutal organization; the officers berated the crew in the crudest of terms and everyone thumped and banged about amid a constant barrage of piping and incomprehensible chatter over the Tannoy system. Meanwhile, we, the RAF contingent, cowered in our various corners as this strange race of men went about its duties in bludgeoning style, hurrying to and fro and up and down holes in the decks like monkeys on sticks. The only stationary humans, it seemed, were the Marines with their sour looks and rifles at the ready; there, no doubt, to quell mutinies.

As the Royal Navy ponderously manoeuvred its iron charges around the Atlantic, the focal point of the Air Force's seaborne existence became the wardroom, towards which we all gravitated unsteadily like nervous dogs seeking the solace of a fireside basket. In the dining room there were white cloths on the tables, something seldom seen in an RAF officers' mess, and my first meal was ruined by the sight of a weathered Lieutenant Commander wolfing down his breakfast clad completely in hat and oilskins. My God! First a set of pirates for a crew, then hats and coats in the dining room! Whatever next?

The wardroom, however, had more acceptable customs, one of which was to serve gin at all hours of the day and night. With grog at only several pence a tot,[1] the allure of

---

[1] Equivalent to about one new penny!

the bar became irresistible and a hard core of at least a dozen in light-blue uniform hung on to it manfully, determined, no doubt, that it should come to no harm as the ship reared, wallowed and creaked its way across the Atlantic. With glistening eyes and lips, they would start off the day quietly benevolent, becoming confidentially chummy by mid-afternoon, garrulously happy by dinner, before lapsing gradually into silence as the night progressed. Finally, owlish with bonhomie and oblivious to the threat of instant destruction posed by lurking U-boats, they could be found in the early hours of the morning, swaying in harmony with the ship's movements, totally and endearingly waterlogged. If some of them ever slept, they managed to do so without my knowledge, remaining at station throughout the entire voyage, a lasting tribute to the endurance of the RAF and its single-minded devotion to a just cause.

There were, even so, some duties to perform for those of us who were not of the ship's company, one such responsibility being to collaborate with the gun-crews, presumably in the belief that we would be more familiar with aircraft of the Luftwaffe than they. We were all allotted stations around the ship and I, to my dismay, found that I had been appointed to one of the larger guns up front. Clad in my most seaworthy garb – an RAF raincoat designed to ward off showers at Royal garden parties! – I struggled forward along the streaming deck until I began to run out of ship. There I found my gun – a whopper![1] – not far removed from the anchor, manned by a huddled group of buccaneers glistening in sea-drenched oilskins. The increase to their number of one officer and high-priced expert from the Royal Air Force left them totally unmoved. I was ignored completely as they went about their various duties with much crashing and banging and harsh, wild cries.

After a time there came a lull and we crouched in a circle like a huddle of gorillas – dripping – as the shuddering prow

---

[1] Two whoppers, in fact; it was a twin turret.

79

of the *Furious* battered its way into the Atlantic and vast showers of spray enveloped us in cold, stinging douches. Meanwhile, a crackling voice on the Tannoy directed questions at us, one of them being: what was the speed of the Stuka dive-bomber? My circle of faces was blankly silent; no-one, other than myself, had the slightest idea and I, by that time in a totally uncooperative mood, was determined to keep quiet. Then, further questions about other aircraft and, finally: what German aircraft was large, had four engines, and could be expected to attack us even in mid-Atlantic? The pirate in charge, a large, shapeless mound of thuggery straight from the seamier end of Liverpool's Scotland Road, thrust a red-eyed, dripping face in my direction.

'Wassat, whack?'

My spirits rose – my chance at last. 'A Lysander', I replied firmly. Then, seeing a look of total bewilderment on his and five other faces, I added convincingly, 'Long-range, of course! Very good aircraft.'

The days dragged by. Whilst we pilots were making our modest contribution towards ensuring the safety of HMS *Furious*, the hangar below was a hive of industry. Hurricanes by the dozen, lashed to the deck, were being prepared for our journey to the Western Desert; long-range tanks were being fitted and electrics tested. Crossey, who was in the habit of visiting my cabin to escape the congestion and bedlam of his own quarters, reported that when the time came, he doubted that there would be sufficient pilots to fly off our allocation of aircraft; several had already fallen down the suicidal ladders that abounded throughout the ship and there had also been casualties among the hammock-dwellers, who, in their first moments of consciousness, were apt to raise their heads smartly, forgetting the existence of a steel deck immediately above.

In groups, we all visited the vast shifting cavern below the flight deck in which our aircraft were tightly quartered like kennelled animals. It was harshly lit and a maze of wings, wheels, tanks, chocks, ropes, mounds of equipment – and pitot heads! The Hurricane pitot head, face-high to a stooping, unsuspecting person with his mind on other matters, was a gruesome implement. To be poked in the eye with one of those was more than just a painful experience and I was informed that at least several walking wounded had already been led away to the sick-bay.

My own aircraft was plainly brand new, as were all the others, and being a tropicalized version of the mark, had the complicated and ungainly muzzle on the air-intake, designed to limit the amount of sand and dust being sucked into the engine. Besides giving the aircraft a most unstreamlined appearance it, and the two 44-gallon long-range tanks, would, I reckoned, reduce the aircraft's performance to little more than that of a nippy Tiger Moth.

Each of us was responsible for ensuring that the electric pumps in our overload tanks were working properly; however, there were no means of verifying this other than by listening carefully for a subdued hum in each tank – no easy task given the noise level in the hangar. As the system required that the extra fuel was passed from overload to internal tanks before reaching the engine, each pilot would be obliged to use first the fuel in his main tanks before replenishing them constantly by pumping petrol from the overloads. If, in the air, the main tanks showed no sign of being replenished, i.e., the pumps were faulty, the unfortunate pilot then had a problem he could do little about. Happily, my tanks and pumps worked perfectly but Crossey's didn't, so that he spent the next hour or so with his ear glued to his aircraft, like some inquisitive tenement dweller absorbed in a next-door quarrel.

More days and nights of tossing and heaving, the weather unrelentingly miserable.

By this time, the reinforcement plan had been explained to us. We had all gathered in the wardroom to be told that we would be tying up at Gibraltar alongside the carrier,

HMS *Ark Royal*. 249 Squadron's Hurricanes would then be man-handled across planks on to the *Ark* where they would remain on the flight deck. Because the Hurricane's wings would not fold and as the *Ark Royal*'s lifts were too small to accommodate our aircraft, all twenty-three would be disposed in such a manner as to enable the carrier's fighters to operate should there be an air attack. Our time of arrival at Gibraltar was also revealed – 9 p.m. on Sunday, 18 May.

With a rapidly drying mouth, I listened to the rest of it. After the contents of the *Furious* – men and machines – had been successfully off-loaded on to the *Ark Royal*, it was intended to collect a larger fleet so that the three carriers, the *Ark Royal*, *Furious* and *Eagle* could be escorted into the Mediterranean. Arriving within 450 miles of Malta, probably at dawn on 21 May, we would be flown off, after which we would be on our own. Then, after a refuelling stop at Malta, there would be a further 850 miles of sea to negotiate before landing at Mersa Matruh, in Egypt. Mersa Matruh! I had never even heard of the place!

The plan finally explained, I thought of the 1,300 miles of water, pretty well all of it in hostile territory, causing me to speculate sombrely that if anything dropped off my aircraft or stopped, I would be *in*, with little hope of ever being rescued. On the other hand, each of us had a dinghy. Even so, the more I thought about it, the less I was enthused, and all the time a mental picture kept appearing of dear old North Weald, our brand new Hurricane 2s, a blazing fire in the ante-room, and quiet games of snooker after dinner. Fool that I was, what was I doing here?

Meanwhile, the weather showing little sign of abating, we plunged and hammered our way southwards at a steady twelve knots. The *London* continued to sit steadfastly abreast of us, and ahead, astern, and on either side, the destroyers put in an occasional appearance above the waves. From time to time, there would be a brief winking session between the ships, otherwise, there seemed to be little communication or fuss.

Regularly, around midday, the Navigation Officer would appear in the wardroom, looking very wise and authoritative, in order to pin up a chart showing our position and those of the U-boats believed to be in our approximate area. The procedure thereafter seemed routine but nonetheless disturbing; wherever the U-boats were, there we made for, presumably in the belief that those were the spots we would be least expected.

As the days elapsed, strange faces in the wardroom became familiar and even friendly and the different rank stripes – straight, wavy and others – together with their colour code, began to make sense. Padres, 'pussers', doctors, engineers and 'real sailors', seemed all on an equal footing. And rightly so; when all was said and done, when the ship went down they *all* went down, regardless of rank or calling. Not a bit like the Air Force where some warriors I could name were likely to pass the entire war without coming within earshot of even the smallest bang.

It was early on in the voyage, too, that I and others had been invited to assist in censoring the mail, as the result of which a new dimension was added to my education. The lower deck, God bless it, was totally uninhibited when it came to discussing its more personal needs and more than once I found myself wriggling in embarrassment as my fellow countrymen revealed to me the activities that were clearly taking place the length and breadth of Britain. Brought up in the belief that my sceptred isle was the home of knights, gentlemen, honest yeomen and virginal maidens, I was harshly introduced to reality; gentlemen were clearly at a premium and virginal maidens as scarce as hens' teeth.

After an endless ten days at sea, we were somewhere south-west of Gibraltar. By the eighth day, the weather had improved considerably and it was an emotional moment for me when I first glimpsed the faint and distant outline of the Atlas mountains in Morocco. As we edged northwards and to the east, the Rock of Gibraltar eventually appeared and in the gathering dusk, we threaded our way in silence between scores of buoys and ships before gently jostling alongside the quay, back-to-back with the towering *Ark Royal.* I consulted my watch. It was 9 p.m. on the button!

5   Flight to Malta

In the warm and sultry blackness of the Mediterranean night, Gibraltar was a blaze of light, a stirring and nostalgic sight for those of us who had lived in conditions of blackout for almost two years. Gathering our meagre belongings, we bade farewell to the *Furious* and stumbled along the debris-strewn dockside towards the *Ark*. Above us, planks had already gone down and the first of our aircraft were being trundled across.

The *Ark Royal* was as different from the *Furious* as chalk is from cheese; it was bigger, cleaner, brighter, more orderly, more civilized and, above all, more comfortable. I was shown to my cabin in which the bunk, though dauntingly hard and with a hump down the middle, seemed positively inviting. Also, thank God, there were no sepulchral noises – no bangs, clatters, howls, anchors being dropped or subterranean gurgles. Only a decent civilized hiss, which no fair-minded chap could possibly object to.

In the wardroom, huge by comparison with that of the *Furious,* we were greeted formally by officers in mess-kit and regaled with drinks before dinner. From our hosts we learned that we would be sailing as soon as the transfer of aircraft had been completed. Later, much later, with pink gins fairly slopping around inside, I returned to my cabin, my morale restored absolutely by the sophistication of my surroundings and the courtesy of my new-found friends. Then, in the wee small hours, tremors and subdued grumblings started up somewhere underfoot and, in a cosy, gin-induced stupor, I concluded that we were once more heading seawards and about to embark on phase two of our death-defying journey to the Western Desert. Good ol' Navy, I thought; Cap'n Bligh, or whoever, would probably know the way. Two points to starboard, if you please, Mister Christian! Dear God! If only the sides of this cabin would keep still.

The following day was warm and bright and the Navy being resplendent in whites, we donned our tropical kit, most of us I suspect, a little self-consciously. I ascended to the flight deck, a vast aircraft-strewn platform, and sniffed the salt-laden south Atlantic air. Mmmm! Delicious! All around, the sea was blue and calm and, in every direction, there were light-coloured ships, proceeding at a leisurely pace and heading more or less in a westerly direction. A truly magnificent sight.

That, of course, was the trick. Because the German consul sat at Algeçiras, a stone's throw from Gibraltar, and spied on all the port's activities, if it were necessary to go into the Mediterranean, the Royal Navy invariably sailed into the Atlantic, only to sneak back through the Straits at dead of night. The Germans, needless to say, were well aware of this simple subterfuge and the game of bluff was apt to become so involved, it became a problem to decide who was fooling whom.

However, after the liquid entertainment of the night before, my mind was in no fit state to dwell upon anything more involved than sunbathing and counting the vessels as they appeared over the horizon. Which they continued to do throughout the day as, in a gentle, swaying meander, we picked up two battleships, the *Rodney* and *Renown,* at least one elegant Sheffield-class cruiser, and a further clutch of white-moustached destroyers which served as a screen as far as the eye could see. There were smaller cruisers, too, of what I always chose to call the *Aurora* class, that ship itself becoming all too familiar in the months ahead. The faithful *London* was also there, together with the carriers *Furious* and *Eagle,* the former giving more than a hint of the First World War cruiser from which she had been converted, whilst the angular *Eagle,* poor thing, was reminiscent of nothing more exciting than a floating shoe-box. In all, there must have been twenty ships, a mighty display of naval strength, enough to make any Englishman's heart swell with pride. No enemy force in its right mind would dare attack us. Even so, I was glad to be on the *Ark*. Good old *Ark*; almost the largest ship in the fleet – and furthest away from the water!

On the night of 19/20 May, we crept silently through the Straits of Gibraltar heading east. When dawn broke, we were well into the Mediterranean, with the Navy visibly dry-mouthed and nervously on edge.

After twenty months of often bitter strife, Britain's war effort in the Middle East, and especially in the Mediterranean, had not been too successful. There was scarcely a blob of pink left on the map between Gibraltar and Egypt; in the Western Desert, what would be called the 8th Army cantered to and fro on what was sportingly referred to later as the Benghazi Handicap; Greece had fallen only weeks before, and a savage battle for Crete was in progress, soon to be lost.

Throughout this unhappy period, the Royal Navy suffered grievously. Two battleships, *Warspite* and *Valiant,* together with the carrier *Formidable,* were within days of being put out of action around Crete; the cruiser and destroyer force was still reeling from a stunning series of losses; and *Illustrious,* one of Britain's latest carriers, together with its supporting force, had been severely damaged when reinforcing Malta several months earlier. Small wonder, therefore, that the Navy had an almost obsessive horror of bombing attacks. They hated all aircraft and were apt to fire without warning at anything that moved, asking no questions and offering few excuses if the unfortunate target happened to be friendly.

The Fleet Air Arm, too, was beset by problems. Very much a Cinderella service, it was poorly equipped with Fulmars, as fighters, and Swordfish, as torpedo-bombers. The Fulmar was a large two-seater and a direct descendant of the Fairey Battle, a name which struck a chill in the heart of any RAF pilot who had had the misfortune to fly one during the first year of the war. With a performance considerably inferior to that of the Hurricane 1, the Fulmar was outclassed by almost everything used by both the Germans and Italians. As for the Swordfish, a biplane which would not have looked out of place even in 1918, it was alleged – apocryphally no doubt – that their comparative immunity during the successful battle of Taranto was due to the enemy not having gunsights capable of accommodating anything that flew quite so slowly.

Fortunately, however, and with outstanding bravery, the pilots of the Fleet Air Arm ignored the unfitness of their mounts and roared into battle with the stoutest of hearts, tolerating their Fulmars and positively doting on their 'Stringbags'. This quite extraordinary loyalty, to the Swordfish in particular, came to the fore when, over a large pink gin, I was commiserating with a group of the *Ark*'s naval aviators on the shortcomings of their aircraft. I was rewarded with silence and such icy stares that for a moment I thought I might be given a taste of the lash. On what other aircraft, I was coldly asked, could I carry ashore a fully-laden motor-cycle, strapped between either the undercarriage legs or the interplane struts? To which I was tempted to reply, in what circumstances would I ever wish to? Thankfully, I had the good sense to keep quiet.

Throughout the daylight hours of 20 May and beneath a solid cloud bank, the Mediterranean, anything but blue, streamed by, every ship trembling with apprehension as we ploughed towards the east. Up on the flight deck we ran our engines, tested everything we could lay hands on, and attended briefings.

There were 23 Hurricanes of 249 Squadron and about a similar number for each of the squadrons on the two other carriers, *Furious* and *Eagle*. Those of us on the *Ark* would be taking off in two batches, one of twelve and the other eleven, the first to be led by 'Butch' Barton and the second by myself. I was happy to afford 'Butch' pride of place; he would be twelve aircraft nearer the sharp end!

We were also faced with the pressing problem of where to store our belongings, including the two ridiculous pith helmets, which, though light, were extremely bulky. Each of us had 30 lbs of clothing and essentials to find a home for but the Hurricane, being a fighter, had room for little more than a couple of maps. In the event, our kit was crammed anywhere and everywhere – in the radio compartment behind the armour plate, tied to the 'floor' in the rear of the fuselage, left and right of the pilot's seat, and in the ammunition boxes in the wings, the 3,000 rounds of .303 being removed for that purpose. This last arrangement had us chuckling; if the enemy were sighted en route, we would be able to give them a quick squirt of McLean's toothpaste from all eight guns, followed by a little of the hard stuff – a few bars of Lifebuoy soap!

In the operations room in the island of the carrier, we drew lines on maps and wrote down courses. For reasons of security, we would be flying just above the water and maintaining RT silence throughout, and each group of Hurricanes would be escorted by a Fulmar; as the naval fighter carried an observer-navigator in the back, this was felt to be a prudent measure. Which led to a rather odd discovery: besides whatever else the observer carried in his cockpit, the beneficent Navy provided him with a Thompson sub-machine gun, one of the Al Capone variety. We discussed this choice of weapon with incredulous laughter. A Tommy-gun, for heaven's sake! With a range of about 20 yards! What on earth was that for? Then, on second thoughts, we decided it was probably for the observer to shoot the pilot, then himself, if things got out of hand.

The route we were to take was anything but straightforward. After take-off, we would fly for about an hour before sighting Cap Bon on the northern tip of Africa, where, more than likely, we would be intercepted by the Vichy French with their Curtiss Hawk 75s, an aircraft they had recently bought from the Americans. That our ex-allies were hostile, we knew; whether or not they would attack us, remained to be seen.

After Cap Bon, there would be a dog-leg to avoid the island of Pantelleria, inhabited by Hun Me 110s we were told, taking care thereafter to skirt both Lampedusa and Linosa, both enemy-held. Finally, with God's grace, we would hit Malta, whereupon we were to circle Filfla Rock, to the south of the island, in order to identify ourselves, before landing, one-third each, on the airfields of Ta Kali, Luqa and Hal Far. In all, we would be flying about 450 miles over a period of two and a half hours, a journey well within our maximum range and endurance of just over 1,000 miles and six and a half hours, respectively.

The decision that we were to fly off at dawn the following day was greeted with glum disapproval. Dawn! The Air Force seemed obsessed with dawns, whereas I, not being a dawn person, heartily disliked them. Dawn patrol brought to mind Errol Flynn and the old Sopwith Camel, with life at its lowest ebb. Why not mid-morning, or mid-afternoon, even? If I had to risk my neck, I always felt I should be permitted to do so on a full stomach and after a good night's sleep – preferably both! But, dawn it had to be, apparently. On Wednesday, 21 May.

The early morning of the fateful day was anything but welcoming, being damp, chilly, heavily overcast and as black as a boot. Four hours flying-time to the east, the battle for Crete was raging to a desperate and tragic conclusion.

Silent and yawning, we went in single file to one of the deserted dining-rooms and were each handed a fried breakfast through a serving hatch by a member of the kitchen staff whose bare and bulging arms were liberally garnished with red-and-blue pictures referring to *Love, Mother,* and a lady called *Doris.* The malevolent yellow eye of an egg stared back at me unwinkingly. There was little conversation as we ate and all the time the ship trembled in spasms with the exertion of maintaining twenty knots.

Up on the flight deck, the wind tore at our clothes and hair as we assembled, shivering, in the operations room for a final briefing. Then out into the darkness again, threading our way between a mass of wings and propellers, maps and papers in hand, feeling empty and not at all happy. Lord, it was chilly! And damp! And miserable! Suddenly, another nostalgic vision of dear old North Weald, so far away now but so very, very desirable.

I climbed into my Hurricane and once in the cockpit felt rather better. The one small map-pocket already stuffed tight with some anonymous garment, I wedged my maps and the all-important paper on which were written the courses we were to follow, into the windscreen crevasse to the left of the gunsight. All around me were towels, shirts, my raincoat and service dress hat and some of the essentials of day-to-day living. Between me and my parachute proper, was the new pilot-type dinghy with its rock-hard gas-cylinder already very much in evidence against one bone of my backside. Some judicious wriggling helped a little, but not very much. Safety demanded its price!

For a time, nothing; the carrier slowly swayed in trembling surges, left and right, up and down. Then the twelve aircraft ahead of me were starting up; no appreciable noise, just airscrews dissolving into blurs as the reflected light caught them with a ghostly sheen. After that, a weirdly attired officer with illuminated wands in his hands, his head nodding and his face mouthing some incomprehensible instruction, was motioning to me. I turned on the fuel, primed the engine, set the throttle and flicked up the mag. switches before pressing the button which turned the airscrew. It moved around, jerked once – twice – before the engine caught with a sudden surge, acrid blue smoke spouting from each side. I throttled back to 1,200 revs and let her warm up. Ahead, pink and blue tongues of flame rippled from the exhausts and the Hurricane rocked slightly as a gusting 30-knot wind plucked at its sides. It was quite dark still but with a growing greyness.

Suddenly I was aware of the ship moving ponderously to the left as she turned into wind and the tremors and shaking grew to a minor frenzy as she wound up to 30 knots. A thin pencil-line of white smoke trailed backwards from the prow, soon to come directly down the centre-line of the deck. The *Ark Royal* was ready. Waiting!

With the coolant temperature showing 60 degrees and with encouragement from the man with the wands, I ran up my engine, exercised the constant-speed unit, and tested the switches. Everything sweet and even. I then set my compass and direction indicator, checked my gauges and settings several times over, adjusted the tail trimmer and lowered the flaps fifteen degrees. Finally, with a swift tug at my straps, I nodded to the wandsman beneath me. I was ready for off.

For several minutes I was kept waiting. Ahead, the first of the twelve Hurricanes began to take off. Spotted in groups of three, each aircraft moved first to the centre-line, then, under the influence of full throttle and with each rudder giving a brief but defiant wag, one aircraft after another surged forward, tail raised, and took off, rising like a lift in a climbing turn to the left.

Then the wandsman again, waving urgently and beckoning in exaggerated gestures. My turn! My mouth dry, I opened up and taxied forward, straightening on the centre-line. The wands gyrating, urging me to rev up. *Up! Up!* Then suddenly, with a sweep of the arm – *Down*! I was *off*!

With full throttle but only a modest 6¼ lbs showing on the boost-gauge and my tail up almost immediately, I set off down the deck at a smart walking pace, my Hurricane feeling ridiculously light. The island drifted by, faces gawping. At this rate I would be airborne in seconds. This really was a stroll!

A moment later I was in the air, despite the extra 88 gallons of fuel, the deck dropping away beneath. In my left hand, I grasped the throttle and clutched a duplicate of the paper on which were written the various compass headings that would take us all to Malta. Veering immediately to the left and away from the ship's prow with its great curving bow-wave – wouldn't do to drop in front of that charging brute! – I changed hands on the control column in order to retract the wheels, the selector being on the right-hand side of the cockpit.

I had barely slipped the knob into the 'UP' position when there was a loud bang, as though a paper bag had been exploded in my left ear. The aircraft dropped a wing sharply and began to fly sideways in an alarming manner. Horror-stricken, I grabbed at the throttle and as the Hurricane continued to slew wildly to the left, was assailed by a flurry of white missiles. The paper on which my courses had been written and which I had released involuntarily when diving for the throttle, zipped past my head to disappear into the great wide world beyond, and with a disconcerting 'whap', the maps and other papers I had so deftly tucked into the windscreen crevasse were sucked out of their hideaway to wrap themselves briefly round my head before being snatched away by the slipstream.

My first and instant diagnosis was that I had lost the port wing-tank. The aircraft, at low speed, was barely controllable even with hard right rudder and full stick and was slipping sideways and downwards disastrously. For one terrible moment, I thought I was bound for the water some 50 feet beneath, but the briefest of glances to my left enabled me to recognize that, although the tank was probably still in place, something almost as unpleasant had occurred. The largest of the gun and ammunition panels on the top surface of the port wing had come adrift and a piece of metal several square feet in area was sticking up at an angle of about 45 degrees, having jammed in its triumphant moment of escape. Obviously, the McLean's toothpaste and Lifebuoy soap had tried to make a break for it with the result that I now had an unwanted third aileron fully applied, as well as a very effective airbrake on my left side. Rigid with fear, I raised the flaps and climbed away with tight and trembling hands, thinking wildly that I would have to land back on the *Ark* immediately and wondering how on earth I was going to do so without a hook and with two overload tanks bulging with fuel and just aching to catch fire. Moreover, there was the aerodynamic effect of the breakaway panel to consider, which meant that I would have to approach the deck at a much higher speed than would otherwise be necessary. Whichever way I looked at it, the outlook was bleak. Engrossed absolutely with keeping the Hurricane out of the water, I dismissed from my mind completely the maps and other papers. To hell with them, they could swim!

As I laboured around the *Ark* in a wide circle at about 300 feet, the other members of my group of eleven began to catch up and formate on me, silent, gawping and totally unaware of my predicament. Below, the carrier's deck looked no bigger than a handkerchief and, on its far side, suddenly – a Fulmar. Our Fulmar!

The engine now well throttled back to 0 lbs boost and 1,800 revs, my Hurricane behaved a little more reasonably. With the gun-panel resolutely rampant, at the higher speed of 170 miles per hour, surprisingly, a little less opposite stick was required but, without a rudder bias, the load on my right foot was painfully tiring after barely two minutes, so that the prospect of two more hours with it in that position was mind-boggling. But – and it was a big but – the alternative was to land back on, and that was even less attractive. The decision, therefore, was not hard to make: it was Malta for me, with or without a usable limb at the end of the journey. In a loose gaggle around the Fulmar, therefore, and with me in the lead, we turned eastwards and set off; with luck I would not even need my sheaf of maps and courses. Shaking and breathless still, I gazed around; the gently heaving sea was endlessly grey in every direction, glittering like molten lead in the early morning gloom.

After about 30 minutes, when my main tanks had emptied sufficiently, I tried transferring fuel and was gratified to see that everything appeared to be working normally. My right leg, which was awkwardly pushed forward almost to its full extent, had long since begun to tremble and grow numb but as I was able to keep changing hands on the control column, my arms did not tire unduly. Those first

30 minutes, though, seemed endless. I consulted my watch regularly, listening and watching for strange happenings up front, but the big Merlin engine was buzzing away quite happily, obviously determined to be cooperative, so that after a time I forgot about it, the wretched gun-panel, my own acute discomfort, and the possibility of missing Malta altogether, being problems of much more immediate concern.

Shortly before the hour, some rocks appeared far off to my right which I concluded were part of Cap Bon. We could expect to be intercepted here by the French and I considered what we might do if attacked. Minutes passed in watchful expectation but no aircraft were seen. Then, when I was just beginning to relax, quite inexplicably and without warning, the Fulmar suddenly began to accelerate and in the space of a mile or two, having left us all standing, pulled up steeply and disappeared into cloud. One moment it was there, the next, it wasn't! *Gone*!

It all happened in seconds. In horrified silence I sat and watched, stunned by the awful significance of its departure. After which, I flew in an aimless curve to my left, my mind grappling weakly for an explanation of its precipitate departure and, more to the point, as I had neither maps nor a list of courses to steer, what I was going to do. Meanwhile, ten Hurricanes, uttering not a word, dutifully followed me about like a trail of lemmings looking for a cliff, wondering, no doubt, what on earth I was up to.

With RT silence to be broken only on pain of death, I flew in a circle without uttering a sound, my mind numb with foreboding. Apart from knowing that Africa was somewhere to the south and Malta approximately to the east, I could have been in Tibet. All around were thousands of square miles of very inhospitable looking water and mist, and immediately overhead – at about 500 feet, in fact – unbroken cloud as far as the eye could see. Behind me trailed my ten disciples, observing my every movement and clearly unaware that I was nearly demented with worry and on the point of tears; a modest 20 years of age and my account barely in credit with the bank of experience, there were precious few resources to call upon.

Then, God-given resolution. To heck with RT silence, we were probably too low for our conversation to be picked up, anyway. Thus reassured, I called up Pat Wells, who was deputy leader, and briefly explained my predicament: would he care to take over the lead? His reply was prompt and devastatingly succinct. *No,* he wouldn't! Then I spoke to the formation at large. Was there anyone capable of leading us to Malta? Silence! Not a word! I can only assume that at that precise moment, *all* their radios suddenly went unserviceable!

I suppose it was the lack of response from my companions that generated a spark of rebellion somewhere beneath my parachute release-box. Bugger it! We couldn't just keep flying in circles in the middle of the Mediterranean. There were only three possible courses of action: to fly south and make a present of ourselves to someone in Africa; to go east for Malta with the probability of missing the island altogether and finishing up in the water; or to go west and return to Gibraltar, using the coast of Africa as a guide. The first option was out of the question, the second I didn't like very much, but the third was a possibility, provided we had sufficient fuel. Desperately, I totted up the miles in my head: a day and a night's sailing at twenty knots – that would be around 650 miles. Add to that an hour's flying at 170 miles per hour. Total, 820 miles, or thereabouts. We could just about do it. Well, almost! Gun-panels and footloads forgotten, I turned my brood about and set course for Gibraltar. And to my everlasting surprise, they all followed, without so much as a word.

As we headed westwards, to describe my feelings as low is to liken a molehill to Everest. I was devastated almost to the point of being physically sick. But, so resilient is the spirit of youth that, after a few minutes, I actually began to perk up. Right or wrong, we were going back to Gibraltar and, God willing, we would all make it safely. In my mind's eye a picture of our arrival took shape. Stap me, they would say when eleven Hurricanes suddenly appeared out of the mist, where have you chaps come from? And I would ask – all innocence, of course – whether we had landed at Ta Kali, Luqa, or Hal Far. This *was* Malta, wasn't it? No? Well, I'd be blowed – it would seem I had flown in the wrong direction! A mere 1,500 miles in the wrong direction! I even managed to raise a smile at the thought of it.

My morale rising as I went, I flew for about 30 minutes on a course of 270 degrees; a little later I would veer south and pick up the African coast, after which it would be easy. There was no turning back now, the die was cast. With my engine running smoothly and everything other than my right leg and backside in fairly good order, my confidence grew by the minute. All we needed now was time.

It was about then that I noticed a change of colour in the water beneath, a streak of lighter green, barely perceptible but there. Immediately, I sensed that I had come across the wake of our returning fleet, sailing hot-foot for safer waters no doubt, and like a hound on the track of a particularly odoriferous fox, I flew with my nose to the trail for some minutes until, there, in the distance and scarcely visible in the haze, the British fleet – pounding for home!

As we approached low down, my aircraft radiating goodwill, our presence had what might euphemistically be described as a stimulating effect on His Majesty's ships. Suspicious as ever of a low-flying attack, every vessel assumed action stations and at least a dozen wheels were thrown about, causing destroyers and cruisers alike to heel over crazily and disperse as quickly as their throbbing screws could urge them. Half-expecting a rash of shell-bursts in my immediate area, I thought desperately of how I could indicate friendly intentions, RT communication being most definitely *out*. I then remembered my downward identification light and my eight-words-per-minute of highly individual Morse Code. What did I say? 'SOS'? 'Don't shoot'? 'Wotcher'? Or just plain 'Friend'? I half-decided that 'Friend' seemed the most appropriate but, in the tension of the moment, couldn't remember 'F' in dahs and dits. Then, it was all too late; we had been recognized.

The *Ark Royal* being somewhere in the middle of all the careering, heeling ships, I climbed up with my silent gaggle of followers and circled it at a respectable height and distance. Far beneath, the carrier's decks were littered with aircraft.

I decided then that we would all have to land-on, hooks or no hooks, and the thought chilled me to the marrow. As the *Ark*'s lifts were too small to take the Hurricanes below, after landing, each one would have to be pushed forward in front of the heavy wire barrier which would then be raised in order to catch the next aircraft should it overshoot – which was more than likely. Not only would it all take time, even assuming there were no accidents, but space on the deck would be severely limited when it became my turn to land-on, the responsibility of leader naturally demanding that I should see everyone safely down and be the last. As I circled and looked down, the more I thought about it, the less attractive the whole business became.

And it was at that point that an aircraft appeared – level with my shoulder before dropping like a hawk towards the *Ark,* landing without ceremony, and clinging on for dear life. It was a Fulmar – our Fulmar. Later, I learned that an oil pipe had burst in front of the pilot, spraying him with hot oil, and anxious to get as far away from the sea as possible and back to the carrier before his engine seized, the unfortunate man had decided to leave us in haste, climbing through the cloud and heading for the fleet. As if we didn't know!

For ten minutes or so, we circled the *Ark* whilst the deck was cleared, an agonizingly slow procedure for all of us looking down. Malta, at that stage, could not have been further from my thoughts as my mind was already attuned to our landing-on.

Then, to my considerable surprise, a Fulmar – another Fulmar – from where I was looking down exactly like a model, crawled to the rear of the ship, turned, then slowly took off. I followed it instinctively and, certainly with no clear idea of what either I or the naval pilot was intending to do, formated on it. The Fulmar then waggled its wings in a friendly fashion, the chap in the back pulled a cheerful face and waved, and ten Hurricanes surged up, left, right and behind me. Looking down at my compass I saw we were heading roughly east again. I then consulted my watch. We had already been airborne for rather more than two hours.

It is sometimes difficult to explain later why one takes a particular course of action. I had no clear idea of what we were about to do or even that the Fulmar was intending to lead us to Malta. But, follow it I did and, thank the Lord, it was. Back again at 300 feet and still maintaining strict RT silence, we clustered around it and with engine settings well reduced and 175 miles per hour on the clock, we settled down on our second attempt to reinforce the Middle East. By the roughest of calculations, there were now about 600 miles between us and Malta, a further three and a half hours of flying for everyone and for me and my right leg, an extended period of pure, undiluted purgatory.

Meanwhile, I had been regularly topping up my main tanks from the overloads and wondering if I might possess a couple of the legendary cornucopias; they seemed bottomless although common sense reasoned that they would soon be empty. And indeed, they were. After two and a half hours of flying, the main-tank contents showed signs of reducing, which meant that I then had less than 90 gallons of fuel remaining.

With the disturbing prospect of landing back on the carrier removed and my Hurricane showing no signs of temperament, I was able to concentrate on my own physical misfortunes. The gun-panel remained stoically obstructive and my right leg ached to the point at which I would have happily agreed to it being sawn off – without an anaesthetic! The metal cylinder in my dinghy-pack, too, was doing its best to cripple me permanently and, to relieve the pressure on the left-hand bone of my backside, I undid my straps and, opening my hood, bounced up and down as far as flying the aircraft and safety would allow. I then rooted about in the bottom of the cockpit and found a towel which I attempted to stuff between my rear and the dinghy-pack. But, to no avail; all my efforts provided only fleeting relief so that I resigned myself to having an insoluble problem for the remainder of the flight. I didn't allow myself even to *think* of the next leg to Mersa Matruh which would involve a further five hours of flying over 850 miles.

When hope of ever seeing land again began to fade, Cap Bon appeared for the second time on my right and we changed course in order to skirt Pantelleria. Meanwhile, the cloud still sat on our heads in a grey and forbidding layer – so much for Mediterranean sunshine! – and we had been flying for so long, it was difficult to comprehend that it was little more than our normal breakfast time. On and on. On and on. Interminably. The Mediterranean couldn't be this big! Then, off to my right, a low mound that I presumed was Pantelleria, at which point I recalled my own firm instructions that no-one was to straggle. I need not have worried; at the first sign of the island, the ten Hurricanes behind me fairly scuttled past so that for a few minutes I actually found myself last in the formation. But of the Hun 110s we saw not a sign, and forty years later I can still raise a rash, speculating on what they might have done to us had they known we were limping past within fifteen miles of their airfield. One German aircraft, a twin-engined bomber, did sail over our heads however, but if the pilot saw us, he had the good sense to ignore us, as indeed with empty guns, we were obliged to ignore him.

From then on, my main preoccupation was considering my fuel state. As leader, I would be better off than the rest of my formation so that the bleats, when they came, would undoubtedly be from those at the rear. As I watched, the two main tanks in my aircraft slowly emptied and I switched on to reserve knowing that only about 30 gallons stood between me and a ditching. From horizon to horizon there was nothing but an endless vista of sea and mist, whilst above, the cloud, though lightening somewhat, still completely obscured the sun.

At this stage we had been airborne for about five hours and I began to pray very earnestly that Malta would materialize. Or, had we already missed it? I had no idea what Malta looked like and visions of the island kept appearing like mirages, only to fade just as quickly into vaporous oblivion. The fear that we had already passed it grew like a cancer.

With a bare fifteen gallons remaining in my reserve tank and little more than a smell of petrol in the mains, I decided to break RT silence. The Fulmar had to be told that we were almost finished and if the enemy tuned in, good luck to him; all he would find would be eleven patches of oil in the sea. I put it as briefly as I could; if we weren't down in fifteen minutes, I announced sombrely, we were all in the water. To this I added a personal and silent message to the duty angel, something to the effect that we would all appreciate a little assistance – if he had a moment or two to spare! But, for some minutes there was no response, no shaft of light, no heavenly revelation, nothing other than mist and sea in every direction.

Malta, when it came, appeared with magical suddenness and in the form of cliffs adjacent to my left ear. They loomed white and brown out of the mist and sea and were almost within touching distance. At the same time, the sun broke through, warm and brilliant, as though to crown our discovery and arrival. A miracle – *the* miracle – had happened!

Filfla rock being just ahead, I made a token dart at it before turning north in order to climb up over the cliffs that formed the island's southern boundary.

As I approached the precipitous edge, my aircraft rocking violently in the up-currents, red tongues of flame darted out all around me. How odd, I thought, cliffs don't usually behave like that! Then I was over the top with barely 50 feet to spare and above the island itself – ochre-coloured sandstone, glaringly bright, tiny brown stone-fringed fields the size of pocket handkerchiefs, everything hot and lumpy and harsh to the eye, a searing landscape of brown and white, utterly different from the Malta of my imagination.

Low that I was, I had no difficulty in picking out the airfield of Luqa; it was dead ahead and I could see the hangars, the pale runways and a scattering of light-brown buildings. I flashed a glance at my fuel gauges. Less than ten gallons remaining. I would go straight in, to heck with a circuit!

Down with the wheels – two green lights. Airscrew in fine pitch – the engine-note rose. Everything bouncing, lurching and bumping. Heavens, was Malta *always* like this? Then the flaps. The aircraft slewing sideways and difficult to handle with the jutting gun-panel, I pulled up the port wing firmly but with the greatest of care and found myself going much too fast. Whoaah! Slow down you brute! About 100 feet up now and the Hurricane fairly jumping about in the convection currents of heat. The runway directly ahead, tilting obliquely. Almost there now, thank God!

Not until I had reached that point did it dawn on me that all was not as it should have been. On the far side of the airfield, the nearest edge of which was about 400 yards away, flame-centred puff-balls exploded into silent flowers of black and brown and a large twin-engined aircraft directly ahead of me disintegrated as if by magic in a violent bubble of flame and oily smoke. And in the several seconds it took for me to interpret these strange goings-on, a stick of bombs came marching towards me with measured strides across the parched brown earth and white streaks of something-or-other flew past my starboard wingtip to curve away into oblivion. I gave a startled glance upwards; so keen was I to get my wheels on the ground, I had never thought of looking in that direction. Immediately above, the sky was filled with white-grey anti-aircraft bursts and pale-bellied aircraft, clearly unfriendly, raced over my head, fortunately in the opposite direction. Great God! I was right in the centre of an air attack! No wonder there had been tongues of flame on the cliffs; they had been anti-aircraft fire, with the gunners obviously not too concerned about my being in their line of sight.

Galvanized into action, I opened up hard and lifting my wheels and flaps in almost frenzied movements, fled away southwards at tree-top height towards Filfla, our planned point of assembly in the event of any such attack.

Within seconds, however, and still hugging the contours of the ground, concern overcame panic. Ten gallons of fuel! What was the point of rushing out to sea if the engine was going to stop as soon as I arrived! If victim I was to be, better by far to be a victim over land rather than in – or under – the water. Without so much as a second thought, I hauled my aircraft about and headed back to the airfield.

Approaching Luqa for the second time, I saw that the raid had passed, although stark evidence of it remained. The twin-engined aircraft I had seen hit was producing a pillar of smoke that could probably be seen in Cairo and there were other fires, too, billowing their filth into the atmosphere, all forming a vast and almost solid pall of drifting dust more than 1,000 feet high. Luqa lay silent, inert and in a way pathetic, like an animal which had just been run over!

All this I noted in a glance but, with surprising and calculated indifference, dismissed it as incidental to my own immediate predicament. My aircraft still bouncing around like a mad thing, I lowered the wheels and flaps yet again and prepared to land on as much of the runway as I could see remained undamaged. Then, with the gun-panel rampant to the end and masses of aileron and right rudder, I shot across the airfield boundary, skidding and slewing and a good twenty miles an hour too fast, and plonked the Hurricane down amid a huge swirl of dust-devils. As the wheels screeched on the hot tarmac, my heart lifted and a prayer of thanks came audibly from my lips. What glorious, wonderful, rock-hard earth! God bless Malta! God bless its drystone walls and tuppenny-ha'penny fields! God bless its bomb-holes! God bless everything about the place! Joyfully, I allowed my

Hurricane to race ahead, its tyres singing in tune with my feelings.

Braking to a stop at the end of the runway and with my engine ticking over as though it hadn't a care in the world, I looked about to see which way to taxi. Not a soul in sight! It was breathtakingly hot, blindingly bright, very quiet, and very still. Except for one other Hurricane, in the middle distance and buzzing faintly around the circuit, I had Luqa entirely to myself – fires, burning aircraft, pillars of black smoke, dust, corruption, stench, the lot!

Undecided, I opened up and moved towards some low buildings half a mile away and after some minutes a solitary khaki-clad figure appeared – with a pipe in its mouth. Running towards me with a hand clutching his hat, the man, a Flying Officer, jumped on to my wing and put his face to my ear. 'Over there,' he screamed, hanging on.

Nodding, I opened the throttle, whereupon the slipstream caught the burning embers of his pipe and whipped them straight into my left eye, which clamped tight, like an oyster, as though someone had poked it with a stick.

There followed several moments of exquisite pain during which I sat there half-blind and streaming, exercising all the self-control I could muster. This *bloody* man! – I even thought of punching him. Then, with bowed head and my remaining good eye, I found myself taking in the clock on my instrument panel and doing some quick mental arithmetic. We had been airborne five hours and twenty-five minutes; probably the longest operational trip ever made by a Hurricane.

I parked my aircraft and, with a trembling sigh of relief, switched off. The airscrew tottered to a clanking standstill and after almost six hours of noise, physical discomfort and tension, the silence and blistering heat were in stark and unforgettable contrast. In the distance the other Hurricane was landing.

And it was then that I found to my embarrassment that I could scarcely move, my right leg being locked in spasm and the left bone of my behind, where the steel CO_2 bottle had impinged for more than five hours, painful beyond description. I tried to rise but couldn't and for a moment thought I would need to be lifted out – except that there was no-one around to help other than the single officer who, by this time, was looking up at me from below and hopping agitatedly from foot to foot.

After a few moments, he shouted truculently, 'You'd better get out, there's an air-raid on.'

To which I shouted back, equally testily, 'I know there is, chum, I've just landed in the middle of it!' – thinking as I did so, that after almost six hours of what I had been through, what was an air-raid?

All the same, some of his concern transferred itself to me and with a determined effort I managed to haul myself to my feet and clamber down, looking like an advertisement for Sloane's Liniment. Immediately, I was grabbed by the arm and hustled, limping, towards a hole in a wall from which stone steps disappeared downwards into the darkness. My guide gave me an unceremonious shove and down I went, stumbling into the gloom.

At the bottom of the steep steps was a mass of hot, sweating, garlic-flavoured humanity, mostly dust-white, chattering Maltese workmen and khaki-clad airmen. However, among the many faces dimly visible in the half-light were several I recognized, one of them belonging to Crossey, who had flown in 'Butch' Barton's group.

'Hello!' I heard myself saying. 'What a perfectly blood-stained journey.' I then explained briefly what had happened to me, and added, 'I'm not looking forward to the next leg one little bit!'

Crossey replied without a smile, 'You needn't worry, there isn't going to be a next leg. Haven't you heard? We're staying here.'

'Staying? Here?' My voice rose to a cracked falsetto. 'You mean we're staying in Malta?' I had an instant mental picture of millions of square miles of sea in every direction, minuscule brown fields, stone walls everywhere, and nowhere, but nowhere, to put down a Hurricane in the event of engine trouble or battle damage. Malta, for God's sake, when all I wanted was miles of open desert!

Crossey nodded. 'The AOC wants an experienced squadron to stay on the island because they've been getting hell. 261 Squadron will take our aircraft on to Egypt and we'll take theirs, or what's left of 'em. We're to get unloaded as quickly as possible!'

Minutes later the 'all clear' sounded and still in a mild state of shock, I found myself once more in the heat and glare of the Maltese sun; although I seemed to have been flying for a week, it was still not yet noon. With others, I limped back to my aircraft and for the next 30 minutes supervised the removal of my possessions. By degrees they all emerged – parachute bag, towels, shirts, raincoat, rolled-up this and that, everything – including the pith helmets. At that stage the pith helmets were becoming something of a joke.

Finally, it was all stacked in a pathetic little heap on the dusty concrete; everything I possessed, which wasn't very much. I looked around with hands on hips – resigned – crushed – defeated. Malta! Who would believe it? And what about our troops, would we ever see them again?[1] And all my other kit, which was going the 'long way round'? No, it really was too much!

An hour later, the eight of us who had landed at Luqa – one-third of both 'Butch' Barton's group and my own – were on our way to Ta Kali airfield by bus. Ta Kali! I had no idea where Ta Kali was exactly or what it looked like other than it was a landing ground and several miles to the north. By that time, however, I was past caring. Hot, running with dust-caked sweat, tired and ravenously hungry, reaction had set in and I was in a depressed frame of mind. Malta, for God's sake! Of all places, Malta! What would my parents think of this arrangement?

[1] Pilots, ground crew (and luggage!) never were reunited.

The bus was unique, reminding me of pictures I had seen of those taking the French army to the battle of the Marne in 1914, although it must have been more modern – just! It roared off, shaking, banging and creaking abominably, being driven by a lunatic Maltese who careered wildly around dusty, unpaved tracks barely wide enough to accommodate the width of the vehicle, the man hooting his horn and shouting at each bare-footed urchin, peasant or herd of goats that cringed into doorways or flattened themselves against stone walls as we hurtled past like a careering collection of tin cans. And it was at that early stage of my stay in Malta that I learned that 'Ar-right!' was the password for everything; 'Ar-right' started the bus and stopped it, it meant yes, no, thank you, good morning, I want to get off, slow down you half-wit, everything! 'Ar-right!' Wonderfully ubiquitous! In front, the driver demonically cheerful, kept turning round and crying 'Ar-right!' to us in the back, driving meanwhile with one hand and seeming hell-bent on suicide. In the rear, gripped by speechless apprehension, we all hung on like clams.

The events of the next few days remain a kaleidoscope of fleeting memories and impressions. The officers' accommodation, within half a mile of Ta Kali airfield, was a large stone building with a courtyard and spiral steps rising to the section used as an ante-room. There, I found 'Butch' Barton and others who had landed at Hal Far and Ta Kali, everyone looking resignedly dazed by our sudden change of circumstances. My flight had not been the only one to suffer misfortune, apparently; only half the complement of Hurricanes had managed to take off from the *Furious,* and other aircraft from both the *Furious* and *Eagle* had turned back, there being a story – untrue as we later learned – that one whole flight had landed in North Africa. Of my own group, all had been critically short of fuel, one pilot having his engine stop when still in the circuit, obliging him to land with a dead stick, whilst another had insufficient fuel even to taxi in. What a scrape! And what a shambles!

Then, an anonymous voice in my ear: 'By the way, why didn't you turn back when the *Ark* came on and said that we couldn't make it?'

I turned, questioning and astonished. 'You mean the *Ark* said that?'

'That's right. Fifteen minutes after we'd set off again, they broke RT silence and said we were all to return and land-on because we wouldn't have the fuel to get here. We thought you pressed on because you didn't think much of the idea.'

I looked blankly at the speaker with an expression of genuine amazement. 'I didn't hear that,' I said limply. 'Honestly I didn't!' And I hadn't, although I doubt that anyone present really believed me.

After a thoroughly indifferent meal, which I hardly ate, I found myself confronted by a number of familiar faces including those of several ex-members of 56 Squadron, whom I had known at North Weald, and Worrall, who used to be in 249. I formed the impression that most of 261 were mad keen to get off the island, which was not exactly encouraging. Then someone was asking if my aircraft was all right. I replied that it was fine, provided he was looking for a Hurricane with three ailerons – which left my questioner a bit perplexed.

But it was that first night that has always loomed large in my memory. Unable to be granted a room because of temporary overcrowding, I found myself on a camp-bed in a stone corridor down which, it appeared, the whole population of Malta – stark naked – pushed past at two-minute intervals en route to the single lavatory situated within feet of where I lay. Furthermore, as there was high incidence of what was termed 'Malta dog', a particularly nasty form of dysentery, the noises-off were as unpleasant as the other manifestations of the affliction.

All this, however, was but a minor inconvenience when compared with the onslaught of the mosquitos which, relishing this latest import of sweet, new English flesh, circled me throughout the night, singing like choristers and imbibing voraciously. Driven almost demented by their persistent biting, I struck out blindly in the darkness and awoke to find myself a mass of red bumps which itched abominably. Indeed, in the months to come, I found the mosquitos much more of a nuisance than the Germans and the Italians combined as, with none of the present-day insecticides available, they proved to be a remorseless and seemingly indestructible enemy.

As I crept miserably towards the bare, stone dining-room on that first morning-after and viewed with distaste the plateful of fatty bacon, fried bread and the rest, all curling at the edges and swimming in congealing grease, my morale was as low as ever I had known it. Malta, for God's sake! What malevolent angel had decided that we should be holed up in this . . . this *dump*?

Having landed on 21 May, for several days thereafter we did little other than settle in and find our way about. Malta, although a great shock to the system initially, gradually began to take on a more favourable aspect despite the oppressive heat and lack of facilities in the mess.

We officers were quartered in a rather sombre castle-like building known as Torre Cumbo, situated less than a mile from Ta Kali airfield. Looking as though it had been erected at the time of the Crusades, it was formidably built of large stone blocks, a method of construction with which we were soon to become all too familiar and which later proved to be a greater threat to life than the enemy bombs themselves, as a collapsed building caused by a near-miss invariably meant death – or at least a braining – for those within, unless they had the good sense to dive beneath the nearest table or bed. During my seven months in Malta, I was to spend a good deal of time under my bed.

Thankfully, I was soon able to vacate my camp-bed adjacent to the musical lavatory having been offered a room on the other side of the courtyard, which I subsequently shared with 'Ozzie' Crossey. A largish, rather sepulchral place, it was reminiscent of a monk's cell, gloomy but cool and with a single shuttered window. However, as all the bedrooms led off each other, it too was something of a thoroughfare, there always seeming to be a trail of pale, naked forms padding sleepily to yet another lavatory just beyond our door, a scene once picturesquely described to me by a colleague as looking like the production line in a black-pudding factory.

With our new accommodation went a shared batman, a little boy of about twelve called Charlie, whose duties were to keep the place clean, look after our laundry, and fight off the mosquitos. This last named task he attempted by closing the shutters and laying down a fog of 'Flit', which did considerably more damage to Crossey and to me than ever it did to the mosquitos, as scarcely a night passed without my being bitten to pieces, the little brutes not only surviving the almost solid veil of insecticide but worming their way through even the most scrupulously inspected of mosquito nets.

And Charlie had other qualities, too. One of a family of twelve – the Maltese were (and probably still are) practising Catholics! – he had the face of an angel and the voice of a fog-horn, his vocal chords honed, by endless competition at home no doubt, to produce a sound not unlike a distress signal at sea. Despite his choirboy looks, he could also be a savage little animal at times and, on one occasion, it was only by the grace of God that murder was prevented when Crossey caught him brandishing a knife and about to slit the throat of another of the child batmen who had apparently upset him.

With little that was modern about the place, such as electric bells, the only means of communication was by voice. Requiring assistance, we simply howled 'Charlie', and kept on howling until the little lad appeared, and as everyone else did the same and Charlie's answering voice was more strident than all of ours in total, the volume of sound across the courtyard could, on occasion, be considerable.

It was also on my second full day in Malta that I went into Valletta.

Valletta, the principal town on the island, was the seat of government, the site of the Citadel, the dockyards, the Army, Navy, and Air Force headquarters, our own fighter control centre, everything. About six miles away, it was normally reached by bus – Maltese bus! – and in order to catch the bus, those of us at Ta Kali were obliged to walk into Mosta.

In 1941, the village of Mosta represented perhaps the most blatant example of poverty and wealth in juxtaposition I had ever beheld. The massive Roman Catholic church, its hugely magnificent dome decorated internally with the most breathtaking display of marble and gold, was the focal point of a village that was primitive and deprived almost beyond description. The streets between the unkempt ruins of houses were mere rutted paths streaming with urine and excrement through which dark, bare-footed children shouted and played and goats dragged their bloated, milk-heavy udders as they scavenged among the filth and rubbish, the whole area buzzing with clouds of green-bodied flies all seemingly mesmerized by the summer heat.[1]

And the bus, in its way, was scarcely better. At least as ancient as the relic we had travelled in from Luqa to Ta Kali, it was crammed with flat-hatted, black-robed priests and Maltese peasants, all squat, bulky, work-stained, pungently sweating and garlicky – and vociferous! The driver shouted and gesticulated, the passengers shouted back, and all this before the bus had even started! Then with loud 'Ar-rights', we were off, hooting, clattering and roaring through the narrow stone-walled lanes and unkempt villages until eventually, and miraculously, we entered the outskirts of Valletta. By this time I was alive with fleas donated by my earthy, malodorous companion in the next seat and being bitten almost into a solid lump. My oath, what a place! How long could I stand it?

Valletta was a distinct improvement, however, many of the buildings and streets of grand dimensions and possessing an ordered and noble air. With several others, I inspected the one-street shopping centre, Strada Royalle, looked out over the many harbours and inlets crowded with warships and other craft, examined from a safe distance the Gut – the

[1] Mosta has since been transformed.

naughty place! – and finally entered the Union Club, a cool and pleasant haven cast in the mould of a St James's gentleman's establishment. There, among other civilized services available, I could have my hair cut and washed – an absolute necessity in Malta, as I was soon to learn – and be offered delicate turkey sandwiches with my afternoon tea. An oasis in the midst of a desert of sandstone, smells, mosquitos and fleas, I signed the appropriate application form immediately and became a prospective member, although I never recall paying my subscription! Later still, I was introduced to Monico's and Maxim's, where a bulky but extremely amiable ex-ship's steward, who was to become a great friend of us all, served cool John Collinses and other multi-coloured concoctions – plus hot pork sandwiches! In the months to follow, and although I never saw a pig on the island – they were alleged to share each farmhouse with the farmer and take precedence over all his family – the hot pork sandwiches remained in constant supply despite the severe food shortage that resulted later in the year when the Axis besiegers tightened the screw.

But if my spirits had been raised by my excursion into Valletta, they were dashed absolutely when 'Butch' and I, with others, gathered on Ta Kali airfield to inspect facilities and consider how best to arrange ourselves.

The facilities were soon inspected – there were next to none! A single 12-foot square tent, with its sides rolled up, constituted the operations room and pilots' accommodation, and there was another to shelter the NCOs and airmen forming the first-line servicing crews. Around both, roughly dispersed, were about six Hurricanes, some tropicalized, others not, all of them patched and grey with accumulated dust, some with metal De Havilland airscrews, others with wooden Rotols. With not a squadron marking in sight, the dejected-looking aircraft sat there with hung heads like hounds exhausted by a fruitless chase. Alongside, several starter-batteries, their chattering chore-horses 'putt-putting' away endlessly, trailed their hoses to a few of the defeated hulks, whilst on the hill several miles to the south and west, the yellow walls and towers of M'dina and Rabat[1] looked down hotly and impassively in our direction, the afternoon heat rising in breathless, shimmering waves from a jigsaw of intervening drystone boundaries and dusty, postage-stamp fields. And as we formed a lack-lustre group, running with unaccustomed sweat and with our white knees blinking in the near-tropical sun, we all became aware of the subtle but unmistakable aroma of Malta, half Middle Eastern, half – something.

A group of 261 Squadron pilots, yet to embark on their journey to Egypt, clustered around us and a gharry, hauled by a decrepit-looking nag, its ears protruding through a squashed straw hat and with a young officer at the reins, creaked past on the dusty track which ran across the end of the airfield and adjacent to dispersal. Another of 261, I was informed, as mild cheers and waves were exchanged, a pastoral, totally incongruous scene when contrasted with the violent air attack I had landed in only hours before.

I found myself in conversation with someone. How many of the squadron were airborne? None, I was told. I wondered incredulously if those six, clapped-out Hurricanes were all there were? No, not quite, they could usually muster around eight or nine – one Mark 2 and the rest Mark 1s. Seldom more than nine, though, and they were all pretty tired. Tired! I remember looking at them in dismay – euphemism taken to extreme!

With so few aircraft available and more than 26 pilots in the squadron, 'Butch' and I decided to operate as two groups, one led by him and the other by me. We would use the same aircraft, of course, and share the daily task of defending the island which, at that time, was a 24-hour job as we were also expected to operate at night, when required. We were encouraged to learn that there were about the same number

[1] I never knew which was which, learning later that M'dina was, in fact, the Arab name for Rabat.

of Hurricanes in 185 Squadron, stationed at Hal Far, some ten miles to the south and east, the total available force of fighters on the island being eighteen at best. With 185's Hurricanes about as impressive as our own – as I was soon to find out! – the defenders of Malta towards the end of May 1941 had about them a distinctly jaded air. Who comprised the enemy in Sicily I had no idea, except that they were Germans with Italian assistance, the whole force being pretty effective, having succeeded in making a mess of 261 Squadron in recent months and putting the fear of God into the Royal Navy. But what of it? We had dealt with Huns and Eyeties before and could lick them again, of that we had no doubt. Our only concern was the quality of the rubbish we had to fly and the real fear that our aircraft might not be up to catching the blighters. Why couldn't they give us Spits or some decent Hurricane 2s at the very least?

We also learned that we were to take over 261's duties the following day, 25 May. None of us had flown since arriving on the island, nor would we have the opportunity to do so before being thrown into battle in aircraft totally new to us. Moreover, apart from our brief glimpse of Malta on the day of our arrival, we had not even seen it from the air. Still, what did it matter? All places – all Huns, in fact – were the same to us.

After deciding on how we should organize the squadron, I wandered out to the parked aircraft in order to select one that looked even half-way decent. I was not encouraged. God, what a rag-bag set! Tomorrow? We'd just have to see.

Meanwhile, the sun beat down with tropical intensity and it occurred to me that as the Air Force did not provide us with any sort of flying suit, I would have to go into battle in shorts and shirt or, more precisely, bare arms and knees, unless I wore my own black overall, purchased privately during my training days at Barton in 1938 and made of a heavy and most untropical linen. Still, better that than nothing; only too well were we aware of the Hurricane's proneness to catch fire and its unpleasant habit of barbecuing its pilot in the cockpit. Memories of poor old Nick's[1] hands and face, and those of a hundred other victims, remained a terrible reminder.

Sunday, 25 May: stiflingly hot with most of us bathed in sweat and uncomfortably aware of the brassy sun overhead. Through narrowed eyes I found myself gazing skywards. Talk about Huns in the sun; we were going to have a hard time of it here, I could see.

'Butch's' group had taken the first stint of duty starting at dawn, but nothing much had happened. By noon, the whole island was wilting in a breathless, humid heat. On the white drystone walls, tiny lizards basked unblinking in the midday glare, to dart off at lightning speed when threatened, or lose their tails when pinned down by amused fingers. Away on the hill, the ochre-and-brown walls and castellations of Rabat and M'dina stared down with the serene gaze of two thousand silent years. No birds. No movement. Just stillness, oven heat, and talcum-powder dust. A lone gharry with its drooping straw-hatted horse and somnolent driver, creaked wearily across the end of the airfield as though we, and the war, were a million miles away.

I had arrived with my group shortly before 1 p.m. to begin the ritual of change-over. There were nine aircraft, all hooked up to starter batteries whose chore-horses puttered away endlessly.

The pilots' tent and so-called operations room was merely a cover to keep off the sun, the four sides rolled up to enable even the smallest breeze to fan a dozen lolling forms. A bored airman sat at a table confronting a small battery of telephones connecting the airfield to the control centre in Valletta, six miles away. The equipment was primitive, instruments that had to be held down and wound, with wires everywhere. All day long the airman on duty was obliged to listen in frustrated silence to 'officer' and 'pilot' talk, much less spicy, no doubt,

[1] Our former colleague, Flight Lieutenant J.B. Nicolson, V.C., shot down on 16 August, 1940.

than the conversation to which he was accustomed. There were compensations, however; he at least knew what was going on and could spread the word among his mates later in his own quarters. The airman-of-the-watch that day was a non-smiling, faintly truculent Scotsman with a Glaswegian accent that would have curdled milk.

For ten minutes or so, we sorted ourselves out. I took over V4048 and, leaving my plugged-in helmet hanging on the gunsight, draped my parachute over the tail – I disliked having it in the cockpit seat and being trodden on all the time. Making the brief ritual inspection to satisfy myself that all the main parts were in place, I ran my hand over the tailplane and found the metal almost too hot to touch. Well, we had bleated constantly about too much cloud in England; now we had the sun – and how! I walked back to the tent; our first spell of duty in Malta and about seven hours before we were likely to be 'stood-down'.

For more than half an hour, nothing; no excitement, no tension even. We sat around, fanning ourselves and trying to keep cool. Waiting. Outside the chore-horses chattered on monotonously and the sun continued to bake the acres of glaring white sandstone beyond our canvas cover so that the heat rose in shimmering eddies, making Rabat on the distant hill wobble and shake. And all around was that subtle smell – of Malta.

I had already spoken to control some fifteen minutes earlier and been assured that nothing unusual was happening, so that when a distant air-raid siren began its whooping dirge, it came as a surprise and an unpleasant shock. Air-raid siren! What were we doing sitting here if the Huns were within even 50 miles of us? I jumped to my feet, as did everyone else, and went outside to waken myself up and to observe. Nothing though, or nothing that I could see. Even so, I didn't like it – some sixth sense. We wouldn't be hanging about like this at North Weald, by George!

Anxious to be in the best possible state of preparedness, I ordered everyone to 'Standby', which meant that they sat, strapped up, in their cockpits, after which I spoke again to control.

We could hear air-raid sirens, I observed tersely. What was going on?

Hearing voices in the background and discussion, I sensed uncertainty. Then their reply: nothing as far as they knew. As soon as anything developed they would let us know. OK?

Still suspicious, I went out into the sun again and, walking back to my aircraft, climbed in and strapped up, leaving off my helmet.

Minutes passed. Nothing. Then another air-raid siren, this time very much closer.

Hell's bells! What *was* going on? I flung off my straps and, jumping down, ran the fifty yards back to the tent. By God, I'd give them what-for!

Jogging into the tent, I had barely ordered the airman-of-the-watch to: 'Get me control!' when it all started.

First, the shrill, deafening scream of racing engines and the ripping, tearing bedlam of machine-guns and cannons. All hell let loose!

I dropped the telephone like a hot plate and threw myself to the ground, only to find the airman-of-the-watch had beaten me to it and, knees to chin, was clutching his head like a hear-no-evil monkey. Lying on my left side, with my face to one open end of the tent, I had the briefest glimpse of a small aircraft, which I immediately recognized as a German 109, about 50 feet up and pointing, it seemed, straight at me. *Firing!* Shocked absolutely into a numbed paralysis, I closed my eyes and cringed, waiting for the impact of bullets and shells, wondering quite stupidly meanwhile whether they were likely to go right through my body or only partly so, and if they would penetrate that of the airman as well. For all of four seconds.

Then, with a final explosion of sound and fury, they were gone, their lightning departure marked by the rapid 'clump-clump-clump' of the several Bofors guns around the airfield and the chatter of defending machine-guns.

Scrambling to my feet, I ran outside to see the rapidly diminishing silhouettes of at least three aircraft, their wings glinting in the sun as they sped away to safety in the direction of the area later known to me as St Paul's Bay. In their wake streamed curving clutches of red balls as the Bofors gunners strove to catch them before they finally disappeared. But, what a hope! Within seconds, the last of them had gone and a breathless, trembling peace had been restored, a terrible, stunned and pregnant silence.

My first impression was that we had lost at least one aircraft and that several people had been either killed or wounded. One Hurricane in the middle of the dispersed group was already on fire, though in a small way, and at least one other had been hit and was shedding smoke.

Then, out of the small group of people moving about urgently but seemingly without purpose, a figure hopped almost comically in my direction. It was Pat Wells and he was calling out to me; he had been hit, it seemed, and was apologizing. Apologizing! Obviously in shock, he was shouting: 'Ginger? Sorry, Ginge! Sorry about this. I really am sorry. Before we've even flown, too. Always seems to happen to me. Sorry!'

I moved in his direction, still nervously on edge, steadying him with an arm.

'Where've you been hit?'

'Here. In the foot.' He painfully proffered a leg like a puppy with a sore paw. 'Saw them coming but couldn't do anything about it. Didn't feel it happen; didn't even know anything about it until I got out.'

Then Crossey, Harrington, Palliser and others were crowding round. Everyone tense but relieved, talking excitedly, laughing even. Christ! That was a close one; everyone strapped in and unable to move, looking straight down the muzzles of those guns. No more of *that*, if you don't mind! But why hadn't we been told, for God's sake? Those stupid sods in Valletta. They *must* have known! And if they didn't, *why*? – all the rest of Malta seemed to. Then more relieved laughter and experiences being recounted. A few yards away, the second Hurricane was beginning to burn, but there was nothing available to put out the flames so we all watched impotently as the fire spread; I even thought of throwing handfuls of sand at it but it seemed a silly thing to do.

In minutes both aircraft were massively alight and black smoke was billowing to the heavens in two almighty pillars. Then other people approaching from everywhere with rising dust and the noise of several vehicles, including an ambulance; everyone urgent, questioning, helpful. MacVean, one of the NCO pilots, was badly damaged apparently; having been in the Hurricane nearest to the Huns when they had opened fire, he had scrambled over the side in double quick time, breaking – or badly damaging – both his legs. Bit of a joke really, as MacVean was a portly youth and not given either to moving or thinking quickly. Not until today, that is!

Anyone else hurt? Several airmen, apparently; no-one killed though, which was a miracle. What a thing to happen! Our first stint of 'Readiness', and none of us off the ground yet. The smoke from the aircraft towering columns now that could probably be seen in Sicily! In seconds our whole squadron neutralized – demolished! Well, almost!

Harrington, our tall, scholarly colleague from the Bank of England, was bewailing the loss of a pair of polaroid specs; wearing them when the shooting started, he was explaining querulously. Terribly expensive, old boy, wouldn't want to lose them. His was one of the two burning Hurricanes and he had been hit in his parachute, too. Right under his bum! Pretty close, what?

People swirling about now and, amid the sound of laughter, things being done in some semblance of order. The two aircraft, burning still with a vicious red-and-black intensity, were collapsing and stinking, their ammunition exploding with zipping cracks, which made some of us jump. I suddenly became aware that Crossey and I were standing directly in front of one of them and I pulled him away. Suddenly aware of his vulnerability, he jerked in response before controlling himself almost sheepishly; not really dangerous, said he, until I reminded him of rounds 'up the spout'. We both moved away – just in case.

I had a brief situation report from the senior NCO, whom I did not even know. Two aircraft burnt out and two others badly hit and goners he thought, a total of perhaps five out of commission. Then the ambulance was moving away to hospital, carting off the wounded. The smoke was now billowing densely to at least a thousand feet, the two Hurricanes merely embers, each with engine intact and propeller pointing ridiculously to the heavens. Harrington, still worrying about his polaroid specs, was circling the ashes of his aircraft, trying to get at it to make a search but being forced back by the heat. He was sure he was wearing them when it happened, he was telling us endlessly.

Finally, calmness and order. Everyone back to normal. But, what a thing to happen! And all before we had made even our first take-off. What had got into those clowns down the hole? They must have known *something*.

Later that same afternoon, leading the three remaining aircraft, I was scrambled twice, whether in response to genuine Hun activity or as a reflex action by control to show that they were still alive and in charge of our affairs, I do not know. Whatever the reason, we encountered no enemy aircraft, my recollections of the flights being mainly of my Hurricane lurching more violently than I had ever known in the convection currents of heat, and the dust-storm we created when taking off, a grey and ochre pall that rose to 500 feet and hung in the air for minutes like a drifting balloon. With such conditions, no wonder the Hurricanes were falling to bits!

That seemingly endless first day drifted to a limp conclusion. Knocked for six before we had even made a move! Who'd have thought it?

Unable to produce more than four aircraft, we were ordered across to Hal Far the following day to use 185 Squadron's

Hurricanes, an arrangement that would continue for about a week. Initially, we made the ten-mile journey by bus.

Hal Far was another dishing patch of worn grass at the southern end of the island. Arriving for the first time with my half of the squadron, I set about organizing the 'state'. On an airfield I had never seen before, aircraft we had never flown before, and with groundcrew who were friendly enough but quite foreign to us, our first period of 'Readiness' was endured in an atmosphere that was neither homely nor cheerful.

Selecting one aircraft for myself – about as wearily decrepit as any of those at Ta Kali – I arranged my parachute and equipment, and waited.

After a short time, we were scrambled. I raced out, started up, and fled to the end of the airfield, streaming dust in every direction. My tattered mob following me, I roared off towards the south in a typhoon of rising filth and in a wide turn climbed away towards the north and in the direction of the enemy.

Information began to come up to us. Fifty-plus bandits approaching from the north; climb to Angels 15 – the usual stuff. Fifty-plus! And eight of us! But, what the heck? We had heard it all before.

We were just south of Valletta and at around 6,000 feet when I noticed that the little pointer on my oil pressure gauge was registering about 30 lbs instead of the usual 70. And sinking! Oh, no! A duff gauge? I hoped so.

My eyes glued to the instrument, I continued to climb hard at the head of my swaying formation but by the time we had reached 8,000 feet the pressure was down to about 10 lbs, and as I sat there watching in torment, the pointer dropped to the bottom of the instrument before disappearing altogether. Oh, God! What did I do now? In front, the Merlin engine sounded cheerful enough but, as the book said, if I had a complete oil failure, I had only two or three minutes before the brute seized. I climbed on, submerged in despair. Then, as though to confirm my worst fear, the oil temperature needle

121

began to march around the dial; no doubt about it, it was a failure right enough and it looked as though I was due for a forced-landing. Bloody aircraft! Bloody Malta! What a hell of a place to have come to!

It was at that moment that the voice of an angel rose up from below with news that the fifty-plus plots had now turned away and that we should pancake without delay. Pancake! Thank God for that! My dilemma resolved, I dropped my nose and started back towards Hal Far.

The airfield about twelve miles distant, I began to have doubts that I would make it when there came a powerful smell of hot Hurricane and a haze of blue smoke began to rise around my feet. Throttling right back, I coarsened the airscrew pitch lever down to the full extent of its travel and half glided towards the hangars now well within sight. Praying! Hang on you brute! Hang on! I felt myself urging the aircraft forward against my straps, willing the airscrew to keep turning.

To my great relief it did, and with a glad heart I swished across the top of the hangars and almost threw the aeroplane at the ground. And barely had the wheels touched and with the Hurricane still racing ahead, than the propeller jerked to a halt, the engine stopped with an ominous, juddering click, and lots more blue smoke rose up from below. Wow! Close shave! Thank God for that!

Even before it had rolled to a standstill, I had climbed over the side and dropped off the wing-root. Then, retreating to a safe distance, I stood watching, half-expecting the whole thing to explode. Nothing much happened though, apart from the smoke and lots of hissing and ticking as the vastly overheated engine cooled down. Then, as there seemed little I could do, I walked the half-mile back to dispersal, limp but greatly relieved.

As I trudged on, I ruminated wearily. What else could happen to me? After the longest Hurricane trip in history and nearly being written-off in an air-raid on arrival, I had survived a near-lethal strafing attack before I had made even

122

my first trip. And now, here I was with an engine failure after less than two hours of flying! All this in five days! It only remained for some lunatic Maltese driver to maim me in the aircrew bus and my week would be a sparkling success.

Back in dispersal, I sought out the crew of my machine but managed to locate only one youth who warily described himself as a fitter. Our encounter was unforgettable.

'My engine's just seized,' I announced crossly. 'Where's the Form 700?'[1]

The youth – grass-green by the look of him – stared back.

'Well, where's the 700?' I repeated.

'700, sir? There isn't one.'

Me, dumbstruck: 'No 700? But there *has* to be a 700! Every aircraft in the Air Force has a Form 700. Where's the one for this aircraft?'

The boy shifted uncomfortably. 'This one doesn't,' he asserted vehemently. 'We haven't had a 700 for this aircraft for ages.'

I was almost beyond responding. 'But you must have signed the 700 after the DI[2]. Before you declared it serviceable. You *did* sign for it, I take it?'

But even as I spoke, the terrible truth dawned on me that in the heat of the change-over and amid our other distractions, none of us pilots had signed for any of our Hurricanes; we had simply taken the few that were lying around – and gladly at that! Nor had we signed any Authorization Book, a truly terrible omission as, even in war, things had to be 'done proper'; their 'Airships' didn't mind their pilots being killed but they did insist on the paperwork being in order.

Sensing defeat but determined that the youth should accompany me so that we might investigate the cause of the

[1] Form 700 – Servicing record.
[2] DI – Daily Inspection.

engine trouble together, we tramped out into the sunshine and heat.

Having twisted off the oil-tank cap in the wing-root – no easy task as it was still barely touchable – the lad gave an experimental poke into the depths.

'There's no oil in it,' he announced triumphantly, as though it were all my fault.

I said ominously, 'That doesn't surprise me. The point is, there should be eleven gallons.'

'Well, there's none now. There must be a leak.'

'Leak! When did you last fill her up?'

The other looked vague. 'Can't remember, sir.'

'Well, was it today? Yesterday? Last week? When?'

'Not today, sir – I don't think.' Then with a perplexed but almost engaging frown, 'Can't remember, really. Someone else might have, though.'

I experienced a terrible weariness. No Form 700 and he couldn't remember when he last put oil in the engine. No, it was all too difficult: the hopeless aircraft, the heat, the mosquitos and revolting food, chaps like this who hardly knew which way was 'up', the lack of almost everything. Malta! What a bloody awful place to come to!

We both turned and left the aircraft standing there. Right in the middle of the airfield.

6 Action Commences

Malta!

The present-day island with its package-tour image, crowded holiday apartments and lobster-coloured tourists, bears few similarities to the Malta of 1941. Indeed, little of its former primitive character remains and such places as St Paul's Bay, Mosta, Ghajn Tuffeiha, and even the old airfield at Ta Kali, are hardly recognizable. But then, as now, the Maltese, never a warrior race, were kindly, gentle folk, with a few exceptions darkly Mediterranean in appearance and much given to the Roman church, its priests and trappings, and the business of warding off the evil eye.

On the whole, they were very pro-British, although being so close to Italy and with many of the more educated speaking Italian and having links with that country, during the period of the siege there were naturally some who felt more emotionally if not politically aligned with their next-door neighbours. Even so, there was never a noticeable undercurrent of resentment towards us and, as far as I am aware, never any activities even remotely subversive. At the time, the Anglo-Maltese family of Strickland, who seemed to own almost everything on the island including the single newspaper, the *Times of Malta*, were an obvious and powerful influence.

Quite a few Maltese traditionally joined the Navy, many of them being employed in the kitchens and messes, and those who took to soldiering formed the bulk of the Royal Malta Artillery which manned the ack-ack defences. Those who weren't militarily inclined went about their business as usual in what was primarily an agricultural community, the bare-footed peasant farmers and their families tilling the meagre fields with impassive indifference as the tracer soared and the air battles raged above their heads, the pregnant women among them delivering their squalling infants in the odd moment between hoeing a line or two in the brown earth, bending always with straight legs, so that one of my more vivid memories of Malta is the sight of backsides of all shapes and sizes pointing defiantly towards the enemy. Some of the more affluent members of the populace, who normally lived in the grander suburbs of Valletta, had taken the precaution of evacuating themselves to Rabat and other such places in the centre of the island, so that in the summer of 1941 it was possible to rent a magnificent four-storey furnished house in Sliema for as little as £5 per month.

Even under the greatest stress, the Maltese menfolk of whatever class, were courteous and helpful to the point of being obsequious and the young and attractive ladies of courting age were as obliging as their religion and hawk-eyed parents would allow. Maltese mothers, in the main, tended to be less favourably disposed towards us, warning their daughters that these handsome RAF officers would not *always* be around and *then* who would be willing to seek their favours?

Despite our initial difficulty in locating the island and our not undramatic arrival on 21 May, to say that I had not known where Malta was, would not be strictly correct. Along with Hong Kong, Singapore, Zanzibar and Manila, the precise position of Malta had been the subject of a question on the geography paper of my mock-Matric examination in 1936. Moreover, the more recent exploits of Faith, Hope and Charity, the three Gladiator fighters which had earlier defended the island, had been headline news at home, as indeed had the Mediterranean war in general. No, I knew where Malta was all right and the unpleasant things that were happening there, as did my family and friends, who were horrified when they learned that the squadron had been retained in its defence.

I was also tolerably familiar with its history and was aware that the inhabitants, far from being fifty per cent priests and fifty per cent goats, as was facetiously alleged, were not only heavily involved in the Crusades in medieval times but were descendants of the Phoenicians, who were civilized traders when we Ancient Britons were carrying spears and daubing ourselves with woad. And, of course, there was the Bible and those worthy saints, Paul and John – wasn't Paul shipwrecked somewhere on the north coast of Malta? So, what if their language *was* all 'exes and vees upside down' and if, at one time, my mother did harbour the unspoken fear that my new Maltese girlfriend might be black and have crinkly hair?

It was this slightly patronizing ignorance of Malta and the Maltese, coupled with their national reverence for dogged resistance, that led the British people in 1940 and later – me included – to believe that the island was totally preoccupied with defending itself, which was far from the truth. Throughout the period of the Mediterranean war, Malta was a vital base from which offensive action by air and sea caused such crippling losses to the enemy that, in 1942, the Germans seriously considered invading it in order to maintain their supply lines to General Rommel and his forces in North Africa.

The three main centres from which this offensive action was launched were the airfields of Luqa and Hal Far and the port of Valletta. For this reason, all three came constantly under attack by Axis aircraft for more than two years, the airfield at Ta Kali – in my time the home of at least half the fighter force on the island – being merely a secondary target which was bombed and strafed more or less for good measure. In particular, Valletta – its harbour, dockyards and installations – came in for a terrible drubbing, requiring it to be heavily defended by anti-aircraft guns of all types and sizes, whose soaring tracer, fiery balls and formidable, crumping barrage, provided constant and colourful entertainment for those of us at Ta Kali, who often took our after-dinner coffee and sat in the darkness on the flat roof of the mess in order to enjoy the free firework display.

Until the eventual rout of the German and Italian forces in North Africa in the late autumn of 1942, the Royal Navy viewed Malta with scowling trepidation and only lodged its ships there when it had to, although from time to time this became necessary as the naval vessels themselves had to be supported and the island, with few resources, had to be supplied constantly with aviation fuel and oil, ammunition, food, and almost every other type of commodity. At regular intervals, His Majesty's submarines would creep in and out in such sinister silence that we seldom knew of their presence until the familiar, cheerful and bearded faces of their commanders turned up in the hotels and bars in Valletta. Without exception, they were proud and splendid men whose exploits were to inspire the nation, the names of Wanklyn VC, and others, becoming household words.

The main group of naval surface ships in Malta, known as Force 'K', consisted of one or more six-inch gun cruisers of the *Aurora* class of which HMS *Aurora* herself, and occasionally HMS *Penelope,* were the representatives, and around six destroyers, all of wh: :h, like the submarines, came and left with great stealth, going about their deadly business with such secrecy that we in Hurricanes were occasionally despatched into the Mediterranean to find them, as often as not being shot at for our pains immediately we ventured within range. To Force 'K', indeed the Royal Navy in general, every aircraft was a German aircraft, which in one respect was a bonus as we knew that whenever ack-ack bursts began to pock-mark the sky around us, we need go no further as they were the chaps we were looking for!

The small Navy air contingent, in the form of Fulmars, Swordfish and Albacores, operated from Hal Far and carried out torpedo attacks and mining operations, mostly at night and over a wide area, the Fulmars specializing in intruder work. The Fulmars and crews who had escorted us to Malta had been incorporated into this hardy group and those of us in 249 were able to renew our happy association with them. And our sympathy, too, as they were obliged to fly their obsolete and barely serviceable aircraft on the most hazardous of sorties, always over the sea and often well

One of Cecil Beaton's much publicised photographs of the author.

Most of 'the other half of 249 Squadron' – December 1941.
From left to right: Tedford (American), Branch, Owen, Matthews, Beazley, Mortimer-Rose, Davis, Smith, Harrington.
Behind: Parker, Leggett, Rist. *(C. Bowyer)*.

Left to right: Crossey, Davis (C.C.H.), and Beazley at North Weald. Davis was later killed in the Middle East.

Left to right: Munro (Rhodesian), Thompson, and Wells (South African). Munro was the first 249 fatality in Malta.

'Dicky' Wynn (holding Wilfred, the duck), with American visitor and Cassidy (with Pipsqueak, the pup). Wynn was tragically killed shortly after this photograph was taken.

Squadron Leader R.A. (Butch) Barton, Officer Commanding 249 Squadron, December 1940 to December 1941. *(C. Bowyer).*

This type of tropicalised Me 109, E-4 was much in evidence over Malta and in the Western Desert throughout 1941. This aircraft of JG 27, is seen over the North African coast in September of that year. *(Aeroplane Monthly).*

Torre Cumbo – the officers' mess at RAF Ta Kali. The courtyard and the spiral staircase to the ante-room – the door on the right.

A Fulmar, similar to those which led 249 to Malta, preparing to take-off; with HMS *London* behind, 'trotting alongside it like an Old English Sheepdog!'

The Hurricanes of Flying Officers Wells and Harrington after the German attack of 25 May 1941. The pilots' tent 'with the rolled up sides' can be seen between the two aircraft with the first-line servicing crew's tent to the right. *(F. Etchells).*

A captured Savoia 79. This was the most numerous and effective Italian bomber/torpedo-carrying aircraft operating over and around Malta in 1941. *(Imperial War Museum)*.

The Me 109F, which first appeared in numbers over Malta in December 1941. It was so superior in performance to the Hurricane that combat was grossly one-sided. This aircraft was captured in Sicily some time later. *(Aeroplane Monthly)*.

A Martin Maryland of 69 Squadron. For the most part stationed at Luqa, they were fast and pleasant to fly but with neither armour-plate nor self-sealing tanks, were highly vulnerable to enemy fighter attacks. *(C. Bowyer)*.

The Macchi 200. This Italian fighter was the one most frequently encountered over Malta in 1941. Most flew with an open cockpit but some had wind-deflectors incorporated, as seen here.

The Macchi 202, which made its first appearance over Malta in October 1941. With a performance comparable to that of an Me 109E, it could outstrip the Hurricane and, with its .5 inch machine guns, carried a formidable punch.

A naval Fairey Swordfish with torpedo. The Swordfish force operated from RAF Hal Far.

The Bristol Beaufighter. Throughout 1941, Beaufighters were either 'high-jacked' when flying to and from the Middle East, or brought to Malta for special occasions. With four cannons and six machine-guns, they were marginally faster than the Hurricane low down and often created havoc when employed in the low-flying, strafing role.

The Bristol Blenheim. Based at Luqa throughout 1941, the Blenheims did sterling work at low level against Axis shipping but at very great cost to themselves, casualties occasionally amounting to fifty per cent.

HMS *Furious*, in full war paint. 'Cripes! Are we going to war in THAT?'

HMS *Ark Royal*, in life. *(Aeroplane Monthly).*

HMS *Ark Royal* in death – 13 November 1941. *(Aeroplane Monthly).*

into the harbours and airspace of Sicily, seldom returning without some sort of mishap.

Luqa, the airfield on which I had first landed, was the only one with runways and accommodated the reconnaissance and bomber force. 69 Squadron carried out the reconnaissance work and flew Martin Marylands, an American twin-engined aircraft, one of whose better characteristics was a high cruising speed enabling it to outdistance most of the opposition. In the capable hands of Warburton, Devine and others, the Marylands ranged far and wide, providing vital intelligence on enemy shipping and other activity in the greater Mediterranean area. An irrepressible group, some of their antics around Ta Kali did not always meet with our approval.

Also at Luqa were the Wellingtons and Blenheims, the former making nocturnal trips to Axis-held North African ports – principally Benghazi, Tripoli and Tobruk – plus other targets in mainland Europe, whilst the latter carried on a remorseless and bloody war at mast-height against all Axis shipping within a 300-mile radius, in the course of which their casualties were little short of catastrophic. At Luqa, too, the occasional Beaufighter squadron, passing through to or from the Middle East, would be 'hijacked' and obliged to make attacks on one or more of the Axis airfields and ports in Sicily, some 60–100 miles to the north of us. And then, of course, there were the slow-motion Sunderlands, like the submarines, creeping in and out of the island under cover of darkness and using Kalafrana Bay as their alighting area. Although I was well aware of their presence and activities, I never once saw a Sunderland during the many months I spent on the island.

All of this – the sharp end of Malta, so to speak – we in Hurricanes were there to defend, although our role was to develop considerably later in the year. However, it would be many weeks before I became aware of the full extent of the island's offensive activities and even then more through personal contacts in the bars and hotels of Valletta than as the result of formal briefings or intelligence summaries; not only were we ignorant of what the enemy was up to, we knew very little of what our own side was achieving, other than by accident and word of mouth.

Furthermore, despite it being a very small island, I was painfully ignorant of those in control of us early on, and not much wiser by the time I left. Lieutenant General Sir William Dobbie, the Governor and senior military personage, was a distant and venerable gentleman known only to me by photograph and through the medium of the *Times of Malta*. The Air Officer Commanding, however, an appointment soon to be filled by Air Vice Marshal H. P. Lloyd, was someone I came to know a good deal better and about whom I was to harbour mixed feelings. Air Headquarters, Malta, together with the Sector Operations Centre and the controllers, were, and would remain, anonymous bodies and occasional names, existing somewhere below ground in Valletta in what was darkly referred to as 'the Hole', a place to which I was never invited nor encouraged to visit. And finally, although I sometimes encountered Wing Commander John Warfield, my Station Commander at Ta Kali, who seemed a nice enough man, in no way did I feel that he was actually in charge of my destiny, whether even he would be there the following day when I turned up in the mess for lunch. However, one notable officer who had arrived on the island about the same time as ourselves was Wing Commander 'Bull' Halahan, a man who had served with No. 1 Squadron in France in 1939, and who, looking very much like his name, had earned himself an impressive reputation as a man of action. By the end of our first week, I had met him several times without knowing precisely what his responsibilities were although he appeared to have some sort of authority over us, which seemed a step in the right direction.

Somewhere beneath this shadowy and uncertain command structure, we operated – at first anyway – in an atmosphere of mild bewilderment. Officers and NCO pilots of other units arrived out of nowhere announcing they were now part of 249, all with such lack of warning and explanation that there were times when I did not know who was in my flight much less my squadron. Instructions and information materialized, from where exactly was often a mystery, so that on occasion we felt that we were merely pawns in a game beyond our understanding. With our 'troops' somewhere in Africa, our first-line and maintenance crews at Ta Kali were totally foreign to us; moreover, for a lengthy period we were without an adjutant, intelligence officer, or even an engineer officer, our only shared possessions being the tent with the rolled-up sides and a distinctly part-worn, sit-up-and-beg Austin 16, painted a sand-yellow, which served as squadron transport and which 'Butch' drove mostly and I occasionally. My one and only task as flight commander, it seemed, was to organize as many as I could of the dejected-looking Hurricanes dispersed around the airfield's edge and adjacent walled fields into some sort of dog-eared fighting force, lead them into the battle, and land them back in one piece – if at all possible.

Still mildly resentful about our own 'hijacking' into Malta, the unaccustomed summer heat – then in the high 80s and 90s – our lack of kit, the mosquitos and other more personal wildlife, and the type of food and insanitary messing conditions which had many of us beating a path to the musical lavatory, all these I found additional, morale-sapping sources of irritation. After the staid and ordered comfort of North Weald, everything was strange, disorganized and uncomfortably new. On the other hand, would we have fared any better in the Western Desert? Perhaps we had had it altogether too easy thus far.

At the end of May 1941, the German star, if not in the ascendant, was certainly not on the wane. Crete, only a few hundred miles to the east, had just fallen to their airborne forces with heavy loss to Britain in ships, men and material, and the taciturn but admirable General Wavell was in process of being thwarted in his effort to relieve Tobruk in Libya. In the Atlantic, too, there had recently been set-backs, HMS *Hood* being sunk by the *Bismark* with almost the German battleship's first salvo. The *Hood,* for heaven's sake! – just about the biggest warship we had. All right, the *Bismark* had been sunk, too, but that was to be expected, wasn't it? – the Navy being the Navy and all that. No, things were definitely not right and it seemed that at least in part, our equipment was letting us down. In the Western Desert, British tanks were a joke, being completely outgunned by something called a German Mark 4, and the Air Force there seemed to be fielding all sorts of obsolete or obsolescent aircraft, of which, in my view, the Hurricane Mark 1 was a prime example. The Huns were running rings around us and must be laughing themselves sick. Even the new American Tomahawk, which had recently been used in the Desert, was said to be a poor climber and generally lacking in performance – another American streamlined brick, it seemed.

Much of this we knew, if only vaguely, the business of flying and fighting tending to concentrate our minds on events of more immediate and personal import, such as scrambles, ropey engines, forced landings, and staying alive! But what we did not know, although others no doubt did, was that Germany's plans to invade Russia were well advanced and that massive forces, including those of the Luftwaffe in Sicily, were being assembled in eastern Europe for that purpose. Soon, the Hun units which had dealt so harshly with our ships and aircraft in and around Malta, would be departing for the borders of Russia, leaving us only the Italians with whom to wage war. Had we known of this at the time, we might have felt rather better; the Germans we could just about cope with, the Eyeties we regarded as easier meat. After all, were they not the chaps whose tanks were said to have one forward gear and four reverse, and who boasted that nothing could *catch* their cruisers and destroyers? None of us in 249 had ever encountered an Italian aircraft, despite being involved in the raid off the Essex and Suffolk coasts the previous November. On that occasion, 249 had shot down the accompanying spotter and rescue aircraft – an unpleasant task – after which, from the other North Weald squadrons, we had heard all about the Fiat

BR 20 bombers and CR 42 fighters. Biplane fighters! – I wouldn't mind fighting those chaps any day of the week; even the old Hurricane would be good enough for them!

Thus was it during the last week of May 1941. In the glaring, humid heat of Malta. With most of us turning lobster-pink and being bitten to a standstill by plagues of mosquitos and fleas. For fair-skinned me, they were the main enemy; something had to be done about *them*!

I was at 22,000 feet, some fifteen miles north of the island, my shirt sticking clammily to my body where the sweat had congealed to form a chilling adhesive. Alongside me, well spread out in battle formation and properly alert, were three others of my section, everyone more than aware of a sun so glaringly bright that it was impossible to look in its direction even with our newly issued sunglasses. Some fifteen minutes earlier we had scrambled in a lather of excitement, but disappointingly, there was little news, the enemy plots having either evaporated or turned away.

Far below and to my left, the island of Malta appeared brightly, almost luminously, sand-coloured. Not a trace of green; just light brown and white, surrounded by the sea, a million square miles of unending, shadowed blue. On every side the dark azure of the heavens paled into the whitish haze of a horizon which encircled us in a straight, unbroken line. Not even a small cloud. Anywhere.

There were three islands, I observed – Malta itself, lying roughly south-east/north-west, Comino, a little north of the main island and hardly more than a rock, then Gozo, about half the size of Malta but sparsely inhabited and used, we had been told, for sheep, goats and prisoners-of-war. A ferry normally ran between the two major islands in peace-time but only occasionally in war. I hardly gave Gozo a thought; we were never expected to go there.

Away beneath, on the northern side of Malta, was the toothy huddle of Valletta, with its rectangular inlets forming Grand Harbour, its bastions, berths and dockside buildings, all of them heavily protected and accommodating naval and other vessels, all details of which were obliterated by distance. In one respect our job as defenders was easy; there was little doubt as to where the enemy was heading, quite unlike in Britain where there were targets galore.

I tilted to my right in a wide sweep, my gaze alternating in disciplined movements between the heavens, the horizon, and the sea below. Emptiness – nothing but emptiness, enough space to conceal a thousand enemy aircraft which could quite easily stream past us, silent and unobserved. In the distance, some fifty miles to the north, the pale mass that was Sicily was plainly visible, merging left and right into the mists of distance. A parched and arid place it looked from 22,000 feet, much the same as Malta and of the same colour.

We were still operating from Hal Far, journeying to and from Ta Kali by jolting, rattling bus each morning and afternoon. It was my fourth trip from that airfield and in the same aircraft – Z4043 – a tropicalized Mark 1, the engine tolerably smooth at 2,600 revs but with a slightly worrying oil temperature which was consistently higher than the normal 60–65 degrees. After my first engine failure three days earlier, I had watched my gauges like a hawk, looking and listening for the smallest deviation of the pointers or sound of trouble. Never before had I cause to doubt the old and trusty Merlin – not until now, that is!

We flew around in wide figures of eight. On guard. Watchful. With gradually lessening suspicion. Until finally, the pancake instruction.

Tilting towards the south, we dropped our noses, the roar of the slipstream rising to a hissing scream as our descent quickened, until we jolted finally and very uncomfortably into the hard-edged eddies of rising heat some 3,000 feet above the glistening ochre of the sandstone. My Hurricane lurched and shuddered as the waves of convection pummelled and snatched at it. God Almighty, what bumps! Always the same in summer we had been told.

134

Then, everything much quieter and, with the hangars drifting past on our left, we landed. And taxied in. I glanced into the mirror above my cockpit hood. Our airscrews were whipping up vast clouds of dust which followed us about in dark, drifting curtains. Thank heaven I was the leader and ahead of all the others. How the engines were expected to keep going in these conditions I would never know. I looked quickly down to check that the shutter of my Vokes filter was correctly positioned.

Another trip completed. It was 31 May, my ninth day in Malta, and my eighth flight in anger. And I was still in one piece, thank God, which, after our rude welcome the week before, was something of a surprise.

There had been bombers overhead throughout the previous several nights and much waving of searchlights and tonking of guns. If there were bombs dropped, none had come near to us at Ta Kali so that we viewed it all with little more than casual interest. That was one thing about Malta; there was a performance laid on every night – better than going to the theatre. A little less comforting was the news that we would be expected to take our turn at night flying almost immediately; which concerned me more than a little as I didn't trust some of our aircraft even in daylight!

First of June, which was a Sunday. The weather hot and sticky still, the Sabbath's silence almost tangible, the black-robed, flat-hatted priests more than ever in evidence.

Having been bitten miserably by mosquitos the previous night, I awoke, covered with red bumps and scratching like a terrier. As we slept naked, after their aperitif of Flit, the brutes had masses of warm, damp flesh on which to disport themselves. Positively bloated with blood, they would then hang on the sides of the net like bats, so that the first five minutes of consciousness were always devoted to swiping them vengefully to the accompaniment of muttered curses, after which the place looked like a miniature slaughter house. After that, the next five minutes

135

were spent looking for the holes in the net where the little blighters had made their entry.

My flight was on duty that day and when I had struggled into my thick black flying overall, I found it unpleasantly pongy and clammily cold with congealed sweat. Did the dhobi deal with overalls? I would have to find out.

I was scrambled almost immediately but brought down after 25 minutes. In fact, we were seldom kept up longer than that. There was a lot of enemy activity over Sicily, it appeared, but after drawing us into the air, the Huns, or whoever, seemed always to lose interest. Or was it control being hypersensitive because of our harsh words following the massacre at Ta Kali on the 25th? Whatever the reason, we seemed to get masses of scrambles but no interceptions. Apart from looking into the business-end of those 109s during their strafing run, thus far I had not seen a single enemy aircraft.

On 3 June, we were back at Hal Far for the day, this time going by air. If on the dawn stint, we usually left our aircraft there for 'Butch's' half of the squadron to use, before coming back by bus. That ten-mile rattling, bone-shaking return journey in the midday heat and behind those lunatic drivers, I found far more wearing than flying the clapped-out Hurricanes.

By then I was beginning to know the geography of the island quite well, including the names of the places. Kalafrana Bay, next door to Hal Far, was a very picturesque area; the Sunderland flying boats operated from there on their nocturnal comings and goings, but even when they didn't, a dummy flare path was usually laid down in the bay to confuse the enemy. Whatever its effect on the enemy, it certainly confused some of our own heavy boiler chaps, as more than one had already landed in the water by mistake – and others would continue to do so. Mostly inexperienced OTU boys and freshly out of England, it must have been a great surprise for them to be dunked in the water, having spent hours creeping around the Mediterranean in the darkness.

Flying across that day, I had looked down on the new air-strip being created at Safi, situated half-way between Luqa and Hal Far. We were told that we were likely to disperse our aircraft there in the future, anywhere to get them away from the three airfields where the enemy could blitz them.

There were some Swordfish and other naval aircraft in evidence at Hal Far that day. The night before, apparently, one of them carrying a mine – an Albacore, I was told – had hit a wall on take-off and had exploded. Instant dispersal! A terrible way to go, though.

I did not fly for the two days between 3 and 6 June, my flight being on duty for only half of that period. However, 'Butch' Barton, flying Z4043, the aircraft we often shared, was vectored on to an Italian Savoia 79, a three-engined bomber and multi-purpose aircraft which, having taken off from Sicily, was apparently en route for Libya. No doubt believing that the ardour of Malta's defending fighters had been sufficiently cooled by the attacks of previous weeks and perhaps a little over-confident as a result, the Italians chose to fly too close to the island, enabling 'Butch' to make an interception a little to the north and west of Gozo. Almost predictably, the little man, with his usual zeal and efficiency, shot it down into the sea where it fell a blazing wreck. None of the crew was seen in the water, nor were any bodies found later when the air-sea rescue launch reached the spot. Feather number one in 249's cap, the first of many in the months to come.

It was about this time, too, that on one of our afternoons of freedom, a group of us went swimming at Ghajn Tuffieha, our first such party in Malta. On the south-west side of the island and pronounced, we were advised, 'Ein Tuffewer', it was the only place where there was any sand.

'Butch' drove us there in the ochre-coloured Austin and six of us had the elderly springs well and truly bottoming as we crept along the lonely cratered lane that led down to the beach. The bay, at the bottom of a steep decline, was a small and almost deserted curve of sand, the water uninvitingly grey and tepid. Not exactly Torquay!

As we descended with our swimming trunks and towels, I saw in the middle distance several people in a huddle, one of them bending over what appeared to be a seal lying on the sand. I wandered over to look, and others followed.

It was no seal, unfortunately, but a large man who was leaking water and very dead. Drowned. A worried-looking Maltese in shorts and with dark curly hair was applying artificial respiration but to no avail, and two youngish women were weeping quietly and plainly in shock.

I spoke to them. The victim was English and the captain of one of the visiting merchant ships, the ladies local 'companions'. Against advice, apparently, he had ventured too far out and got into difficulties, the rest being obvious. He was bloated, green and very unpleasant looking. I turned away, feeling slightly sick.

Later, after we had moved away, the body was carried off on a stretcher, a large lolling mound, an arm hanging. The ladies, still weeping, followed at a discreet distance and I was sombrely reminded of the two Marys at the Crucifixion. And we hadn't even started *our* swimming!

Even so, we took to the water, which felt much as it looked, like warm, grey glue, and after splashing about for several hours, towelled ourselves dry and moved off, our feet gritty with sand. Not a very joyful afternoon. I felt miserable and never wanted to see Ghajn Tuffieha again. Nor did I throughout my seven-month stay in Malta.

The days limped by, hot and breathless. Several more frantic scrambles, one of them on 7 June to the far end of the island in pursuit of a mob of Macchi 200s which had attacked Hal Far. We raced down full of the offensive spirit but by the time we had reached there, the birds had flown. I was in Z4043 again, the aircraft in which 'Butch' had shot down the Savoia a few days earlier; I did not like it particularly but felt that a little of its good luck might rub off on me.

138

But, we saw not a thing. Even so, we chased out to sea in pursuit, ending up some 30 miles north of the island, in all 50 minutes of near full-throttle flying. Only later did the penny drop; they were probably after a large batch of reinforcement aircraft which had flown in the day before.

We had had news of the newcomers several days earlier. More Hurricanes, we were told, some Mark 2s this time, at least half of them going on to the Middle East. Included in the group, we were surprised to learn, was 46 Squadron, which was to remain in Malta. 46! Our old mates from North Weald, with 'Rags' Rabagliati, Pete Le Fevre, 'Bert' Ambrose, 'Chips' Carpenter, MacGregor, and the rest; it would be nice to share the burden of defence with some old and trusted companions.

I did not see them arrive; escorted by Blenheims, they were mercifully spared the problems caused by the decrepit Fulmars and all of them landed unscathed. But, like 249, in no very cheerful frame of mind; their airmen, too, with their luggage and some of their pilots, were traipsing around the Cape, never to be seen again. Why, oh why, did the powers that be do such things? Wasn't there *anyone* who understood that a squadron was like a family, that squadron spirit was a delicately nurtured plant, and that to disregard it was to deal the unit a body blow from which it could take ages to recover?

It seemed that we were flying constantly, but for every hour we spent in the air, we spent five on the ground, fanning ourselves in our no-sided tent and blessing Malta, its noisome discomforts and its sweltering heat. And a particular source of irritation – very much a personal hate, this – were the chattering chore-horses which recharged our trolley-acks.

Our Hurricanes were normally started using external accumulators which were moved about in wheeled trolleys and plugged in when required. In order to keep them properly charged, a petrol motor was attached to each and kept running as long as was necessary. During the interminable hours of 'Readiness', there could be up to half-a-dozen of these abominable manufacturers of noise clattering away incessantly within yards of us. For an hour it was tolerable, after two the nerves began to jangle, but after four to six, everyone within twenty paces was contemplating murder. Moreover, with the chore-horses in full voice, very little else could be heard, which in Malta could amount to a death sentence.

It was on one such occasion, with the chore-horses chugging and rattling remorselessly, that someone chanced to look up to see a twin-engined Junkers 88, about 50 feet up, bearing down on us from the shallow valley alongside M'dina and Rabat. As it was less than ten days since the Hun 109s had attacked us with catastrophic results, we were in no mood to treat the matter lightly. In an instant we were all on our feet and running like stags in as many directions as there are spokes in a wheel, expecting all the time to hear the ripping, pulverizing chatter of cannons and machine-guns, everyone frantically seeking some place of sanctuary – hole, wall, equipment, anything in, or behind which to hide.

In the space of seconds and with a shattering roar, the aircraft had swept over our heads, revealing itself to be not an 88 but a Maryland. From 69 Squadron at Luqa. That *bloody* man Devine!

With a mixture of relief and anger, we rose to our feet, dusted ourselves off, and congregated, presently to be joined by the crumpled, bloodied and sorry-looking figure of the tall and usually immaculate Flying Officer Harrington – Harrington of the Bank, the pilot of one now burnt-out Hurricane and the late owner of a pair of apparently priceless polaroid spectacles. His face was a picture. 'I say, old boy' – the usual preface – 'who was the stupid *bastard* who did that? Did you see who it was?' There was more, but unprintable, and murder in his eyes. And for good reason. Covered in scratches and blood, he had flung himself head-first into a rectangular hole in the ground – crammed with refuse and a mass of barbed wire!

That was *it*! I ordered all the chore-horses to be switched off immediately – we couldn't hear the approach of 50 Huns with all that din. But barely had the noise of them died away when a newly commissioned engineer officer appeared from the far side of the airfield, in high dudgeon, wanting to know who had had the temerity to interfere with his chargers. In a savage mood, I was not about to be lectured by anyone, least of all a junior I regarded as a non-flying, paper-qualified, ex-university nonentity, and we nearly came to blows. But the chattering was silenced, at least for a time, although finally, because even I recognized the need to keep the batteries charged, we came to an arrangement.

It was around the dispersal tent, too, that we had a drains problem, or so we thought. For several days we wandered about, complaining of the terrible smell and rooting around for the cause. But there were no drains, it seemed, or not in the immediate vicinity. What on earth was it? A dead rat? Another rotting animal, perhaps?

On about the third morning, the answer was provided by the slightly truculent airman-of-the-watch who had joined me on the floor of the tent at the speed of light when the 109s had attacked us a fortnight earlier. He had just come on duty and was listening to our conversation.

He turned and faced us, his mouth working. 'It's that other bloke's feet, sorr. He stinks us out in the billet.'

We all looked up, stunned. 'Whose feet?'

'That bloke I've just relieved, sorr. The other feller. It's his feet a'right. He never washes 'em, or his socks. Drives us all mad in the billet.' He pulled an agonized face. 'Terrible it is, sorr.' The boy's Glaswegian voice was thick with pent-up indignation.

Amused, faintly shocked but happy to have the matter resolved, the airman with the cheesy feet was dealt with the following day, after which there were no more 'dead rats' or searches.

*   *   *

It was early in June, too, that our new AOC, Air Vice Marshal H.P. Lloyd, arrived at dispersal to meet us all.

Referred to familiarly as Hugh Pughe, the Air Marshal was a middle-sized man of stocky build, who cultivated a rather Cromwellian sternness and brevity of speech. With bright blue eyes, he also had the slightly disconcerting habit of thrusting forward his face until it was within inches of one's own, and staring wordlessly, a fire-eating affectation I found rather childish. After all, we didn't need to be impressed by such theatrical mannerisms; most of us had been fighting continuously for almost a year and knew only too well what was required of us.

But the Air Marshal was friendly enough. We subsequently learned that he had been briefed to bolster morale and to be a thorn in the side of the enemy by cutting Axis supply lines to Africa, using every air resource at his disposal, which he seemed determined to do. Needless to say, we expressed our willingness to play our part, adding vehemently that we wished we had something more serviceable and with a better performance than the lame-duck Hurricanes we had been lumbered with. The poor quality of our aircraft, and the need for something better, was our theme on that occasion and indeed on every occasion for the duration of my stay in Malta.

Then, on 8 June, more unproductive scrambles during the day followed by night flying, 'Butch', several others and I being called upon to defend Malta in the dark. Despite the uncertain quality of our mounts, I actually found myself looking forward to the event.

Ta Kali airfield being merely a flat dust-bowl of worn grass, the flare path was laid out by hand and consisted of about a dozen glim lamps, which could barely be seen above 2,000 feet. There was also a Chance light – when it could be persuaded to work – but no such luxuries as lead-in, exit, or other perimeter lights. In fact, they were seldom needed as in full moon conditions one could almost read a newspaper, and even on the darkest nights – and they could be very dark in Malta – the searchlights proved a useful means of orientating oneself.

Over an area approximately fifteen miles by eight, our system of defence was simple and effective. The bombers usually arriving singly and invariably aiming at Grand Harbour or one or other of our three airfields, the searchlights could normally be expected to illuminate each one as it approached from the north. Meanwhile, up to two Hurricanes, patrolling to one side, would wait for the tell-tale grey-white object to be revealed. Thereafter, a single fighter would scuttle swiftly into the line-astern position and let fly – very straightforward and usually very effective. Or, on an order to us to get out of the way, the guns would take over, Valletta would shake with the crash and crump of a hundred salvos and the sky would be filled with flying shrapnel. In the strictest sense, we were never controlled on to the target, although there were few occasions when we were not given a height and vector, after which we just followed the searchlight beams like cats waiting to pounce.

As good fortune would have it, on that first night we had instant success, 'Butch' Barton – who else? – being lucky enough to be on patrol when a BR 20 was illuminated. Sliding quickly into position, he opened fire and was rewarded immediately when the Italian aircraft was set alight and plunged into the ground, killing those of the crew who were unable to bale out. Despite flying for several hours, however, and positively willing an Eyetie to be illuminated, I had no luck, a particular disappointment as, later, another BR 20 was attacked by two of our aircraft, flown by John Beazley and the diminutive 'Titch' Palliser, and claimed as a 'probable'.

On the whole a most successful night; if this was night-fighting, it was dead easy. Not only was the target area small and the searchlights more than adept, but the BR 20s were most obliging, catching fire almost at the first strike. Not a bit like England, where one flew endless sorties with hardly a sniff of a Hun, and even when an interception was made, the

Junkers 88s especially being as tough as boots and seemingly impervious to scores of strikes.

I was on duty again at dawn but having just flown for almost two hours and been up most of the night, I elected not to lead the first section off, to my everlasting regret. It was a hazy morning with the promise of a blazing sun and scorching day.

Fairly early on, we received a scramble order but with little information of what was afoot. The stately Harrington, who had never before seen an enemy aircraft, took off with three others, Sergeant Rex, formerly a member of 3 Squadron in England, the young and inexperienced Sergeant Lawson, and a recent addition to 249, Sergeant Livingstone, a fair-haired non-smiling Scotsman who had been with 261 and had only recently moved across to us via 185 Squadron. Off they roared in a vast pall of dust and fled away to the south. After which – silence.

About fifteen minutes later the telephone rang and I was informed in a terse sentence that the section had intercepted some 40 miles south of the island and that there were people in the water. Some Savoias had apparently been skirting Malta en route for Libya and at least one had been shot down. One of our Hurricanes had also gone in.

I immediately arranged for a further section to take off and search, and hardly had my instructions been given when a single Hurricane approached from the south and landed without ceremony. It was Harrington, as animated as ever I had seen him.

They had suddenly come upon four Savoias low down, he explained. One of the Eyeties had been shot into the sea and Sergeant Rex had also gone in – whether shot down or due to some sort of engine failure he didn't know. At the moment Rex was swimming about in his Mae West, with the others marking the spot. A long way south, unfortunately, it would take ages for a boat to reach him.

144

The adrenalin still racing, 'Harry' was walking round in circles. How he wished I had been leading; probably have done things differently. He was more excited and concerned than I ever imagined he could be.

Amid a welter of questions and answers, we sorted ourselves out, news being received that the air-sea rescue launch had already left. After which, we waited.

Shortly after, the remaining Hurricanes returned and with the assistance of several more, the rescue launch buffeted its way towards Africa.

Two hours later and almost 50 miles south of the island, Sergeant Rex was picked up, not too unhappy with life apparently, having been swimming powerfully in the wrong direction. Also hooked out of the sea was a single burnt and bedraggled Italian, who was clinging to what remained of one wing of the Savoia. Wrapped up and cosseted, Rex and the Eyetie spent the next two hours sitting in the launch, commiserating with each other.

Later, we talked it over. It seemed that everyone had shot at the Savoias but only one had gone in. What about the others, I asked sternly? Shaken heads; they had just flown on, it seemed, one being as many as they could cope with, the Hurricane ditching and all that. Livingstone was claiming it, although others had shared in its destruction, including Rex who was admitting that he did not know whether he had been hit by return fire or had suffered a straight forward coolant leak. Coolant leak! Another engine problem? But, what did it matter; aircraft and offending engine were down among the dead men now!

Later we heard that the little Italian had been taken to Imtarfa hospital, where he was recovering. As for me, I was kicking myself; having missed out on a BR 20 the night before, I had allowed Harrington to lead the first section off, which was something I would never have permitted in normal circumstances. Still, it could have been me bobbing about out there like a cork. No, I would have to learn to be patient and take things as they came.

Everyone seemed very pleased; it was a long time since Malta's Hurricanes had had a success so far away south. Good old 249, was the verdict.

A day or so later, several of us, including Crossey and Harrington, visited the Italian in hospital, having bought him a razor and other odds and ends. We found him in one of the wards, looking very apprehensive. With the assistance of one of the Maltese doctors, who was known to us and spoke Italian, we calmed his fears and tried to cheer him up, until, eventually, he was so overcome by our good nature that he came close to breaking down. Poor chap, he was the only survivor apparently, although he did not seem too upset about it. Pouff, they had *gone,* he said, dismissing his erstwhile companions to purgatory, or wherever Italians went, with a few eloquent hand signals and a Latin lift of his shoulder. We parted finally, with the little man waving like a child and declaring undying gratitude and friendship. As we left, I wondered what would become of him. A pathetic little chap, and very lucky to be alive.

Although, with others of 249, I was scrambled on both the 10th and 11th, I made no contact. More fortunate were some members of 46 Squadron, who, on the morning of the 11th and during their first flight in anger from the island, intercepted a force of Italian fighters who were escorting a single Savoia reconnaissance aircraft. A ragged engagement ensued after which all sorts of claims were made. Good luck to them, we thought; for us, it had been a nothing day. Thus far, I had not even seen an Italian aircraft.

The following day, which was the 12th, was different, however.

Being scrambled mid-morning, I climbed away towards the south and east with my ragged formation of eight, turning north then west around Hal Far, by which time we were at about 17,000 feet. Receiving definite news of incoming aircraft, I soon saw moving ack-ack fire slightly below me and in the direction of Valletta.

I hardly had time to weigh up the situation, when a mob of aircraft in close formation emerged from the splatter of bursting ack-ack, slightly below us and heading in the opposite direction. Then, as they passed quickly underneath, I reared up and dropped down on them, my retinue streaming in pursuit.

I just had time to recognize a three-engined Savoia bomber in the middle of the enemy group surrounded by fighters, the closest of which I identified as an Me 109 with a light-coloured nose. Then, as we charged among them, aircraft began to scatter in all directions, like leaves whirling in a sudden gust of wind.

Hanging on to the one I had perceived to be a 109, I was thwarted momentarily when it reared up and pointed its nose straight to the heavens. I attempted to follow but was losing ground when, to my surprise, it did not pull away as expected but turned over and in the act of so doing, presented itself as an almost stationary target. I fired. My tracer with its familiar flecks of curving, whipping red, reached out and clutched both fuselage and wings in a brief rippling embrace. After which it was gone. Below my tipping wing. Downwards. Turning. Diving steeply.

I followed, violently, keeping it in sight. I was aware of the sea directly beneath and the coastline behind me, Filfla somewhere adjacent to my forehead, looking on impassively. The enemy turning slowly but going straight down. The slipstream screaming, I flashed worried glances to my sides and rear. Nothing. Going like mad now, left foot extended to the limit, everything roaring and shaking. *Firing!* Then a sudden small blob that was a parachute, detaching, a white streak at first, then developing, finally drifting sideways before rushing quickly in my direction and vanishing to my rear. Further below me still, a diminishing silhouette and a sudden slow-motion eruption of water which died quickly into a disc of pale green as the aircraft went in. I pulled away, staring, everything bending and draining. Then climbed, breathlessly elated but vibrantly tense. Isolated aircraft in the distance, flying in all directions, seemingly unconcerned. And the enemy? Gone!

Back on the ground there was lots of excitement but differing stories. Several, including Crossey, were able to confirm the crash of my victim into the sea off Filfla, together with the parachute. Hamish Munro, who had joined the squadron at North Weald in the spring, was one of several who appeared to be missing and someone was explaining how he had been attacked by Macchi 200s. Macchi 200s! What on earth was he talking about? The aircraft I had encountered alongside the Savoia had been a 109; I ought to know as I'd been shooting at the blighters for the last nine months! One or two, including Crossey and Sergeant Etchells, agreed, but others were doubtful. I heard my voice rising. You couldn't confuse a 109 with a Macchi 200, for heaven's sake; one had an in-line engine and the other a ruddy great radial. Then everyone was admitting that there might have been two formations, the second being the Macchis. Macchis! I hadn't seen any Macchis. We went on talking hotly. Arguing, but finally coming to a reluctant consensus. Still one or two chaps missing, although someone was said to have force-landed at Safi. I gave up; nothing was more confusing than air combat. Later, we heard that 46 had also engaged some Macchis. Had they? Well, bully for them!

When we had been relieved and were back in the courtyard of Torre Cumbo, the Station Commander, John Warfield, congratulated me. Thanking him, I added a little peevishly that there had been so much confusion, I was now not sure *what* had happened.

I found myself hoping that the chap in the parachute would be picked up, but by the late afternoon there was no news. I hated the thought of anyone being left in the sea, imagining myself a victim and being drowned by degrees. However, because it was twenty miles away and I had other things to think about, I soon forgot about it. A not too satisfactory morning in spite of our success. Poor old Ham Munro; he hadn't lasted long.

148

Some time after lunch, because there was so much to-ing and fro-ing from the airfield, I walked the mile or so back to dispersal to watch scattered remnants of 'Butch's' flight who were landing and taxying in, surrounded by the usual clouds of dust. Around the pilots' tent there was a babble of excitement and a number of chaps were pointing fingers at each other and claiming that *he* or *they* had done it. On the fringe of things, I was soon to learn why.

Following the morning's activity, a number of Italian air-sea rescue planes had apparently been sent out from Sicily to pick up those of the enemy who had been shot into the sea, and 'Butch' and his men had run into a Cant seaplane low down over the water some 40 miles north of the island. As the red crosses were plainly visible, they flew around but did not attack, reporting the interception meanwhile. Back came the instruction: 'Shoot it down!' But none of them wanted to, and remonstrated. Back came a further instruction: 'Shoot it down – or else!' So, they shot it down – as gently as they could, and it collapsed into the water.

Back at Ta Kali no-one wanted to claim it, hence the pointed fingers and protestations of innocence. Listening to the quite lively exchange and watching the flushed faces, I found it all rather amusing. Finally, several were ordered to put in combat reports, although I don't know even now whose names were eventually associated with the foul deed. It had been a direct order from the AOC, apparently; not a very nice thing to have had to do – or decide.

It had been quite a day for aircraft falling into the water. 46 Squadron had lost several and some time later, over a drink in Valletta, I learned that another of the clapped-out Fulmars from Hal Far had had an engine failure that day and had been obliged to ditch; their aircraft were as bad as ours, if not worse. Were their Lordships, or 'Airships', aware of the strain it was flying over the sea continually, all the time waiting for the engine to conk out or spring a leak? It seemed not.

*   *   *

The 14th June dawned cloudy and continued that way, which was most unusual. My part of the squadron came to 'Readiness' at 1 p.m.

Several large formations of Hurricanes were expected to land in Malta, bound for the Middle East, our journey of 21 May repeated yet again. They were unlikely to affect us, we were told, except that we should be prepared to ward off any attempt to attack them on arrival, as indeed we had been attacked. I discussed arrangements with control and we sat there, waiting.

And scrambled we were, but not to repel the enemy. The controller had spoken to me briefly before take-off. Apparently, the Hurricanes, in several formations, were being led by a group of twin-engined aircraft which had taken off from Gibraltar prior to rendezvousing with the carriers *Ark Royal* and *Victorious*. Unfortunately, RDF plots now indicated that one of the escorting aircraft, with its Hurricanes, was well north of Malta and showing every sign of missing the island altogether. Panic stations! We were to intercept them as quickly as possible and bring them back.

There followed a quite extraordinary series of events. As we raced northwards below cloud, it appeared that the guiding Hudson was ignoring all vectors and instructions passed to it by control, the usual RT silence being thrown to the wind. Soon we were more than 40 miles north, at which point we were informed that the formation was then to the east of Malta and heading south. That sounded more like it; it looked as if they were now on the right track. Round we turned and headed for home, soon to be told that escort and formation were heading away from Malta again. The half-wits! What had got into them? We turned and, for the second time, set off in pursuit.

After about 40 minutes of chasing about below cloud, much of it closer to Sicily than Malta, we had still not intercepted them. However, on being told that they finally seemed to be heading towards the island, we were brought back to land. Panic over.

But it wasn't! Hardly had we landed when it became clear that the whole formation was once more in difficulty, with the Hurricanes now in despair and telling anyone who cared to listen that they were fast running out of fuel. At their wit's end, control ordered us off, this time sending us south-east in order to reach them, hopefully before they fell into the sea, after which we were to assist the air-sea rescue boats. Racing out over Kalafrana Bay, Crossey and I headed in the general direction of Egypt, little more than 30 feet above the waves, each of us with the unpleasant vision of a dozen or more aircraft dropping into the water one by one.

Although we were not to know it at the time, most of the Hurricanes passed us unseen and scraped in on their last dregs of petrol, two pilots crashing, even so, and one being killed, when their aircraft ran out of fuel before they could land.

Meanwhile, some 40 miles south-east and barely above the waves, we had the good fortune to find one of the two pilots who had already ditched. Leaving Crossey to circle the tiny yellow dot in the water, I returned and made contact with the rescue launch, which was crashing and bouncing its way towards us at maximum speed, and after pointing it in the right direction, flew backwards and forwards endlessly, acting as guide. After hours, it seemed, we watched it successfully make the pick-up, after which we left, full of warm feelings. It was nice to be able to save life for a change!

Just before sunset that evening, with others, I flew across to the new strip at Safi to disperse my aircraft in the fields there, the first of a score of occasions. It was blissfully pleasant as I strolled back the half-mile towards our waiting transport – calm, quiet, balmily warm, and with the now familiar and quite appealing perfume of Malta. Even in war there were moments of utter peace and deep, sensual tranquillity. Greatly moved by the occasion, I wrote of it in detail to my parents.

In the next several days, more scrambles but no sightings. Someone was saying that it looked as though the Huns had left Sicily. Had they? That would account for the dearth of activity, but we would need to be convinced. There was no confirmation, however, only speculation. Then, on 18 June, a sad event.

By this time 249 had been in Malta three weeks and at best could muster on average about ten aircraft – eight Mark 1s and a couple of Mark 2s. Most of the Mark 1s were tropicalized but the Mark 2s were not, their open air-intakes, situated under the engine and between the undercarriage legs, ideally placed to suck in every particle of dust and filth whipped up by our whirling airscrews during take-off, landing, and even taxying. Mr Sidney Camm, in his moments of inspiration when designing the Hurricane, clearly did not have deserts in mind – nor Malta!

I never flew the Mark 2s for the most obvious reason; as leader, had I used the faster type of aircraft, the rest of my formation would always have difficulty keeping up. Reluctantly, therefore, but as a matter of course, I led in a Mark 1, and on the first scramble of that day, I was flying Z4048.

As our dispersal was at the southern end of Ta Kali, we mostly took off south to north, which reduced taxying – and the filth – to a minimum. In this direction, we were faced with rising ground at the end of the airfield and a mass of ridges and stone walls. Every time my wheels left the ground, I prayed; prayed that my engine would keep going and that I would not end up ploughing into the hill or crashing through a score of obstructions. There were very few places to force-land in Malta and to bale out was considered to be the only sensible course of action. But, below 1,000 feet, even baling out was a hazard.

On that occasion, as I roared off in the usual panic, I sensed that there was something wrong with my engine, but in the excitement of the moment, I pressed ahead and committed myself to the air with everything shaking and banging. Twenty feet up, I *knew* it was going to stop. This was it! The hill and the walls clutching at me, I did the unforgiveable – I took a chance on turning back towards the airfield. For some moments, and with my heart in my mouth, I thought I would not make it. However, popping, lurching and banging, the Hurricane dragged itself around, and in the space of seconds I was back again on the ground, limp with emotion and breathing thanks to the Almighty that things had turned out as they had. Away in the distance, my companions were climbing away and turning north.

Relief soon gave way to annoyance, however, and whilst the engine panels were being removed and the cause of the trouble investigated, I stood and watched, seething and fulminating. Bloody hopeless aircraft! It really wasn't good enough; what was a formation without a leader? And I was still in a black mood when, an hour or so later, all the others were back and 4048's problems were still being rectified.

As there were hints of further action from control, I suddenly came to a decision; I would fly the only Mark 2 and someone else would have to go without, or fly 4048 if and when it became serviceable. Then, as the new boy Sergeant Livingstone was the weaver and had his kit in the only Mark 2, I instructed him to remove his belongings, which he did, reluctantly, his face registering surly disapproval.

After which we sat. And waited.

Eventually, the scramble order came. We all raced to the point of take-off, rudders wagging. Then turned, facing north. Clouds of dust billowing and rising behind us, the whole formation roughly line abreast to avoid each other's slipstream and dirt. Then – *off*! As leader and marginally in front, I opened my throttle firmly and we surged forward.

Well – not quite! Everyone else surged, I merely trickled. With my throttle lever up to the gate, then through, I should have been getting first 9 lbs, then 12 lbs boost. Instead of which I achieved barely enough power to set me jog-trotting across the airfield at around twenty miles per hour. *What on earth*— ? Covered in a cloud of filth from the remainder of my roaring formation which had overtaken me for the second time that morning, I gaped at the throttle lever in my left hand. It was at maximum stretch and I had no power – an engine malfunction, twice running! I stopped at the end of the airfield and taxied slowly back. Not fuming this time, just apathetically resigned.

Back in dispersal, my Flight Sergeant was almost jaunty.

'Never mind, sir. It's only the boost capsule stuck. Happens all the time. With all the sherbet (a nice euphemism, that) being sucked into the engine, it's a wonder they ever work at all. It'll only take an hour or so to fix.' And as he spoke the engine cowlings were being stripped off and discarded. Boost capsule! I'd never heard of any such device – boost capsules, thermostats, aneroid thises and thats, such technicalities left me cold. All I wanted was the engine to go, and to keep going!

For twenty minutes or so I stood around with my hands in my pockets, watching a couple of fitters, naked to the waist and streaming with sweat, tinker with the innards and call out to each other. Finally, when they had doctored it to their satisfaction, the engine was restarted and run up, the noise and whipped-up sand a deafening and abrasive whirlwind.

Then, amid the turmoil, the telephone. I ran to answer. Excitement! My flight had intercepted, apparently; there had been an engagement, although the result was uncertain. They were now on their way back.

As we all stood outside the aircrew tent with shaded eyes looking towards Valletta, a pair of Hurricanes appeared in the distance, then another, and finally more. One, however, was on its own and approaching slowly. With something wrong, too, a wisp of white trailing in a tiny feather from its rear. We all watched – wondering. Then as it entered the circuit at about 800 feet and half-a-mile from where we stood, I saw a black dot detach itself from the cockpit. The pilot! As the aircraft fell away downwards, I watched the tiny dark figure drop behind. Oh *no*! A small sliver of white as the parachute streamed, but all too slowly. Everything in slow motion. Come on! Come on! *Open*! It did – partially, but not quickly enough. The dot, larger now, fell . . . fell . . . then thudded into the ground, bounced minutely, and lay still, the parachute, a white fluttering shroud, gently subsiding alongside like a cuddling animal seeking affection. Meanwhile, only several hundred yards away, the crashed Hurricane burned in a frenzy of flame and black smoke.

With others around me, I stood and watched – helpless, wordless, and faintly sick. Then, wearily: who was it? In moments, we knew. It was Sergeant Livingstone. In 4048!

There had been a brush with Macchi 200s, apparently, and Palliser and someone else were claiming a 'probable', a 'damaged' – something. But, what did it matter? A man was dead; the poor, sad, unsmiling Livingstone. In that *bloody* aircraft, too! Had he been hit, or was it just an engine problem? No-one could be sure.

The day dragged on. Blighted.

For the next week we seemed to do little other than deliver then collect our aircraft to and from Safi and be scrambled against raids which either did not materialize or were too high for us to do anything about. Between 19 and 28 June I flew on nine interceptions only, being airborne for little more than twenty minutes on each occasion. Except, that is, for the first sortie on the 27th when, leading ten aircraft, I saw ack-ack fire high above Grand Harbour. A little to the north of Hal Far at the time, we were climbing through 17,000 feet with the enemy several thousand feet above us. Turning towards them we gave chase, but the mass of them, mere dots, fled away northwards towards Sicily. They were Macchi 200s apparently, although we did not get close enough to identify them. Escorting a single Savoia reconnaissance aircraft, we were told, which seemed a disproportionate amount of fighter effort in the circumstances. With the Huns clearly gone from Sicily, the Italians did not seem keen to bomb us by day, preferring to do so at night. What then did they hope to achieve, apart from taking pictures of Grand Harbour?

After chasing them almost to Sicily, we returned having spent 80 minutes in the air. Later, we did a second trip with much the same result. Other than in manoeuvrability, the

Macchi 200, which was an open-cockpit aircraft,[1] appeared to be slightly inferior in performance to even our older Hurricanes, their pilots seldom keen to fight other than over their own back-yard. Having the initiative, and height, they habitually made a shallow dive when approaching Malta so that they were moving fairly quickly when they came within our orbit. When caught unawares, mostly during their return journey, they could be dealt with quite easily, in marked contrast to the Hun 109s which were the most difficult brutes to cope with whatever the circumstances, being able to dive or climb away from us almost at will. I was quite happy to chase Eyeties all day long, but knowing they were merely fighters flying at altitude and not intending to bomb or strafe us, somehow there was not the same degree of urgency about our interceptions, although I doubt that any one of us would ever have admitted harbouring any such thought or attitude. With the departure of the Luftwaffe, a little of the hard edge had gone out of our determination to pursue the enemy to the death; combat, now, was more of a dangerous game.

More Hurricanes from the *Ark Royal* arrived in Malta that day, Mark 2Cs apparently, each tropicalized and with four cannons, although for some reason I did not see them land. There was talk that we would all be re-equipped with the Mark 2 pretty soon – they seemed to be turning up regularly now – which pleased me more than a little as I was still flying one of the old Mark 1s, usually 4380. In spite of my prejudice against the tropicalized version of the Hurricane, there was no doubt about it, the untropicalized ones just didn't work. We were constantly having engine problems on all our aircraft but especially the few Mark 2s, so that scarcely a day passed when I didn't sit there during take-off, stiff with apprehension, waiting for the loss of power or stoppage that would pitch me into the hill ahead or the endless rows of stone walls. And, as if to further reduce my confidence in our

[1] Some had hoods but, apparently, the Italian pilots preferred an open cockpit with a wind deflector.

equipment, on 30 June, when engaged in a hectic scramble in 2815, the Mark 2 which had previously let me down and which, even indirectly, was a factor in Livingstone's death, I had a repeat performance of the engine's intractability. Once more, with the throttle wide open, all I could achieve was a gentle twenty-miles-an-hour trot to the far end of the airfield. On that occasion, however, my feelings were less of anger and more a mixture of despair and relief, despair that we would ever get the aircraft right, and relief that something worse had not happened and that I was still in one piece. When I had taxied back to dispersal and met the enquiring looks of my Flight Sergeant and crew, my advice to them was tersely abrupt: 'Burn the bloody thing!'

It was also during the last week in June that we learned of Germany's attack on Russia and that the Russian Air Force had been almost wiped out. So, that's where the Huns from Sicily had got to! Discussing this development in the mess, the general view was that Hitler was out of his mind but that it was a godsend; what had possessed the man to do such a thing, to make the most elementary mistake of all, that of waging major war on more than one front? We had been jolly glad to see the back of those Huns in Sicily though; with the Hurricanes we had to fly, *anything* might have happened!

7 Summer Sets In

The 1st July was a Tuesday. It was still unpleasantly hot and humid although we were becoming accustomed to the extremes of temperature and the discomfort of being alternately kippered in the cockpit low down and frozen high up. I found that temperature alone did not affect me greatly although the sun did; being very fair-skinned my hide took every opportunity to come off in strips obliging me to keep myself covered whenever possible.

Before dawn on that first day we all took the bus to Safi to collect our aircraft dispersed there and minutes later I was kicking myself when I found that I had so organized things that I had left myself to fly 2815. 2815! Two engine failures in three flights! Would this be the third? And at Safi, too, a make-shift strip surrounded by natural and man-made hazards, the area being littered with explosive devices laid down to thwart any parachute or glider attack. Happily the aircraft behaved perfectly and I landed at Ta Kali without incident. Even more happily, it was to be the last time I ever flew 2815; in fact, I flew neither it nor any of the old Mark 1s ever again, a brand new set of Mark 2s being delivered to us. Yes, things were definitely looking up. Even the fresh paintwork cheered us up although we were still without our squadron markings which strangely, I missed most of all, finding that they gave me a sense of belonging and were a powerful link with past successes.

For three days after we were not called upon to fly. I sorted myself out a new aircraft, Z3498, had its spinner painted red and felt altogether better as a result. There were a number of new officers and NCOs posted to the squadron, too, one of them, Graham Leggett, being known to me in England. Otherwise, the newcomers were totally inexperienced and seemed terribly young, although they were barely younger than myself. I thanked God that there was a lull in activities; had the Huns been in Sicily there would have been slaughter on a grand scale. With so many experienced fellows available at home why did they keep sending out these green apprentices? And to Malta, of all places!

It was about 1 July, too, that 46 Squadron, who were now sharing Ta Kali with us, learned that they were to forfeit their squadron number and be known henceforth as 126 Squadron. They were stunned – absolutely – as were the rest of us. *What* a thing to do! Here they were, one of the oldest squadrons in the Air Force and among the most famous, being instructed at a moment's notice to lose their identity. There was near mutiny. Even I was horrified; to me 'Rags' Rabagliati, Pete Le Fevre, and all the rest, colleagues throughout the Battle of Britain and after, *were* 46, as were their illustrious forebears, MacLaren, one of the big aces of 1918, and Victor Yeates, who had written 'Winged Victory' in 1937, a book I had grown up with and one which I considered to be the best description written of aerial warfare during the Great War. We, too, had lost our airmen and others in process of journeying to the Middle East, but we, at least, had kept our name and number. Now they had lost everything. The Air Ministry, or whoever, must be *mad*. In the mess, we all exchanged furious and recklessly undiplomatic comments on the stupidity of those in control of our affairs. *Fools*! They just didn't *understand*!

But whatever these distractions, we were all settling down in Malta; letters from home were arriving spasmodically, but arriving; the food and conditions in the mess were improving; there was talk of a proper dispersal building being constructed on the airfield to replace the tent; and in our constant battle with the mosquito and flea population, we seemed to be gaining ground, although the amount of Flit expended in and around my shared bedroom could have floated a ship.

Crossey and I were also in process of providing ourselves with a new wardrobe, a tailor in Valletta producing an elegant line in shirts and shorts in a rather fetching curtain material which, whilst its qualities of lightness and ventilation might be lacking, at least enabled us to feel comfortable and look like officers, thereby heightening our morale.

Our knowledge of Valletta, too, had widened considerably, but, alas, not always to our advantage. Earlier in June, 'Butch' Barton's half of the squadron had sallied forth into the town-centre and embarked upon an afternoon and evening of good fellowship. Towards midnight and then in the company of Wing Commander 'Bull' Halahan, they had created such a disturbance in first a bar and then an hotel, that the police had been summoned. Unhappily, the upholders of the law had not much relished the task of either reasoning with, or subduing, a dozen or so rowdy Air Force officers in full voice, and had unfortunately shown their timidity. The outcome was, reinforcements were called for and about half the fighter defence of Malta was eventually marched cheering through the streets and into gaol, where several of the more uninhibited among them began running up and down the bars of the cell like caged monkeys, making the appropriate gestures and noises and frightening the police half to death.

And there they stayed.

The following morning, authority's dilemma was plain to see: who was going to defend the island? Without further ado, the squadron was released and arrived back at Ta Kali with thick heads and dry mouths but still enjoying the joke, although Squadron Leader Barton's smile was observed to be more than a little strained. As indeed was 'Bull' Halahan's. Summoned to the Air Officer Commanding's presence that very morning, within hours he had been banished from Malta, his career blighted for all time.

Altogether, a sad and tragic ending to a harmless prank and a reminder that hooliganism did not start in the football stadiums.

* * *

On 7 July, feeling full of bounce in my new Hurricane 2, I led my half of the squadron against a large, fast-moving raid of which we heard a good deal but saw nothing. After racing northwards to within gliding distance of Sicily, we returned in fine fettle, despite encountering nothing other than a wilderness of sea. For a change, it was nice to fly behind an engine which sounded reassuringly healthy.

On my way home, watching the distant sand-coloured slivers that were Malta and Gozo develop slowly into the island's familiar inlets, bays, and ridges and finally the white-brown congestions of Valletta and distant Rabat, I mused on the difficulties of intercepting anything in this vast arena of glaring sun and sea – unless one ran full tilt into the enemy, that is, or we crossed paths within a mile or two and several thousand feet. Knowing that we were dealing with the Italian Air Force only, I found myself in a comparatively relaxed frame of mind; at least we did not have the constant dread of being jumped from the rear by 109s which dived and zoomed much faster than we were ever able to cope with. We had heard that all the Hun fighter squadrons were re-equipping with the 'F' version of the 109, which had a considerably better performance than the 'E', whose potential for mischief we knew only too well; if that were so, even with our improved Hurricanes, we would be back to square one. Moreover, there was news, too, of the Eyeties getting something called a Macchi 202, which had the same in-line engine as the 109 and was supposed to be about as fast. None of us had seen any, but we were not too concerned about the prospect of meeting them; Eyeties were Eyeties, when all was said and done.

Commencing 8 July, 249 spent the next fortnight operating mainly at night, although the change of role did not mean that we had the hours of daylight to ourselves. Apart from being called upon to make the occasional scramble – fruitless, needless to say – it did enable us to indulge in a little practice flying and interception training, the latter exercises being mainly for the benefit of the controllers 'down the hole'. After

161

the tensions of the first several weeks, this interlude, together with our new and more reliable aircraft, brought about a comparatively relaxed atmosphere. Even the mosquitos, the fleas, and the everlasting Flit, seemed lesser irritants.

And on the night of the 8th, we had some success.

Flying Z3498, I took off well after dark with the message ringing in my ears that bombers were on the way. Climbing up to 15,000 feet, I took up my patrol line a few miles to the east of Valletta, and waited, flying meanwhile in wide figures of eight.

For some time, nothing – no word, no searchlights, no activity of any sort. The night pretty dark but with a well-defined horizon which made instrument flying easy, I wandered about, not in the least perturbed or even excited. In my opinion night fighting did not have much to commend it as it was so seldom rewarding; the enemy hardly ever turned up when, or where, expected and most of one's time and effort was spent establishing one's position and getting back to base in conditions of complete black-out. After about 40 minutes, though, a terse sentence with news that one – two – bogeys were ten miles north, angels 14. And almost immediately, searchlights.

The beams materialized out of nothing, blue-white fingers in the darkness, feeling around, sightless, exploring. This was more like it! Suddenly alert, I sorted out my cockpit by feel, dimmed everything – including the graticules in my gunsight – to the faintest minimum, twisted my gun-button to 'FIRE' and surged up alongside a clutch of around six beams which were crossing experimentally like pale scissoring lances. About a mile distant and following them as they probed, I watched carefully. On edge. Expectant.

Then more searchlights, a dozen or so now, concentrating. Over Valletta, about – I found myself praying that they would keep their itching fingers off those triggers far below. The beams now in a steep pyramid, solidly together. They had something, or had they? Unable to see, I dropped down below the cone and looked up. Nothing. Nothing yet, and the thin moving columns of light falling behind – I was going too fast, damn it. I curved away to the left and made a complete turn, picking up the beams again and focusing hard. Still nothing. Then . . . *something*! Fleetingly. Was it? I looked again. *Yes*! I could *see* it!

As the beams caught the bomber, I had a glimpse of the pale undersurfaces of a largish aircraft. A surge of excitement. I turned hard in its direction, flying by feel and instinct in the darkness. The lights moving quickly now and together, but with no bomber in the cone, or none that I could see. Hang on! Hold him! Don't let him go! I hurled my Hurricane in pursuit. Where was it! Line astern now and about 500 yards behind but with nothing visible ahead. The lights moving still as though they were seeing the enemy aircraft from the ground, whereas from directly behind I could see nothing. I dropped down again and looked up hoping to see the pale reflection. Nothing. The fingers wandered about uncertainly, searching again. Then, in a searing blaze of blue and white, they caught me. Oh, *no*! *Not me,* you clowns! I ducked down into the cockpit – for one, two, three seconds – before the brilliant eyes beneath, recognizing their error, shifted their glare and I was straining my own eyes into the red darkness of light-scarred blindness. Damn and blast the stupid . . . ! The beams ahead of me now, but there, to the left of the cone, a small dark shadow that was the bomber. Eureka! I could see it, but those below couldn't! To the left, I felt like screaming. Your *left!* But the beams moved away to the right, missing it, as I followed closely. After which, in a flash – inspiration! I would fire and whoever it was would fire back at my tracer, giving away their position. I did so and my cannons thumped and shook – a short burst, but not a sign of tracer. And nothing in return, either. My aircraft had cannons, hadn't it? – loaded with ball and armour-piercing; no tracer and certainly no de Wilde. What a time *not* to have machine-guns!

I found myself curving to the right in a fast dive but well behind the moving cone of light. Somewhere in the centre of the island, I imagined. I'd missed it! Missed it, after being so close, too. Still searching hopefully, I followed the searchlights like a cat. But they were clearly uncertain now – splitting, moving this way and that, and finally – one by one, being doused, the pin-prick sources of light far below spluttering minutely and fading, until, after a time, I was left in total blackness. Heading – which way? I straightened up and, my DI having toppled, strained my eyes into the gloomy bowl of the compass between my knees. Faintly, the petulantly wandering needle eventually indicated that I was flying north. North! I was way out to sea again, probably. Hell! All over and yet again I had missed a sitter. I turned around and climbing back to 14,000 feet, informed control I was resuming my patrol. They acknowledged my remark dispassionately, adding that there was no other business at the moment. Thereafter, everything went quiet and I had the night – and the blackness beneath that was Malta – all to myself.

Twenty minutes later, I landed. I had been airborne 70 minutes.

Back in dispersal and in the shaded glimmer within the tent, someone was saying he *knew* he had heard gunfire, after which I was voicing my annoyance and 'Butch' was commiserating with me in his quiet Canadian voice:

'Hard luck, Ginger!' He even reached out a hand to touch my arm, which was about the most demonstrative act I had ever seen my squadron commander perform.

Hard luck! I was seething inside. Fancy letting that blighter get away.

Somewhat later, and whilst I and several others were still in dispersal awaiting developments, Flying Officer Cassidy took off to man the patrol line.

Cassidy, variously referred to as Cass, Casserole, or Hopalong, was a small, doe-eyed young man of Catholic Irish ancestry, who had transferred to 249 from 25 Squadron at North Weald the previous autumn. Formerly on fighter Blenheims, during his early weeks with 249 he had mainly impressed himself on my mind as having run foul of his then Station Commander who was himself a devout Catholic and who constantly demanded to know why Cassidy had not been to mass. With members of the Roman church thin on the ground, I sensed that although Cass always referred to the Station Commander's strictures as rather a joke, there was just that hint of outrage in his description of events which suggested they were not quite the joke he alleged them to be.

After the sound of Cassidy's Hurricane had faded into the darkness, I stood around enjoying the mellow warmth and scents of the Maltese night. Other than the dim illumination within the tent, everything was black and silent with only the occasional sound of laughter from the small groups of airmen who formed the first-line servicing party. Stretching away to the north was the flare-path, a dozen or so pin-pricks of light at the head of which was the black stump of the Chance floodlight, its beam extinguished. Everybody waited. Patiently.

After a time, the telephone. At least one bogey approaching from the north. Expectantly, we all looked towards the north and presently the searchlights flicked on – one, three, six, then many more – waving experimentally like the antennae of some giant insect blindly seeking out its prey. Then, as the drone of engines high up drifted in our direction, they began to focus, pencils of pale grey moving in tall pyramids, purposefully now, catching the underside of the occasional small patch of cloud in sudden splodges of reflected light. Had they caught it? We couldn't see. I found myself holding my breath. They should, though. Any moment. And as we strained our lifted eyes into the darkness, the additional sound of Cassidy's Hurricane, an all-too familiar sound. Everyone tense. Come on! Come on! Pick the blighter up!

And they did. A sudden flick of something extra and the beams caught the underside of a twin-engine aircraft. They'd *got it*! Immediately, every lance of light moved quickly on to the target. And held it. They'd got it all right! Now for it!

I estimated the Eyetie bomber to be something over 10,000 feet, the noise of its thrumming unsynchronized engines clear in our ears. It moved across Valletta in our direction then turned away towards the south. Hell! Normally, the night bombers turned north, which would have brought it right across Ta Kali. Now we wouldn't see the interception, unless Cassidy caught up with it in seconds. Where was he, for Pete's sake? Anyone see him? But no-one had done.

Expectant still, we watched the beams follow the now fading sound of engines until they, too, were only dim shafts in the far distance. Probably in the Hal Far area, we estimated. And no interception. Cass must have seen it, surely, or been told. What a shame. Another disappointment. We continued to watch. And listen. Until everything died away into silence. And darkness.

Then, just above the horizon and far to the south a sudden flicker of light. Followed by a tiny shifting flare. Moving. Dropping. Falling. Not unlike a star, but much more slowly. He'd *got* it! Cass had *hit it!* – it was on fire! His first aircraft at night, too! Voices raised in a thin, ragged cheer. Yes, the blighter was a goner, all right. We continued to strain our eyes. The noiseless moving light fell away downwards . . . downwards . . . until, finally, it disappeared. Totally. Extinguished in a second by rocky earth or water, what did it matter? After which, and for the second time, there was only silence. And the mellow, sweet-scented darkness that was Malta.

In less than ten minutes, Cassidy's Hurricane was back in the circuit, an invisible noise. Moving around. Then, much quieter now, we heard the whisper of his engine over M'dina. On with the Chance light! The din of the generator rose to a dull roar as the broad flat beam developed into a pool of light extending down to the fourth or fifth flare. An aircraft emerged suddenly, almost silently, out of the darkness and into the beam, before floating to the ground and disappearing into the black void of the airfield beyond. He'd made it. He was down. Well done! A real hero!

Within minutes, Cassidy was being carried shoulder-high around dispersal, grinning, but feeling much as he looked, totally embarrassed. A BR 20, he thought. Into the sea south of the island. Easy really. Caught fire so quickly, at the

166

first touch, it seemed. Obviously no self-sealing tanks or armour plate. Incredible! None of us gave the Eyetie crew a single thought – dead or alive!

Talk and more talk. A good night, in most people's opinion. Not in mine, though. To think, we might have had *two! Two* in a single night! Some time later, I wrote in my logbook: '8th July. Fired at Italian aircraft; must have missed!'

The following day, we heard that a section of 185 from Hal Far had intercepted a small group of Macchi 200s and a couple of Air Sea Rescue float-planes, which were presumably looking for survivors. Being vectored on to them somewhere to the east of the island, they had attacked, apparently, but to no great effect, although claims of a sort had been made. We all reckoned they couldn't have been trying very hard. Shooting down ASR float-planes didn't come easily to any of us, although the policy was to do so.

What a thoroughly nasty war!

There was nothing much doing for 249 over the next several days. I mucked about in dispersal, was involved in a few abortive scrambles, most of them of less than twenty minutes duration, and went into Valletta, fighting off the fleas en route. In the bars there, we heard that a few of 126 and 185, 'Rags' Rabagliati and 'Boy' Mould included, had made a low level attack on Syracuse harbour and had claimed all sorts of flying boats which had been moored there. Terribly daring, as Syracuse, well up the east coast of Sicily, was very well defended and more than 100 miles distant. 'Rags', with his slow smile, told me about it in his quiet drawling voice, his explanation all the more appealing as he had a slight lisp. 'Boy' Mould, whom I had met several times at Hal Far, was the commanding officer of 185 and had been with No. 1 Squadron in France at the beginning of the war. A most charming, pleasant-faced young man, he was about four years older than myself and had achieved great fame when he was credited with shooting down the first enemy aircraft to fall to the British forces in France. Syracuse! With some of the engines I had flown behind, venturing anywhere beyond gliding distance of Ta Kali was apt to give me the willies!

My 21st birthday being on 14 July, as I thought it would be doubly upsetting for my parents were I to be killed on that day, I arranged not to fly. I need not have worried, however, as nothing much happened. I learned subsequently that to celebrate the occasion, my parents had sent me a greetings telegram – which arrived a fortnight later! The mail, too, was hopeless. At one stage, my family did not receive a letter from me for nearly two months and became almost demented with worry, speculating that I might even have been sent off to Russia. It was terribly cold in Russia, my mother observed in one unhappy letter – forgetting no doubt that it was mid-summer – adding that she *did* hope I wouldn't be sent there as I hadn't the proper clothing. I had a hollow feeling that she might decide to complain to Air Ministry.

To all of which I eventually replied that I wasn't in Russia and, as regards correspondence, I was doing my best. Malta *was* a bit isolated at the moment, didn't she understand, and I wasn't really responsible for my letters turning up in batches of five and six. In England, press reports were suggesting that we were having a terrible time, which was far from the truth. Now that the Huns had departed and our engines and aircraft were newer and rather more reliable, I was moderately happy. There was the nightly, ever present threat of being hit by a bomb, of course, and there were more sea and stone walls than I would have wished for, otherwise things were more than tolerable.

For the next several days I continued to race off the ground on half a dozen dust-streaming interceptions, all of them abortive as we saw not a thing. Then, as luck would have it, on the 17th, a day when my half of the squadron was not on duty, 'Butch' and seven others ran full tilt into a minor swarm of Macchi 200s a little north of Valletta, a group which had become separated from the main Italian formation of something over 40. In the brief, running fight that ensued, 'Butch', with his usual combination of skill and good fortune, disposed of one, and a further Macchi was shot down by several other members of his flight. Unhappily, one of our own Sergeants was lost, a young man called Guest, who had joined the squadron just before our departure from England and of whom I knew only a little.

With the squadron still operating in two parts, some of the family feeling so carefully nurtured over the past twelve months and so splendidly evident during the summer and autumn of 1940, seemed to be slipping away. I was barely acquainted with half a dozen of the pilots in 'Butch's' group and even in my own, there were several who were merely names and faces. A sad business, as I always felt that morale, to a large degree, was founded on example, continuity, and personal association, none of these elements being able to flourish in an atmosphere of constant change and uncertainty. The incident resulting in the death of Livingstone remained poignantly in mind; as his flight commander, I wished I had known him better, Sergeant Guest, too, for that matter.

The AOC, Hugh Pughe Lloyd, came to visit us again about this time, treating me, as leader of those on duty, to his now-familiar stern, Cromwellian glare from a distance of about nine inches. Our conversation was pleasant enough, however. I pointed out that in spite of a substantial number of reinforcement Hurricanes arriving in Malta, 249 could seldom put up more than eight aircraft, our serviceability state remaining deplorable as we still possessed a few clapped-out Mark 1s and untropicalized Mark 2s, whose engines seemed only to function when the spirit moved them. In terms of performance, whilst we could cope with the Macchi 200s, Savoias and other Eyetie aircraft, if the Huns returned with their 109s and 88s, or if the new Macchi 202s put in an appearance, we would be hard put to hold our own. Were there no Spitfires available? Or Tomahawks, even?

Fixing me with a fierce stare, Hugh Pughe explained that we should all be more offensive-minded. Carry the fight to the enemy! Strike them everywhere! Bomb them out of their stride, that was the ticket! And that was what we would have to do.

I listened to his fierce exhortations in mild wonderment and dismay. Somehow there seemed to be a credibility gap between my AOC's expectations and our own capabilities.

Meanwhile, in addition to our daylight activities, we were still operating at night and on 24 and 28 July, I was airborne again, the first occasion being especially memorable.

On a moonlit night, it was a joy to fly in Malta; one hardly needed a flarepath even for landing. Moreover, from 15,000 feet, with the horizon a firm line in every direction and the whole island clearly visible, navigation, even without the searchlights, was a simple enough matter. Sadly, my flight of 24 July was not one of those occasions.

Being scrambled shortly before midnight, I found the night sky as black as ever I had known it. For the first time I could recall, I was obliged to climb away entirely on instruments, my head buried in the office not only until I was at height but also as I was wandering about on my supposed patrol-line somewhere in the area of Kalafrana Bay. There was no horizon, no searchlights, not a candle's flicker anywhere, just impenetrable, velvety blackness, a blackness accentuated by the magenta flare of my engine exhausts, visible evidence of the struggle being waged to keep my Hurricane and me in the air. Uncomfortably alone and with only a vague notion of where I was, I kept in touch with control with plaintive enquiries as to what was going on, the reassuring voice from below establishing a welcome link between me and the earth in an otherwise dark and hostile wilderness. At that very moment, my parents would be comfortably and obliviously asleep in far away England; if only they could see me now, I mused. I cruised around at 14,000 feet, watching my instruments like a hawk. If I ran into a bomber tonight, in the excitement of manoeuvring and shooting, I was going to have my work cut out deciding which way was *up*!

Then, the voice from below. Bogey approaching from the north. Vector three-five-zero. I turned in that direction, straightened up, and flew off to greet the enemy. After which, I waited. And searched. And waited. In every direction, nothing but a blank, black wall .

After a time, but behind me – *miles* behind me! – a sudden clutch of searchlights. I turned, very circumspectly, and flew back towards them, my eyes darting in rapid glances away from my instrument-panel. I followed the hesitant beams expectantly, about a mile behind. Cautiously and on edge. Nothing to see, though. The tall pencils of light moving indecisively this way and that, then more in concert. Drifting. Searching. Moving off to my right. But nothing still. I watched carefully the apex of the minutely waving cone of wands. Stalking. Following. Turning with them. More. Then more. Now straightening. Close, very close, almost within touching distance. I began to lose patience. Come on, for God's sake, *show* something! Now, going north again, I sensed. I fell into line astern. Whoever it was was now going home, surely? Then, after some apparent indecision far below, in an instant – *nothing*! The lights disappeared at the snap of a finger, leaving me in eye-searing blackness.

For a full minute, I remained glued to my instruments but after some anxious moments of reorientation, I looked up to see a reddish flare ahead of me. The glow of an exhaust! An *exhaust*! Eureka! A bomber, ahead but slightly higher. A Hun – Eyetie – or whoever, going away northwards. About 500 feet higher, I judged, a distinct exhaust glow, something I had seen at night several times before. Careful though. Didn't want to scare the blighter and provoke a shower of sherbet from the rear gunner.

I opened up and felt my engine and airframe tighten as the throttle lever was thrust forward to the gate and my airscrew fined to a shrill, 2,850 revs. Then everything right forward to obtain maximum power. My gaze raptly focused on the spot of light ahead – mustn't lose it! – I climbed hotly in pursuit, tensely oblivious of the endless void of blackness all around me.

A minute or more of urgent, vibrating flight. A quick glance at my instruments – 250 on the clock at something approaching 14,000 feet – getting on for a Hurricane's maximum speed on the level.[1] My aircraft drumming and shivering in tune with my excitement. Ought to be catching up by now. The Hun, or whoever, still ahead and a bit above, which was rather odd. Going like hell, too! Press on, though. I urged my Hurricane forward. Faster! Faster!

The adrenalin surging, I raced northwards for perhaps five trembling, raging minutes. Until, reluctantly and with a gradual dawning of comprehension, I began to realize that I was not chasing an enemy aircraft at all but one of the Lord's own cosmic creations – a star! Low on the horizon and reddish in colour, was it Mars? Venus? Something to do with the Plough? My astronomy negligible, I didn't know, nor did I care very much.

Closing the throttle – to my Hurricane's immense relief, I sensed – I turned carefully towards the south and after straightening up, called for a fix and homing vector. The now familiar voice came up from below: 'Any luck?' And, after some moments, the same voice: 'Steer, 175 degrees, distance 38 miles!'

I sagged back with relief. Thank God for that! Just the sort of night for me to have an RT failure as well! More composed now, I headed south into the blackness.

Glued to my instruments, I let down gradually, carefully, praying for the companionable sight of the searchlights which, thus far, had seemed eager to give assistance only to the enemy. But, for me, not so much as a flicker. I thought of asking control to have them switched on but decided against it. Having behaved like a half-wit, it was best to keep quiet about it!

That night, I saw nothing whatever of Malta until I was back again in the circuit at Ta Kali, at which point and almost

---

[1] True airspeed increases with height; I was actually flying at a little over 300 mph.

by accident, I caught sight of the thin line of pin-pricks which were the flarepath lights. I had been airborne a mere 40 minutes, which had seemed like hours. And all for nothing.

I wrote home that night, apparently at peace in the remaining period of cool, silent darkness. A very tired letter, though, and a little disheartened and peevish. What was the use of all this harrying and chasing about, I asked querulously? More than two months in Malta, and I had hardly fired a shot.

Having flown three times on the 24th and been up most of that night, I was not on duty for the next two days, 'Butch's' half of the squadron together with 185, across at Hal Far, taking over the responsibility of defending the island. We had heard earlier, via the grapevine, that there was a big escorted convoy of ours somewhere away to the west, but as it was not yet within our orbit, we gave it little thought.

Despite my lack of sleep, I was sufficiently alive and active – most unusual for me! – to be out and about in Valletta during the morning of the following day and was witness to a part of my own squadron in action. The air raid siren having sounded and with people in the streets either scurrying for shelter or gawping into the sky, I joined the watchers and heard the thin, angry drone of invisible engines high above, followed by the faint 'brrrr' of distant machine-guns and soon after, the white, pencil-thin trace of an aircraft heading rapidly earthwards. My vision obstructed by the building next to me, I lost sight of it for a time, but seconds later I saw it again and immediately sensed a plunge to destruction. One of ours? I shaded my eyes. Impossible to say; no flames or anything really dramatic, only faint, minute puffs of white from an aircraft now over the vertical, screaming like a banshee and looking as though it would dive right into the middle of Valletta. Which it did, with a terrible bang, not too far away from where I was standing.

Immediately, there was excitement and shrill hysterical chatter, with people running in the direction of the crash, no doubt wishing to dip their handkerchiefs in the blood.

I halted in disgust. The ghouls! Well, there would be no blood with that one, and very little of anything else. I just hoped it had not been one of ours.

In fact, it was a Macchi 200, the victim of Bob Matthews, a pilot officer in 'Butch's' flight who had joined 249 shortly before our departure from England, the Eyetie fighter being one of several destroyed as the result of an interception made a little north of Valletta. Even more horrifying, the Italian pilot had apparently baled out but his parachute not functioning properly, the unfortunate man had followed his Macchi down to disaster, a pathetic curving stone. Poor chap! Although it was about the fifth such incident I had either witnessed or knew of over the previous twelve months, the latest being Sergeant Livingstone, the stomach-churning unpleasantness of it never diminished. Plenty of time for each wretched victim to watch and wait for his inevitable pulverizing and bloody end. Did nature anaesthetize the mind on such occasions? I hoped I would never be in the position to find out.

But, whatever its immediate effect on me, the memory of the incident soon evaporated. It had been the usual reconnaissance aircraft, apparently, a twin-engined Cant this time – it too being shot down – escorted by a mass of Italian fighters. Silly people; why did they insist on doing the same thing day after day? If all they wanted were pictures of Grand Harbour and Luqa, surely they could achieve their ends more economically. We supposed they had come to photograph Valletta which was bulging with ships, the convoy we had heard about having reached its destination if in somewhat depleted numbers. Now what? we wondered.

Within hours we were to find out.

It was still dark the following morning when I was awakened by bumps, but bumps with a difference. With bombs, one's sleeping ear was cocked first for the drone of the bomber, then the whistle and thump of bombs in the middle distance, until finally, when the whistles became the briefest of shrieks and the ground began to shake, it was over the side and under the bed in a single liquid movement. How

I – and others – achieved this magical transfer of more than eleven stones of flesh and blood, was always a mystery as my mosquito net was always tucked in tightly, yet never once did it impede my lightning progress. Perhaps surprisingly, I was never greatly upset by enemy bombing in Malta, even when the 500 pounders fell within yards of the Mess; quite without evidence or reason, I was always confident that the bombs were destined to drop on someone else.

It was against this background that I interpreted the thumps in the early morning of 26 July as something other than bombs, although earlier there had been the usual noise of bombing in the distance. Naked except for a towel round my middle, my bare feet smacking on the cool flagstones of my shared bedroom, I joined Crossey and several others who were outside, talking in quiet tones on the elevated walk-way that ran one side of the courtyard. It was still quite dark.

'What's up?'

Crossey replied that he didn't know in hushed tones that suggested that he didn't want the enemy to hear. An attack of some sort. Out to sea, he thought. The continuous series of bumps in the distance were clearly more in keeping with naval guns than the anti-aircraft fire with which we were so familiar.

'D'you think we're being invaded?'

'Invaded! I hope not!' An unsteady laugh.

'Have you got your gun?'

'Gun! I think so. Somewhere. It might be an idea to dig it out.'

I agreed – profoundly; the prospect of Max Schmeling's[1] face appearing around the door-jamb behind a Tommy-gun was not in the least appealing.

The first streaks of dawn in the east, there soon came the distant noise of aircraft engines bursting into life and after some minutes, several pairs of Hurricanes rose out of the

[1] Former World Heavyweight Champion; in 1941 a German paratrooper.

night and, dark silhouettes, roared across our front, climbing towards the lightening grey beyond St Paul's Bay. Far away to our right, searchlight beams slanted obliquely across the sky and out to sea. Yes, something was most definitely up!

For half an hour or so, we hung about on the stone parapet in the cool dampness of dawn, speculating, listening, and watching as aircraft left and reappeared with the urgency that suggested battle, the distant noise of guns continuing spasmodically meanwhile. Then, word began to filter through that there had been a seaborne attack on Grand Harbour but that things were now under control; some 'E' boats, or their Italian equivalent, had apparently made a suicide attack but had been beaten off. The Hurricanes of 126 Squadron we had seen taking off from Ta Kali had shot up a number of the MTBs and there were Eyetie fighters about too.

Things not being quite as desperate as we had feared, the tension subsided and I suddenly found myself shivering. As it was still well before 6 a.m. – still time for a couple of hours' zizz before breakfast – I padded back to my bed. No point in hanging about, catching pneumonia.

By mid-afternoon the following day, the picture was more or less clear. Several Italian MTBs and up to a dozen smaller vessels, including one-man explosive craft and human torpedoes, had been escorted to within twenty miles of Malta by a mother ship and launched against Grand Harbour in a do-or-die attempt to breach the defences and get at the ships within. The attack had started, as we well knew, considerably before dawn to the accompaniment of a diversionary bombing attack, the sounds of which we had faintly heard. Then, when the light was sufficiently good, a force of Macchi 200s had flown south in order to cover the withdrawal of the seaborne force.

249 Squadron not being on duty that morning, it fell to 126 and 185 to scramble against what was for them a quite unusual target and also brave the hail of shell and shot that was arcing luminously from the now wideawake shore defences. In fact, those on shore had never been other

than wideawake, being forewarned, apparently, of the Italian attack.[1]

Scarcely believing their good fortune, the Hurricanes had attacked the MTBs and other craft and were in turn attacked by the Macchis. On balance, however, our own side had triumphed handsomely, almost all the MTBs and other craft being disabled or sunk and several Macchis being shot into the sea. However, during the fracas, Denis Winton, who had been part of my flight in 249 during our first days in Malta and had later joined 185, was hit – whether by fighter or ship was unclear – and forced to bale out. Plopping into the sea, he inflated his dinghy and climbed aboard, thanking God for his deliverance.

Some time later, he became aware that he was fairly close to one of the larger vessels he had attacked and put out of action. As the MTB appeared to be harmlessly adrift and deciding that it represented a more secure sanctuary than his bobbing dinghy, he swam and otherwise urged himself towards it and finally clambered aboard only to find himself faced with the product of his own handiwork – eight mutilated and bleeding corpses. Mildly revolted by the carnage around him, he was obliged to stay there for several hours, praying that some other belligerent Hurricanes would not attack the Italian vessel of which he was now the sole occupant. Some time later, after waving an improvised white flag in an effort to convince the crew of a cautiously circling British rescue craft that he needed rescuing, he was picked up by a Swordfish floatplane, a type of aircraft I never at any time saw on the island. Later, displaying his trophies, he was able to regale us amusingly with the tale of his macabre adventure. The MTB was also retrieved, being towed back to Malta with its eight uncomplaining occupants.

A successful day for those of us in Malta, a gory and tragic one for the Italian attackers, their casualties being

[1] From our own intelligence via the captured ULTRA decoding equipment.

fifteen dead and eighteen captured. Such glorious, flamboyant but foolhardy bravery, so typical of the Eyeties; given the circumstances, what did they hope to achieve? All the same, I was glad it had not been Max Schmeling and his mates! Which rather begged the question: what would I have done in the event of a German parachute invasion? Despite the recent airborne assault on Crete, which had had such bitter consequences for us British, none of us at Ta Kali was in the least prepared for any such happening in Malta, nor had we even talked about it – seriously that is. I wasn't even sure of the whereabouts of my revolver!

July drifted to a close with a searingly brilliant sun and humid and oppressive heat. In our primitive dispersal tent, we gasped and fanned ourselves and prayed for rain as we waited for the next scramble instruction, blessing the talcum powder dust that insinuated itself into mouth, eyes and hair whenever a whirling airscrew lifted it in twisting devils from the baked earth and set it in motion as a malevolent wandering cloud. On the track that ran close to dispersal and across the landing run, the occasional horse, cart, and somnolent peasant would wander disconcertingly in front of aircraft in the final stages of touching down, producing screams of invective from outraged pilots who were obliged either to veer away or go round again. There were dire threats uttered about 'giving the idle buggers a squirt' – with eight or twelve Brownings, naturally – but no-one was ever driven to such an extreme. Notices, threats, and even cajolery had little effect; the peasantry grinned, nodded, then went on doing exactly what it had been doing for two thousand years.

On the 27th, I was off on a longish scramble in 612, a Mark 2 I had never flown before. Some 60 miles north and west of the island, we were kept at a low altitude and warned to look out for low flying Savoias en route for Libya. But, either the Eyeties had come and gone or were a figment of the controller's imagination; whatever the reason, we saw nothing. Later, we learned that a section of 185 had had

178

some success earlier in the day, shooting down two of the self-same Savoias. Perhaps it was their success that had prompted control to send us off.

It was more of the same the following day with a long night at 'Readiness', my dreary vigil broken only by a single scramble and a brief but uneventful trip of fifteen minutes during which the searchlights did not even deign to put in an appearance. Our own comparative inactivity that day was, however, in marked contrast with the pulsating comings and goings of the Beaufighters based temporarily at Luqa.

Hugh Pughe, our belligerent AOC, not for the first time and certainly not for the last, had contrived to prolong the stay of one of the Beaufighter squadrons in transit to the Middle East, for the purpose of carrying out a series of low-level attacks on airfields and other targets in Sicily. For this particular duty the Beau was well suited as it had a good turn of speed low down – slightly better than that of our Hurricanes, in fact – and having two whopping great air-cooled radial engines, was far less likely to be crippled by light flak than were our own aircraft with their single engines and exposed radiators. Furthermore, the Beaufighter was an unusually quiet aircraft, particularly at high speed, and had a formidable armament of four cannons and six machine guns. To the enemy, it eventually became known as 'whispering death', a description well merited as it dealt fearful damage on a number of occasions during the summer of 1941, one of the most notable being that of 28 July when about twenty enemy aircraft were destroyed and damaged on the ground in addition to a considerable number of troops on the move and some small craft at sea. Having been on the receiving end of the Hun 109s some eight weeks earlier, my imagination had no difficulty in visualizing the chaos likely to be inflicted by four times as many aircraft, each with massively greater fire power than the Me 109.

The following day, even I thought I was in for some success. Being scrambled with only the briefest information of what was ahead of us, four of us fled westwards at

179

lowish altitude, in search, we thought, of a batch of juicy Savoias en route for Libya. Some 50 miles out and at less than 1,000 feet, I suddenly saw them a long way off, skimming across the wave tops. A wild surge of exultation. *'Tallyho!'* Four of them! This time we'd *got* the blighters! Open with the throttle and up with the revs; a brief and feverish glance at my gunbutton and gunsight, the former properly on *'Fire'*, the range bars on the sight set at 40 feet. Forty feet! That was no good. A twist by feel to 60, click, click – to me, all bomber aircraft had a wingspan of 60 feet, Dorniers, 88s, BR 20s, the lot.

We curved towards them, the blood draining. At about a mile range now, pulling hard in a tightish turn, and with memories of past engagements with Dorniers and 88s vividly in mind, I resolved to attack the far outside aircraft, noting with mild disapproval that I would be unable to take up the comparatively safe position under the tail. Half a mile! I pulled up sharply before diving – at which point my heart sank and all the emotion ebbed away. They were Blenheims. Four ruddy *Blenheims*!

Like predators thwarted of their prey, we veered away, still tense, resentful and scowling. And spread out, two of us either side. What an anti-climax! Still, no point in frightening these chaps to death, they had a hell of a life anyway carrying out their mast-height attacks and suffering terrible casualties; we would give their morale a lift and escort them home. Which we did. Our one good turn for the day.

The next day, too, more fruitless haring about, this time without even a sight of an aircraft. What had happened to the enemy? – they certainly didn't seem to be trying very hard these days. It was a Thursday, I noted; the last day of July.

My letter home that night was cheerful if circumspectly phrased in order to avoid the censor's black ink. I was always vaguely resentful about having my letters read and censored; if as Flight Commander I was allowed to censor other people's, why couldn't I censor my own? A silly business, the system probably starting at Agincourt!

Making up my logbook for the month, I saw that I had made 44 operational flights since arriving in Malta; masses of adrenalin expended for remarkably few results. I was becoming accustomed to flying over endless tracts of sea and operating from an island on which it was almost impossible to force-land safely. On the other hand, having had five engine failures in eight weeks – euphemistically termed malfunctions – I still did not have complete confidence in the Hurricanes I was flying. Even the dinghy, which had contributed so much to my peace of mind and on which I had sat so painfully during my initial trip from the *Ark Royal*, had proved to be suspect. Shortly after our arrival, when a group of us had gone down to Sliema to try out our new life-saving equipment, my dinghy had not only refused to inflate, the CO_2 bottle choking to an immediate stop with a strangled '*fizz*', but had sunk dismally with scarcely a splutter when I attempted to use the little concertina handpump, there being a six-inch gash in the yellow rubber.

But, in spite of everything, I was alive, wasn't I? And moderately happy. For all of which I thanked God!

And as a sign that the Lord was indeed on my side, the following day, 'Butch' Barton had an engine failure on take-off flying Z3492, the aircraft I had used on its previous flight to intercept the Blenheims. His engine stopping at several hundred feet, quite properly he did not attempt to turn back but crashed straight ahead, his Hurricane ploughing through several of the stone walls I had been eyeing so jaundicedly over the past eight weeks. His aircraft wrecked and trapped in the cockpit, the little man was nastily burnt about the face when the aircraft batteries came loose and doused him with acid.

Crossey and I visited him in Imtafa hospital the day after and found him disfigured, shocked and trembling but profoundly thankful that things had turned out as well as they had. Few people had survived such an experience and with so much operational and other flying behind him, he felt that an engine failure of some sort was long overdue. And now it had happened, in Malta of all places, and he was still alive and kicking. Looking tiny and waif-like in his hospital bed, he was childishly relieved at his deliverance.

As we left him behind, I was all too conscious of the squadron's debt to the little man. Small and slight in stature, in no way an heroic figure and unassuming almost to a fault, he was one of the best leaders and fighter pilots it would be my good fortune to meet. Having flown together for more than a year, including the whole of the Battle of Britain, my admiration for his ability and devotion to duty was unbounded.

As he was expected to be in hospital and out of action for some time, it fell to me to command the squadron. And of more immediate satisfaction, to be the guardian of our single most cherished possession – one clapped-out Austin 16!

8 *August 1941*

August, a month of comparative tranquillity, was also one of change and uncertainty. It was a time, too, when, with a considerable reduction in the demands made upon our services, the more amorous of us were enabled to widen our experience in an area delicately referred to as poodle-faking. Now that we were guests of the Maltese people – more or less – it was incumbent upon us (we considered) to keep ourselves in the mainstream of social intercourse, a duty which inevitably involved the civilian population, or, more precisely, the civilian population's daughters.

It had all started early in June when a number of 249 were invited to a swimming party at the Dragonara Palace, a place noted for its magnificent scenic position, its private swimming pool, and the largesse and munificence of its owner the Marquis Scicluna. In addition, as fringe benefits so to speak, there were two plump but pleasant daughters – and a model railway in the basement! Alas, the daughters didn't stand a chance; on the two occasions I was a guest there, the model railway claimed my attention entirely.

At about the same time, I chanced to be in dispersal at Ta Kali when a gharry, with the statutory straw-hatted nag, creaked past in a swirl of dust. At the reins and dextrously flicking a whip with Beau Brummell aplomb, was a pilot of 261 Squadron, whom I knew would shortly be leaving, and alongside him a delectable dark-eyed girl of about twenty whose name I later discovered was Patsy. Patsy was the second daughter of the Chief Justice of Malta, Sir Phillip Pullicino, one of five daughters, in fact, two of whom were later to marry Service colleagues of mine.

183

I also learned that she lived in Rabat, her parents having had the good sense to evacuate their former home in Sliema when the bombs had begun to fall.

Some time later, Crossey, Palliser, Mills, and I, under the guidance of Pilot Officer Cavan, who had earlier been with 261 Squadron and therefore knew the ropes, made our way up to Rabat for the purpose of inveigling our way into the small community of evacuated families who were living there in cool and isolated security. A rendezvous with a bevy of daughters having been arranged, the vivacious Patsy among them, we assembled on that first occasion at a down-at-heel estaminet with leaning, paint-flaked shutters, called the Point de Vue. Shyly and on our best behaviour, we drank John Collinses and tepid soft drinks amid the long dark shadows of the medieval churches, our adolescent conversation and laughter piercing the breathless afternoon silence and echoing among the sombre walls and deserted, narrow streets. On that first afternoon, too, we picked loganberries on the unkempt slopes of a nearby garden with all the playful simplicity of children on a Sunday-school outing. It was an enchanting occasion, utterly at odds with the grim and deadly business on which we were normally engaged, serving to provide us all with a brief interval of normality.

In the weeks that followed, on such free afternoons as we had, a small group of us, limp and panting in the blistering heat, would tramp the dusty two-mile hill to Rabat, arriving at the Point de Vue exhausted, to sink dripping into the rickety cane and iron chairs on the forecourt before being welcomed by the young ladies of Rabat. Their names live on in my memory: Patsy, Ena and Anne Pullicino, Liliana di Georgio, Florence Testaferrata, the delightful 'Janey' whose other name escapes me, and others. Later, when we spread our wings, there were other daughters just as speciously prim, as well-mannered and as appealingly flirtatious. At various venues in Sliema and Valletta, there were the occasional formal parties, with evening frocks and sipped drinks amid the whistle and thump of bombs; decorous dances with foreheads beaded with perspiration and damp palms on virginally slim waists and exposed shoulders; visits to the only cinema in Valletta to hold hands in the half-light and be eaten into a lump by battalions of fleas hopping about like gazelles in the thick plush of the red seats; and breathlessly hurried journeys home to Rabat and elsewhere by gharry – mustn't be later than ten o'clock or *else*! – with chaste kisses on the doorstep, the occasional parent in some shadowy offing, keeping an eagle eye on what the daughter of the house was up to and praying, no doubt, that their offspring's experience was not advancing at too rapid a pace.

Those were simple, uncomplicated meetings as refreshing as they were uncorrupted by crude thoughts of anything even approximating to sex; indeed, had such vile intentions lurked in our minds (and they probably did from time to time), the opportunities for fulfilment were sadly lacking. In Malta, there was neither the time nor the place to do *anything*!

Over an interval of years, our activities might now appear to be juvenile, but near-juveniles we were, each one of us in his way in need of a little love and gentleness as a relaxation from flying and fighting, engine failures, flak, tracer, the endless wastes of inhospitable sea, and the harsh realities of living in a sometimes coarse and turbulent all-male community. The young ladies of Malta played their part in the defence of their island to a greater extent than ever they realized. Moreover, they provided an additional service; as all of them spoke fluent Italian, we heard more from their reports of what the Italian radio had to say about our day-to-day battles over and around Malta than ever we received from our own intelligence sources. If we had shot at a Macchi, a Cant or a Savoia, we simply asked the girlfriend the following day for news of its fate. And usually they were able to oblige.

There was so little doing that August, we decided that the Eyeties had gone on holiday, and good luck to them – unlike the Germans, a most civilized enemy. With the temperature constantly in the 80s and 90s amid a wilting humidity, the respite was more than welcome. Grouped at the end of the airfield in a scattered clutch and all hooked up for action, our Hurricanes hung their heads and almost visibly shrivelled in the sun, their wings so hot that on several occasions, 20mm cannon ammunition exploded within the stifling confines of the baking metal.

The month had started off inauspiciously. In the last days of July, it had been decided to form a new flight, the Malta Night Fighter Unit – MNFU, as it came to be known. Moderately cheered by this decision, as I had been one of a small group who had been flying by both day and night, I was less happy to learn that 249 would be required to provide the bulk of the pilots. In the event, some of our long-serving stalwarts – Cassidy, Thompson and Mills – all of whom had been with 249 since the autumn of 1940, together with Robertson and the experienced and doubly decorated Donald Stones, two more recent additions, left to become part of the new unit. Squadron Leader Powell-Sheddon, a pleasant, rather bulky young man with a slight but most agreeable stammer, arrived from parts unknown to take charge, and around a dozen officer and NCO pilots took possession of a group of the better Mark 2 Hurricanes and went into business, initially at Ta Kali. Thereafter, I was not called upon to fly at night except in an attacking role, which turned out to be a good deal more hazardous than defending the island, our only targets being 100 miles away in Sicily.

This further reduction among the old hands of 249 depressed me not a little, so much so that I wrote of it in a dismal letter to my parents. The squadron was disintegrating, I lamented; only about six of us left of the original group of the summer and autumn of 1940. Why did they keep mucking us about? The spirit of a squadron was the thing, and ours was dying. And indeed it was; and so was I – in terms of fervour, anyway. 'Butch's' accident had marked the beginning of the end, although during that hot and humid August, I suspect that it was then only a

186

subconscious thought. Things just weren't the same any more, which, after more than a year of incessant fighting and flying, was more than understandable. But 'Butch' and Pat Wells, though temporarily incapacitated, were still with us, plus the imperturbable Beazley, my particular mate, Crossey, and the irrepressible little man, Palliser. Were they as jaded as I was beginning to feel? On the other hand, there were brighter, fresher faces, too, new chaps who had joined us in England: the smiling, even-tempered Davis, a little older than most and a David to Beazley's Jonathan; Bob Matthews, with the wry grin and the equally wry sense of humour, who had shot down the Macchi I had so recently seen plunge into the centre of Valletta; the fair-haired Graham Leggett; the tall, aesthetic-looking but mischievous Harrington, the squadron's acknowledged 'character' with the cards; 'Tony' Morello, with his dark Italian looks, who was part of us yet somehow never quite appeared to be so; and the newer boys still, Cavan, Moon, 'Jack' Hulbert, the gentle and burly Stuart, nicknamed 'Horse', plus a batch of NCO pilots, new, expectantly enthusiastic but to my critical eye, pathetically inexperienced – all these now formed the bulk of the squadron. Thank God there had been a lull. If the Huns with their new 109Fs suddenly returned – it was all too grisly even to contemplate!

Of those in the other squadrons, 126 and 185, there were some I had known from my North Weald days and others I knew by reputation and casual acquaintance. 'Boy' Mould, the commanding officer of 185, was an affable young man with dark, wavy hair and a most infectious grin; a most engaging person, I had warmed to him immediately when we had first met at Hal Far in May. And some others of 185, too, had left a lasting and most favourable impression – Jeffries, Eliot, Thompson, and more.

Of 126, formerly 46 Squadron, there was the seemingly indestructible partnership of 'Rags' Rabagliati, Peter Le Fevre, 'Chips' Carpenter, 'Bert' Ambrose, and MacGregor. Also in the squadron was a comparative newcomer, Pat

Lardner-Burke, a no-nonsense Rhodesian who was as laconi-cally tough as his appearance suggested and was to do very well in the weeks to come, together with a Pilot Officer Anderson.[1] Although Anderson and I did not take to each other at first, I came to admire him as an artist of considerable talent, a common interest which drew us together, enabling us in the weeks ahead to indulge a shared recreation. Remarking, though not complaining, that the war had rather upset his career, he spent a lot of his time sketching aircraft and producing vividly realistic portrayals of combat, the victims always being the enemy, needless to say.

Another newcomer to Malta who made a special im-pression on me was Pilot Officer David Barnwell, whose father was responsible for the design of the Bristol Blenheim bomber, the aircraft type which was having such a thin time of it at Luqa, several miles to the south of us. Initially at Ta Kali and later with the MNFU at Hal Far, Barnwell positively radiated a *Boys Own Paper* brand of enthusiasm besides having a most lively and attractive personality. A gilded youth in almost every respect and part of a gallant family which was almost wiped out by the war, his star was to burn brilliantly but, alas, all too briefly.

Concurrent with the flying, the fighting, and our own and the squadron's developing affairs, a whole series of minor happenings occurred during those breathless summer days.

We had learnt on the grapevine that it was the intention to build a dispersal building to replace the miserable tents which formed our only accommodation on the airfield. It was no surprise, therefore, when a small gang of Maltese workmen turned up one morning and set about marking out the site. What did surprise us, however, was that they didn't arrive with bricks, hods and the usual impedimenta of building, but with a cart and straw-hatted horse and little more than a

[1] Anderson was tragically killed later in the war, as were Rabagliati and Le Fevre.

half dozen saws, iron bars, and hammers. Being a handyman from way back and for most of the time bored with hanging about at 'Readiness', I stood around in full flying kit and Mae West, mildly curious to see how it was done.

The workmen themselves were unique; all had bare feet and large flat caps, the type seen at soccer matches in England during the early '30s. In colour, they were all the shade of the dust – ochre-grey – and each had his trousers rolled up to the knee. From sun-cracked faces the texture of crocodile skin, issued not so much as a single word or smile. Clearly, building dispersal huts was pretty routine stuff.

Within minutes they had retired some 30 yards distant and commenced to dig holes in the ground with picks, jemmies, and hammers. Then, when they had levered out vast chunks of the whitish sandstone, they set about sawing it up with handsaws. Sawing up Malta! I had never seen anyone do that before. Finally, after fashioning the quite sizeable boulders into rough but formidable oblongs, they produced primitive planes, which looked as though they had originated at the time of pyramids, and planed everything into smooth, rectangular shapes. Thus busily engaged for about three days, they collected a huge mound of blocks, all regular and of the same dimensions, with barely the flick of a ruler or square. Fascinated by now, I watched in awe and admiration.

After that came the business of constructing the building itself, a long, low bungalow affair with a kind of verandah with pillars, designed to enable us to sit outside but out of the sun, a not unwelcome arrangement bearing in mind the need to keep a beady eye cocked for low-flying attackers.

Finally, over a period of several weeks, the heavy blocks were humped into position by hand, mortar consisting of ingredients that could only be guessed at was heaped and slopped on the ground, the mixers squatting like Arabs meanwhile, using their hands occasionally and spitting majestically into the goo to give it that extra bit of 'stick'.

And up it went, until we had a dispersal building to be proud of, spacious and coolly white within, a place in which

189

to shelter in the event of a strafing attack and to abandon with all haste at the first whistle of an adjacent bomb.[1] I examined the walls and ceiling with a critical eye. Everything was dead straight, plumb-line vertical, and (quite unlike my own wooden creations) exactly square, the workmanship exemplary. Moreover, where the stone had been dug out of the ground, we had yet another natural and perfectly good air-raid shelter on our doorstep.

But, whatever our surprise initially at the versatility and craftsmanship of the Maltese workmen, we were in contact daily with other examples of their expertise.

Although there had been several reinforcement flights of Hurricanes into Malta since our arrival in May, spare parts were always a problem and it was often necessary to cannibalize – strip one aircraft to make serviceable another – one especially vulnerable item being the propeller.

All the Hurricane Mark 2s and some of the remaining Mark 1s were then equipped with Rotol airscrews, the blades of which were constructed basically of laminated wood, covered in a reinforcing metal and plastic sheath. In the event of a crash, forced-landing, or taxying accident, the airscrew blades were invariably chopped off at the roots and damaged beyond repair. Some were not beyond salvaging, however, and although in Britain they would probably have been scrapped, in Malta, where the need was great, they were sent for repair.

Such work, indeed most of the repair work on any Service item, from ships to shoes, was carried out in the naval dockyard in Valletta or in the primitive workshops in the complex of narrow streets bordering the dockyard. There, miracles were worked and airscrews which needed the skills of Houdini and a watchmaker combined, were reconstructed, using the most basic of tools, from substitute materials and with all the elaborate twists and curves that were necessary,

[1] Despite the heavy bombing attacks later, this building survived the war.

so perfectly that not even an experienced eye could detect a flaw. Over the months, we used several such airscrews in 249 and I never ceased to be humbled by the skill of those who had rebuilt them.

It was in Malta, too, that I learned a little about the armour-plate I had been carting about in and around my cockpit for the past eighteen months, how brutally heavy it was and how nearly impossible it was to bend, cut, bore, or otherwise modify, a fact which was to exercise our minds considerably in the weeks to come.

Clearly, there was much more involved in going to war than sitting in the cockpit and firing the guns now and then. The importance of those who supported us with equipment, know-how and nimbleness of finger and hand was beginning to seep through even to my arrogant, prejudiced noddle.

We had been hanging about at 'Readiness' for most of the morning. It was blisteringly hot at dispersal and we were bored and sweating.

I looked up to find two figures approaching through the eddies of heat and dust, one the station commander, the other a small anonymous person in side-cap and long khaki trousers. Khaki trousers! Unusual that; everyone wore shorts in Malta. I rose and went out to greet them.

The visitor, who came only a little higher than my shoulder, was introduced and to my mild surprise I saw that he wore an Air Vice Marshal's stripes on the tabs of his rather crumpled shirt. His name going right over my head, I imagined him to be some 'equipper' or 'plumber' out from Air Ministry. Would I show him round and explain things? Of course – I smiled the patient, rather superior smile I reserved for high-ranking penguins.

For about fifteen minutes we strolled between the aircraft in the sun and dust, my companion uttering not a word. I told him about the squadron, our role, and what we had achieved in the past three months, adding that although we mostly had Hurricane 2s now, our serviceability rate remained pretty awful; we were still having all sorts of engine and other problems and, as if that wasn't enough, just recently even the cannon ammunition was exploding prematurely in the wings. Hurricane 1s were worse than useless, of course, and even the Mark 2s were only acceptable for as long as we had Macchi 200s BR 20s and Savoias to deal with. Why did those of us overseas always have to fly the junk? There were masses of Spits at home and we really ought to have some in Malta if we were to do anything worthwhile – tropicalized, mind you, the ordinary sort would be no good. Or perhaps Tomahawks, even; anything that would enable us to catch the Eyeties or Huns more easily. I warmed to my favourite subject.

When I had just about exhausted the topic, my companion put in a few quiet questions, nodding in response to my replies, otherwise he said nothing that sparked my interest. Odd little blighter, I thought, no decorations or anything like that; still, equippers and plumbers didn't really need that sort of thing I supposed. The little fellow was very courteous, however, and after a time, he thanked me pleasantly and we parted. Back among the lounging pilots, someone asked me who our visitor had been and I had to admit I didn't know. Later, however, I spoke to someone who did.

'Who was that little chap who came round today?' I asked.

'Tedder.'

'Who?'

'A bloke called Tedder. He's just been appointed something or other in the Desert. Can't remember what, exactly.'[1]

And there it was left.

With more time on our hands, there was the opportunity for leave and the right place to go, apparently, was the RAF rest camp at St Paul's Bay.

[1] As Tedder was then C-in-C Middle East Air Force he must have been an Air Marshal.

Strangely, I did not avail myself of the facilities there initially as the main diversions were sunbathing and swimming, neither of which appealed to me much. Although very little affected by extremes of heat and cold, being very fair-skinned, I burned badly in the sun, after which it was pure hell wearing a parachute harness and Mae West and buckling on my cockpit straps.

To a less jaundiced eye, however, the rest camp had much to offer. St Paul's Bay was then (unlike now) a comparatively deserted and very beautiful deep water inlet on the north side of the island, and the rest-centre a pleasant villa whose garden led down to rocks from which one could dive into water that was sparklingly blue and unpolluted. To the water-babies, it was paradise.

There usually being at least six officers from the various squadrons in residence at any one time, the air was invariably filled with the sound of music and song, there being a vast and comprehensive collection of Bing Crosby, Andrews Sisters, Glenn Miller and other big-band records, most of them scattered in chaotic disarray around the various rooms. This constant background of sound plus cheerfully profane conversation and quite decent messing – the food a distinct improvement on that at Ta Kali – proved to be a great attraction for most of my colleagues, though less so for me. Invariably restless after a day or two, I seldom stayed for my full entitlement of leave and was soon to recognize that what I wanted most was solitude – an absence of people, war-talk and din and a quiet haven where I could read without interruption and draw and paint. In spite of its name, the rest camp was not one of those places.

August drifted to a close, though not uneventfully. I made only nine operational trips that month and most others in the squadron did less. At night, there was a fair amount of bombing with constant whistles and thumps far and near, causing me to sleep with a permanent half-open eye, mentally if not physically prepared to vanish under the bed if things

193

got out of hand. MNFU were often in action during the hours of darkness, shooting down two or three BR 20s that month – at the time, everything to us was a BR 20, in much the same way as, during the Battle of Britain, everything the enemy shot at was a Spitfire.

I ran into 'Rags' Rabagliati one evening who said with mild amusement that he had just been on an air-test and had suddenly run into an Eyetie bomber, which he had managed to shoot into the sea. Surprised, I replied that it sounded a pretty rum sort of air-test, to which, with his slow smile and drawling lisp, he admitted it had been – he had been flying alone at 1,000 feet along the southern coast of Sicily, some 80 miles away to the north. I couldn't conceal my astonishment. Since his squadron had joined us in Malta, 'Rags' had never failed to amaze and amuse me. Being a squadron commander, he had rather more freedom of action than the rest of us; even so, he was clearly taking full advantage of his good fortune and opportunities and was not only quite fearless in action but never seemed the least concerned when wandering about over endless wastes of sea in aircraft that were anything but reliable. Days later, with several others of 126, he made a dawn attack on the Italian seaplane base at Syracuse in Sicily, destroying, or damaging, about six of the enemy. We were all full of admiration for his performance; a great morale raiser, was 'Rags'.

Meanwhile, we continued to have engine problems with painful regularity, yet another pilot from Hal Far being forced to bale out over the sea when his engine stopped. There were several other failures, too, details of which we only heard of later.

About mid-month, being invited to give my opinion of an aircraft – not of 249 Squadron – which appeared to be giving trouble, I walked across to 'Maintenance' at Ta Kali to be confronted by an irate engineer officer, a diffident and apologetic-looking sergeant pilot, and between them, one rather haggard-looking Hurricane equipped with long-range tanks. Their story was simple enough; the sergeant had been one of a group of four who had been instructed to fly to Egypt, a distance of more than 800 miles, all of it across open sea and skirting hostile territory. After setting out, the sergeant, who looked about sixteen years old, didn't much like the sound of his engine and turned back. On his return to Ta Kali, the engineer officer ran the engine and almost abusively pronounced it serviceable, whereupon the sergeant, not too confidently, disagreed. Stalemate; there had to be a third opinion.

I took off and flew the Hurricane around for about fifteen minutes, testing all the bits and pieces. The engine unpleasantly rough and the airframe certainly not among the best I had ever flown, I had to admit, even so, that there appeared nothing fundamentally wrong with the aircraft. Nevertheless, my sympathies were all with the sergeant; *he,* not the irate engineer, who by this time was hinting darkly at lack of moral fibre, was the one who would have to negotiate the 800 miles of sea and run the gauntlet of the Huns in Crete and North Africa, this time all on his own. I was desperately sorry for the youth; I felt I was issuing a death sentence.

Some time later the Hurricane took off – and disappeared without trace. In fact three of the group of four aircraft which set off for Egypt that sorry day, were never seen again. But all this I only learned much later, otherwise I would probably have felt a good deal worse than I did at the time.

Feeling that 249 was being discriminated against as regards opportunities to attack Sicilian targets and being aware that there was a considerable force of enemy aircraft on Comiso airfield, I asked control's permission to make a dawn strafing run. Everyone in my flight full of enthusiasm, we even wrote an insulting note to the Italian Air Force which we planned to drop on the airfield via the flare tube of one of our Hurricanes.

Unhappily, or perhaps fortunately, control would have none of it. We hadn't enough up-to-date intelligence, they said; furthermore, it was too dangerous; Malta couldn't risk losing half a dozen Hurricanes on so uncertain a venture. What about an ordinary sweep over the area? That would cool our ardour besides giving us at least an even chance if a fight developed. Meanwhile, I was to do nothing.

The following day, they came back with grudging approval for a sweep, coupled with telephone instructions which I wrote down in pencil on a piece of paper I still possess. These allowed us to fly over Sicily but forbade us absolutely to attack any targets on the ground.

We were totally deflated; if a strafing attack was ruled out, what was the point? – as we had difficulty in catching the Macchis in the air, the object was to catch them on the ground. But, although everyone confessed to being disappointed, I sensed that after so much discussion and argument, the fire in our bellies had died to a smoulder.

In the event, nine of us took off and carried out a long sweep from Cap Passaro to a point some 30 miles north. At little more than 9,000 feet, we were over Sicily and within sight of Comiso for almost half an hour, which was simply asking for trouble. But of that there was none; we saw not an aircraft, a single ack-ack burst, nor any other type of target. As I gazed down on the parched and lifeless undulations of Sicily, I felt inclined to agree that the risks of such sorties far outweighed the likely advantages. We didn't even have the opportunity to drop our rude note!

Then, some days later, a most extraordinary incident.

At 'Readiness' as usual and being called to the telephone, it was explained to me by the controller in conspiratorial tones, that they were expecting a 'visitor' from the north-east – I visualized him glancing over his shoulder as he spoke. Mildly perplexed, I asked what kind of 'visitor', being further informed that it was part of a – er – clandestine operation, if I knew what he meant. By this time a little amused as well as surprised, I tried to pump the man, but to little effect. The aircraft would be coming roughly from the direction of Greece, he explained; it could be any sort of aircraft and at any height and they hoped they would have sufficient warning to send me off with a section of four to intercept. After that, we were to escort it safely back to Malta. All right? Quite straightforward, really.

I was intrigued. Who could it possibly be? Some exiled head of state? King Zog of Albania? Peter of Yugoslavia? Some leader vital to the allied cause? Someone pretty important, obviously, to merit all this fuss. I even had time to fantasize; would I be in line for some exotic foreign decoration – the Order of the Golden Goat, that sort of thing?

There were several comings and goings before we finally received the word to go, after which we were vectored almost due east, which seldom happened in Malta. I was flying 'B' on that occasion, the Hurricane I had used on the sweep over Sicily several days earlier, and I had with me new boys Hulbert and Stuart plus one of the sergeants.

Right at the start, however, a most irritating development. Shortly after leaving the ground, my windscreen began to show the tell-tale sign of a Git's oil-seal leak, a long-standing and apparently incurable fault on the Hurricane which had required a modification in the form of a rim fitted behind the propeller to catch oil which emerged from that area in a fine, yellow spray. On this occasion, alas, my leak was much more than the rim could accommodate, so that by the time I had reached the far end of the island, I could barely see forward. However, as the other members of my section were fairly new and as I didn't want to miss the occasion, the thought of turning back never crossed my mind.

At about 5,000 feet we headed out a little north of east and after about fifteen minutes flying were some 40 miles away from Malta with nothing in sight but open sea and an endless horizon. By this time, almost totally blind ahead, I had my hood open and was looking forward as best I could from the open cockpit and the rapidly yellowing side-panels of the windscreen. Meanwhile, the vectors kept coming up to us fairly regularly with our target apparently dead ahead of us and approaching. I was quietly content; except for being smothered in oil, everything was fine.

Then, I spotted it, a twin-engined aircraft of some sort, low down, dark against the sea and flying in the opposite direction. I gave a rather low-key 'Tallyho' and, crossing over the top of it, all four of us turned and took station, two either side, before straightening up. Then, dropping down a further 1,000 feet or so, we headed back towards Malta.

With yellow goo now completely obscuring my vision, I didn't choose to get any closer, nor was there any need; from where I was, I could see the other aircraft quite distinctly, below and slightly ahead. Down there, I mused, the important personage was probably relaxing for the first time and thanking God for our presence. And sorting out our decorations, too, I shouldn't wonder!

For around ten minutes we flew back together, the four of us providing what was no doubt a comforting escort to the aircraft beneath, control being advised of our progress from time to time and everyone in good heart. In the distance, Malta hove into sight, then as detail became clearer, Delimara Point and Kalafrana Bay.

As we neared the island, I found myself drifting lower until all four of us were barely several hundred feet above the target aircraft which by that time was just above the waves. And heading straight for Kalafrana Bay, which I thought was a bit odd as I was expecting it to land at Luqa. Still—

At this point, although I had no grounds for suspicion, the faintest shadow of doubt crossed my mind, causing me to look more closely at the aircraft beneath. I couldn't immediately recognize the type, on the other hand I hadn't needed to, the information we had been given, both on the ground and in the air, being so specific. All the same—! Then, whilst I was still toying with my doubts and with the 'visitor' entering the jaws of Kalafrana Bay, something splashed down into the water and the aircraft upended itself in a steep turn to the right so that it passed directly beneath me.

My mouth literally fell open, because I recognized at once the nature of the bounding splash – it was that of an air-launched torpedo. A torpedo! This chap was an Eyetie and had just dropped a torpedo! And we had escorted him all the way to Malta to do it! Well, would you credit it? The *cheeky* . . . ! Words failed me.

Right down on the water now, our erstwhile 'visitor' was heading hot-foot in the direction of Sicily; however, having turned with it, we remained 1,000 or so feet above, all of us still unbelieving and in two minds.

In one outraged sentence, I then informed control that their so-called 'visitor' had just dropped a torpedo in Kalafrana Bay, a message which stopped conversation entirely. Then, an uncertain voice: was I absolutely sure? *Of course* I was sure, we had just watched it happen, hadn't we? Silence and more confusion the other end. After which: 'All right. If you're quite sure, engage it! Shoot it down – immediately!'

It took us several minutes to catch the Italian aircraft, and with my hood open and unable to see forward, I dived to sea-level in no easy frame of mind. Irritated but excited and aware that the others were somewhere off to my right, I thought about cleaning my windscreen but saw immediately that my straps would prevent me from reaching forward sufficiently. For this reason, I pulled away to the left and instructed the others to attack without me; unlike me, at least two of them were flying Mark 2 Cs, equipped with cannons, so that even a few hits would suffice. After which, I undid my straps, half rose in my seat, and tried to insinuate my right hand around the windscreen. But only for a second; the 260-mile-an-hour slipstream immediately snatched at my arm and nearly took it off, causing me to recoil and jerk the controls so violently that for one horrifying moment, I thought I would be pitched out. Momentarily unnerved, I pulled away, regained my composure, then dropped down again to sea-level and to within 400 yards of the enemy aircraft, feeling as I did so the twist of the Eyetie's slipstream. But of the aircraft ahead I could see not a thing, only the pink lines and dot of my own reflector-sight against the brown. Damn it! I would have to leave it to the others.

Pulling up again, I then sat above and alongside the Italian aircraft, watching my companions approach in turn and shoot. They did so several times but I could see only the splash and ricochet of their shells in the water, the Cant – for we had all recognized it as such – now so low that its airscrews were whipping up a feathery trace from the waves.

In despair and almost beside myself with frustration, I watched the tragi-farce drift to a conclusion. The Eyetie, certainly hit, began to trail enough smoke to suggest that it had been damaged quite seriously, but there it remained, flying still and heading for home.

Eventually, some 30 miles north of Malta and my section out of ammunition, we all turned and headed back, our 'visitor' meanwhile still limping off towards the north. Almost sick with feelings of failure and defeat, I was hardly aware of the return journey and landing.

Back on the ground, I learned that Stuart had also suffered a malfunction and had hardly participated in the fight. Hulbert and the sergeant were jubilant, however, being convinced that the Eyetie would never be able to get back, a view supported by a later report from other aircraft which had sighted oil and wreckage in the area. A claim was therefore made for one Cant 'destroyed' which I allowed to go forward though with some reluctance, persuading myself that even if the outcome were doubtful, if it boosted the morale of my chaps, perhaps it was permissible. Privately, however, I later confided in 'Butch' Barton that I thought the claim was overstated.

The following day, I heard from several of our lady friends in Rabat that the Italian wireless had reported that one of their aircraft had returned from a daring attack on Malta, in a heavily damaged condition and with the crew wounded. Although hailed by the Italians as an heroic victory, I was comforted by the thought that if the action had been that heroic, the Cant and its crew might well have been put out

200

of action, if not permanently, for a considerable time. Which, I supposed, was a victory of sorts.

Strangely, the circumstances relating to the incident were never discussed nor even mentioned thereafter, a discreet veil being drawn over the whole affair. For my part, I was so furious with Hurricane 'B' that I determined never to fly the damned thing again. And I never did.

9   A Quiet Autumn

September nudged August slowly into the past, the weather unremittingly hot and sticky. Although we did not know it at the time, for the next several weeks, those of us in Hurricanes would do very little, the war from Malta being waged by the Blenheims, the Wellingtons, the Fulmars and Swordfish.

In the Western Desert, elements of our ground forces yet to be formed into the famous 8th Army, were still resisting attempts by Rommel's German and Italian divisions to move forward to the borders of Egypt, and having failed to retake Tobruk, the brilliant Wavell had finally lost the confidence of the Prime Minister and others and had been replaced by General Auchinleck. In a further hotch-potch of advances and retreats, Free-French and British troops had moved into Syria, so that with these and other movements and actions, it seemed that our forces were either fighting or engaged almost everywhere, even in the Far East where the Japanese were already on the move. But by far the most serious news came from Russia, where the Germans were apparently making hay of our new allies, who had suffered astronomical casualties, the invaders moving ominously towards Moscow, Leningrad, and the Crimean peninsular.

All of which made dismal reading in the *Times of Malta* although, with touching faith in Britain's invincibility, it worried me not a jot. At Ta Kali, we were doing all right, we were getting masses of time off, and even if our engines did stop occasionally, things would sort themselves out. Still turning up regularly in Valletta for my hot pork sandwiches at Monico's and my hair-cuts and more refined snacks in the

Union Club, I only wished I could get a decent cup of tea. What on earth did the Maltese do to their water?

I had a week's leave in September, which I spent mostly at the rest camp at St Paul's Bay, a period so forgettable that I made only the briefest mention of it in my letters home and diary. Otherwise, I flew barely a dozen sorties that month, although one was to cause me concern.

Prior to roaring off on one of our dust-streaming scrambles, I had become aware of a nasty smell when taxying out. Then, barely had I become airborne and closed the hood than the whole cockpit was filled with a cloud of pungent white smoke. In a near-panic, I turned for home and almost threw my Hurricane at the ground, expecting all the time an eruption of flame. However, to my considerable embarrassment, it proved to be far less than an emergency. Having removed the side panels, it was found that one of the ground-crew had spilt a gallon can of glycol in and around the cockpit, most of which had percolated down on to the pipes that ran between engine and radiator, producing something akin to a smoke-screen when everything heated up. A great joke after the event, it was not so funny at the time.

Although there were the routine nocturnal dronings and thumps throughout the early part of the month, there was little action for us day fighters, the only serious engagements occurring on about the 4th, when 126 and 185, who happened to be on duty, ran into a flock of Macchis high up over Grand Harbour and shot down several. Later the same day, 'Butch' Barton, with the other half of 249, chased a minor swarm of Macchi 200s towards the Sicilian coast, at which point, to 'Butch's' considerable consternation, the Eyeties suddenly turned and fought like tigers. This development not being at all according to the script, the Italians usually preferring to run for home, 'Butch' and his men were caught on the hop, low down, a long way from home, and against aircraft capable of out-performing the Hurricane in close combat. At a disadvantage and having to run for it, almost inevitably 249

203

lost two aircraft, those of Pilot Officer Smith, whom I hardly knew, and Sergeant Kimberley, 'Butch' himself being quite shaken by the severity of the engagement. His description of events normally so lacking in emotion, I had seldom seen him so affected; he really had thought his number was up.

Thereafter, action around Malta was mainly by night, so that for us, the next period of excitement occurred mid-month when two further batches of Hurricanes arrived from our old friends, the carriers *Ark Royal* and *Furious,* only half of which were to remain on the island.

On leave at the time, I was in the mess at Ta Kali when the second group of Hurricanes appeared and having nothing much else to do, walked up to dispersal to watch them touch down. It was not exactly an encouraging spectacle as, landing north to south on that occasion, several of them overshot hopelessly, two or three careering past us, one at least finishing up on its nose. It was quite heartbreaking to watch brand new aircraft we were so much in need of, broken by inept and inexperienced pilots, and there were loud groans and unflattering remarks about the legitimacy of several of those involved.

Included in the new group were four Americans who had apparently come to Britain via the Royal Canadian Air Force. I had never seen Americans in RAF blue before despite there being a publicity stunt involving a so-called Eagle Squadron in England, so that their arrival created some interest. Two of the four, Steele and Streets, were the long and short of it, one being tall and thin and the other positively wee. Chatting with them in the mess shortly after, I gathered that on reaching England, they had been entertained at Buckingham Palace, on which occasion the small one had apparently asked the Duke of Kent's wife, Princess Marina, for a 'date'. I was wryly amused. What next, for heaven's sake? Were they not *aware*?

The latest influx of aircraft and the dearth of operational activity enabled all three fighter squadrons on the island to be brought up to established strength; in fact, in 249 we had more Hurricanes than we could use. Moreover, it did enable each of the more senior of us to have a personal aircraft, besides giving us sufficient time to paint on our squadron identification letters. Back again came the old grey markings GN, I laid claim to a brand-new Mark 2B, GN-R, and I had my flight's airscrew spinners painted red. After the wrecks we had been flying over the past several months, here were aircraft we could now fight in with confidence. Moreover, they were beginning to look the part, which was so important. My morale positively soared.

But not for long, alas. Word came through that we would shortly be fitting bomb-racks to accommodate eight 40 lb bombs, and that our old 44-gallon long-range tanks would be re-fitted enabling us to carry out three-hour patrols in search of low-flying Axis aircraft en route to North Africa. Bombs! Long-range tanks! What next, mines and torpedoes? What were we, fighter aircraft, or one-engined Blenheims?

Then, in the latter half of the month, a lot of excitement. With the *Ark* and *Furious* in the offing bringing in the Hurricanes and, later still, with the approach of a large convoy accompanied by the *Ark Royal,* the battleships, *Nelson, Rodney* and *Prince of Wales,* together with a clutch of cruisers and a mass of destroyers as escort, not only were the Italian naval and air forces drawn from their lairs in Sardinia and Sicily, but Malta itself was reinforced by Beaufighters from the Middle East.

Much of the action during that two week period was well beyond the range of our Hurricanes; even so we became aware of all the activity elsewhere on the island, word filtering through of what the fleet Fulmars were up to, poor things, plus our own Malta-based naval aircraft and the intrepid Blenheims. Apparently, the Italian navy, perceiving the size and strength of the British fleet, wisely turned about and tip-toed to the rear, but their air force pressed home its attacks with torpedoes and bombs, so that many fierce and bloody engagements took place somewhere south of Sardinia. Between the 26th and 28th, however, the whole convoy and escort came within our orbit and most of us in Hurricanes were sent off in sections to act as look-outs and escort.

My first sorties were strictly defensive, however; being warned of possible air attacks on Hal Far and Luqa, with members of my flight, I roamed about over the sea north of the island for hours on end. But none of the enemy appeared and we returned shrugging our shoulders. Why all the trouble and fuss?

Then, on the 28th, flying my new aircraft, GN-R, I was vectored westwards to meet the convoy and escort, and having arrived was promptly shot at, the flak bursts appearing magically in the sky directly ahead of me, though fortunately not too close. Thinking there were enemy aircraft around that we had not seen, we fairly hopped about for a minute or two until it became clear that the shots were aimed at us. However, they proved to be no more than a greeting as we were able to continue our patrol for more than an hour, the fleet spread out in long lines some 4,000 feet beneath, white moustaches creaming from their bows – a truly magnificent sight.

Later, I defended Luqa again, patrolling the area in wide, bored curves. None of the enemy appeared, however, which left me reflecting that a fighter pilot's life, even in Malta, was much like that of the ordinary bloke in the army – ninety-five per cent boredom and five per cent blistering, blood-curdling excitement.

The month slid to an undramatic close. Pat Wells, who had rejoined us briefly having recovered from his wounds, left in company with Tony Morello, bound, it was said, for Khartoum. Khartoum! None of us wanted to go to Khartoum, which was the current dirty word, an Operation Training Unit being located there. Everyone thought in terms of England – and Spitfires! Oh, for some really decent aircraft and somewhere to make a forced-landing without either being drowned or breaking one's neck. I was getting bored with Malta and didn't think I wanted to stay much longer.

Earlier in the month a fellow called Barnes of 126 Squadron had had his engine stop and had ploughed through a couple of stone walls, miraculously surviving, someone jocularly remarking at the time that he had discovered the quickest possible way of slowing down. Such macabre humour was always in vogue at Ta Kali.

It was also towards the end of September that a PRU Spitfire arrived with a Flight Lieutenant Messervy at the helm. Messervy was a ginger-haired, balding man, rather older than myself, who, though pleasant enough, did not give very much away. His journey of 1,250 miles from England, straight across Hun-controlled France, had taken almost five hours and he was in Malta to carry out some rather special reconnaissance flights, it appeared. His unarmed Spit, painted a light blue, looked delicious, provoking nostalgic recollections of our own Spits in May and June of the previous year. As we chatted, I decided against ever applying to be in the PRU business; the flights were far too long and the whole thing too coldly and calculatingly brave for me.

October, and a dismal beginning.

We had been scrambled and were climbing up southwards along the coast towards Hal Far. It was a dull day with a fair amount of medium cloud in layers so that we were kept fairly low. After a time, control appeared to lose interest in us, leading me to conclude there was nothing much doing. Then, after a little more than 30 minutes in the air, we were instructed to land.

Back on the ground little was said, so that later it came as a complete surprise when I learned that 185 Squadron had been in action and that their commanding officer, 'Boy' Mould, had been shot down and killed. I was very unhappy, not only because of 'Boy's' sad and tragic death, but because of our own non-involvement; if there had been that much action, why hadn't we been allowed to take part, or even been told? The Eyeties had been in their new Macchi 202s, apparently, and had moved around pretty smartly.

For the following two days, I found myself north of the island flying first at 22,000 feet, then at 27,000, on each occasion watching the enemy stream overhead in silent, pencil-white curves, always much faster than ourselves it seemed and well beyond our reach. Finally, on 6 October, smarting with frustration, we paraded at full Squadron strength at 31,000 feet, whereupon the enemy, either prudently or because they never intended to come anyway, turned back. I heard this information from control with some relief; I never liked fighting in a Hurricane much above 30,000 feet; it was so cold up there and the aircraft tended to fall away and stall in anything more than a gentle turn.

Then, the following day we heard that we were to bomb Sicily – at night!

Never having bombed anything since FTS, when I had thrown 8 lb smoke bombs from Hawker Audaxes in the general direction of the Montrose basin, I didn't rate my chances of hitting anything as very high. In fact, there was a story, apocryphal no doubt, that when the farmers living on the borders of the Montrose basin became aware that it was our day for bombing, they would take the day off and disappear into the foothills.

My target being the railway station at Gela, I took off towards midnight and flew northwards, expecting to find the place without too much difficulty on a night that was dark but clear.

Fondly hoping that the Italians would reveal their known defensive positions by shooting at me with their red balls, they did nothing of the sort, obliging me to wander about endlessly over Sicily trying to discover where exactly I was. In fact, I never did find the railway station but, by sheer good fortune, came across the railway line that presumably lead to it, which I saw dimly beneath me from a height of 1,500 feet. By this time, remembering the thousands of tons of bombs that had been dropped on London to such little effect and deciding that dropping my eight insignificant bangers was a howling waste of time, I did a gentle dive in that direction and disposed of my load. Observing one faint flash in the blackness below, I flew the 100 or so miles back home.

Two days after, for reasons I cannot recall, I was obliged to make an emergency landing at Luqa, my first time on that airfield since the day of my arrival in May. There seemed lots of aircraft parked there which was probably the reason for the low level dawn attack on the 14th, carried out by a small formation of Macchi 202s, which raced across the airfield at first light with banshee screams and glistening beads of tracer. One of several of 249 who were scrambled in pursuit, I was too late to catch the Macchis, which, by that time, were half-way back to Sicily. Several aircraft of MNFU were, however, more fortunate, having taken off before us, and an interception was made some miles north of the island by David Barnwell, who gave a 'Tallyho' then apparently made a successful attack. Shortly after he was heard to say that his engine had failed and that he was baling out – after which, nothing. Dispatched immediately, the air-sea rescue boat combed the area for the rest of the day, but without success.

So perished one of the golden boys of Malta, like so many gifted airmen of the past, disappearing in circumstances that were never entirely clear, although the Italians were subsequently to claim a victory during the course of that attack. But, as so often happened in air combat, although on the verge of being an active participant, I knew little of what had taken place until later.

In all, a sad, sad day. David Barnwell had been in Malta only a matter of weeks but even in that brief period, he had distinguished himself greatly. We all felt the chill of his passing, which was not usually the case.

The day was also something of a landmark for me in that, two days before the Barnwell incident, I received what I regarded to be the ultimate insult. Scrambled in pursuit of a small group of Macchis approaching from the north, I climbed hard with my section towards Grand Harbour, eventually crossing out to sea at about 20,000 feet. Then, as we continued to claw for height, I saw several bursts of ack-ack in the distance, after which came the instruction, 'Clear the area to the north. The guns have been ordered to engage.' Or, as I chose to interpret the message: 'Hop it, you useless creatures, and let someone else have a go!' Outraged initially, I had half a mind to ignore the instruction but not wishing to confuse the gunners below, with my three followers, I slunk off in the direction of Gozo. My God, things had come to a pretty pass when ack-ack was considered more effective than fighters!

I landed that day in a bitter frame of mind, although I was soon to realize that my anger was wasted; in the weeks to follow, there were many similar instructions which various members of 249 were only too glad to carry out to the letter.

The next day, I was involved in three more such scrambles, all inconclusive, one being just that little bit different.

I was at about 2,000 feet, climbing hard, when there was a bang somewhere to my left and something whipped past in the air. Not knowing quite what had happened, I pulled away and returned to Ta Kali to find that the landing light had disappeared, leaving a sizeable gap in the leading edge of my port wing.

It was quite extraordinary; for a whole year in England, I had frequently flown the Hurricane at more than 450 miles per hour throughout one of the most intensive periods of fighting ever known, and apart from the occasional oil leak, never had cause to complain about my engine or my aircraft. But in Malta, in less than five months, I had suffered five major engine malfunctions, any one of which could have resulted in my death, plus sundry other leaks, failures and difficulties, the latest being the loss of the landing light, which had broken away from a newish aircraft at something less than 150 miles per hour. Moreover, my experiences were not untypical – the evil eyes were certainly hard at work, it seemed, and not only around Ta Kali!

*   *   *

In line with our instructions to 'take the offensive', the second half of October saw 249 engaged in lengthy flights in search of transport aircraft en route from Sicily to Africa. As the chosen path for these aircraft appeared to be some 50 miles to the west of Malta, this was regarded as being the most fruitful area in which to operate. There was no question of our being controlled on to known targets, it was all a business of guess and hope. Four of our Hurricanes being fitted with two 44-gallon wing tanks each, Crossey and I were the first to go.

I had mixed feelings about the arrangement. The prospect of shooting down a few juicy Savoias or Cants was appealing enough, but going into action carrying what amounted to a primed bomb under each wing was less attractive. Our long-range tanks were simply not meant for fighting: they could not be jettisoned, they reduced the Hurricane's performance very considerably, and even when empty, contained a lethally explosive mixture. Were we to encounter enemy fighters, our number would almost certainly be up as we could neither fight nor run, dire possibilities which sharpened our minds considerably when making plans.

In the event, nothing much happened on that first trip. We took off in fine weather with just a little cloud at around 4,000 feet and flew low over the sea until we reached Linosa then Lampedusa, after which we wandered further south and west until we were almost within sight of the African coast. I was not too keen on going in the direction of Pantelleria, knowing full well that Macchi 200s and CR 42s were based there; I had never encountered a CR 42, a biplane admittedly but a remarkably nippy in-fighter, and in a Hurricane with long-range tanks, I didn't particularly want to.

After almost three hours we returned, our concentration flagging and our backsides numb from the malicious pressure of our cushionless dinghies, having seen neither enemy air-craft nor vessel.

Three days later, on 19 October, 'Butch' Barton and Palliser, flying exactly the same route, ran into a single Savoia 81 transport aircraft which they promptly shot into the sea, the aircraft exploding in a huge ball of flame and smoke. A very ugly sight, 'Butch' reported with a sad shake of his head, but with the heartlessness of youth, I can't say that the plight of the victims worried us very much. Cheered by yet another success for 'Butch', I couldn't help being a little envious even so; where was the enemy when Crossey and I were around?

On 30 October, Crossey and I tried again, this time taking the bull by the horns and flying directly to Pantelleria. Initially beneath a friendly bank of cloud, by the time we reached Pantelleria the sky was completely clear. Not too happy with this development, we skirted the island on tip-toe – Savoias were one thing, fighters altogether another! Suspiciously on edge, we drifted slowly to the south then east until we were back in the area of Linosa and Lampedusa, once again seeing nothing but a wilderness of open sea.

Thereafter, our long-range trips in that area petered out, our efforts being mainly concentrated on attacking targets in Sicily and on defending Malta. In fact, it was the last long-range sortie I was to make in the Mediterranean war zone

In the intervals between these offensive exercises, we were back on the treadmill of scramble, climb and patrol as the carrier *Ark Royal* plus the cruisers and destroyers of a reinforced Force 'K' approached the island from the west. Leading a section of four, I flew out to protect them, being shot at once again for my pains, the end result being masses of flying but no Eyeties. In spite of this lack of success, however, I was not at all unhappy; my new aircraft, GN-R, was pleasant to fly, with the smoothest of engines and a reassuringly tight airframe. Then, on 22 October, which was a Wednesday, I had the first of two days off.

It was on that morning that I went into Valletta but finding myself at a loose end by lunch time, on impulse I suddenly decided to spend the rest of the day at the rest camp at St Paul's Bay. There being no transport available, I ran the whole eight miles at a jog, reducing myself to a grease-spot but thoroughly enjoying the unaccustomed exercise.

Arriving in the early afternoon and finding Crossey and several others in residence, I joined them on the rocks alongside the water. It being a beautiful scene, peaceful and bright, we all lay back and relaxed. Super! Malta wasn't such a bad place after all.

After a time, we heard the thin sound of aircraft high up and straining our eyes against the glare, caught the occasional glimpse of wings flashing in the sun. 249, probably. Doing what? we wondered.

Then faintly, the noise of engines wailing and the distant 'burrrr' of machine guns. A fight, by George! Right above our heads, too. We all sat up and took notice. Twenty seconds or so of noise and unseen movement aloft, then a blink of light followed by a thin trail of smoke. Someone hit!

We watched the dot that was the doomed aircraft begin its dark pencil-line trail towards the sea – it would crash somewhere towards the entrance to the bay, we decided. And following the aircraft, the tiny white canopy of a parachute, moving slowly sideways, far, far away. Silently, we all followed the aircraft's progress as it fell towards the water. Until it disappeared. No noise. Just a small eruption of white and silent oblivion. High above, the parachute continued its feather-like descent. Poor bloke, we all commented comfortably from the safety of our ringside seats, someone in for a ducking.

As we sat there gazing through shaded eyes, it never for a moment crossed my mind that it might be my new aircraft, GN-R. But it was, flown by Sergeant Owen on that occasion, who was later picked up – the third personal aircraft I had lost when being flown briefly by someone else.

Back at Ta Kali on the 24th, I chose another aircraft, GN-J, of unhappy memory,[1] persuading myself that I couldn't possibly have two mid-air collisions in aircraft similarly marked.

---

[1] I was forced to bale out of GN-J on 7 November, 1940, after a mid-air collision.

With Grand Harbour full of the 'grey funnel line', we carried another long patrol over the sea north of the island then a panic scramble in the defence of Luqa, nothing being seen on either occasion.

It was also on the 24th that six aircraft of 126 bombed the Eyetie airfield at Comiso, escorted by 'Butch' leading half of 249 at 12,000 feet, and me with the rest at 21,000.

The trip was almost a bore. I was far too high – and preoccupied – to see the bombs delivered and roamed about miles into Sicily, mostly above cloud. But not one single enemy aircraft did we see. Or flak burst. Or anything else, in fact. Just massive banks of white beneath us and rolling brown countryside through the occasional gap. I recall thinking: if I had to force-land in Sicily, which part of me would the Mafia cut off? But not even such sombre speculations succeeded in livening me up.

After which, suddenly, it was November.

10   The Year Dies

The Air Force normally went into blue in November; the weather was cool enough and although some did, most didn't. Also it was cloudy, which encouraged the warlike to think in terms of 'mosquitos' – low level strafing attacks on targets of opportunity in Sicily. Plus bombing, of course. Bearing in mind the minute size of our bombs and the lack of penetration of our Brownings, I thought it all a waste of time. Still – if this was what our masters wanted.

Between the 1st and 4th of the month, I did four trips over Sicily, roaming around at nought feet or in the fringes of the cloud, looking for something to shoot at but with only trifling success. Sicily, at close quarters, being more of a brown desert than ever I had imagined, on the first of the trips, my section of two was intercepted four times by – I judged – the same pair of Macchis. Fortunately, with enough cloud about for safety, they did not get close enough to do any damage and I was not in the least interested in fighting Macchis at 500 feet over Sicily with 100 miles of enemy territory and water between me and home. On the fourth trip, when I was carrying eight 40 lb bombs, the weather became so miserable in my particular area, that after wandering round for what seemed an age, I became fed up and dropped all eight of them on a man with a lorry a little to the north of Cap Passaro. I doubt that he enjoyed the experience.

The day following, feeling the need to do something a little more constructive with my bombs, I ordered a programme of dive-bombing, which my flight and I carried out off Filfla rock. With happy memories of Montrose, it turned out to be rather fun, all of us diving steeply from about 8,000 feet

215

and letting go when our noses were lifted through the target smoke-float we had dropped in the water. Moreover, with electrical releases, it was a good deal easier than struggling with the mechanical toggles and pieces of bent wire, as we had been obliged to do on the old Hawker Audaxes.

But my rising spirits were firmly depressed when, the same day, one of the new De Havilland Mosquitos flew into Ta Kali from England and I was persuaded to test the performance of my Hurricane against it. I should have known better!

The Mosquito, a Photographic Reconnaissance Mark 1, was a visitor from Benson and, lightly loaded, was by the standards of the time incredibly fast and agile. Having taken off together and sorted ourselves out, the fight thereafter developed into a chase, with me desperately but unsuccessfully trying to remain in the same piece of sky. Unable to hang on to it and with my engine raging away at maximum boost and 2,850 revs, I finally retired – gracefully, I hope. Clearly, the 'Mossie' could walk away from me any time it liked, my ability to turn inside it meaning very little as I could never get sufficiently close to initiate a dog-fight. I had long suspected that our Hurricanes were clod-hopping carthorses, my flight that morning merely confirmed my suspicions.

The following day, 8 November, I wasn't required to fly but on hearing sounds of activity on the airfield around noon, walked up to dispersal from the mess. 126 Squadron were on duty and the majority of their aircraft had already been airborne for some time. Then, high up and in the direction of Valletta, the splattered smudges of ack-ack and the usual signs of activity although the aircraft themselves were invisible. Then, as I stood and chatted, a number of Hurricanes returned and I idly watched them approach then circle the airfield, first one, then several, touching down and taxying in, dust streaming.

My interest quickening as I saw that the gun patches were missing, I found myself attracted to one Hurricane which was moving slowly and rather aimlessly in my direction. Then I noticed the battle damage and began to run.

The propeller was still turning as I pulled down the retractable step and climbed on to the wing-walk, the slipstream clutching at my face and hair. The pilot still had his face mask attached but I recognized him immediately as Pat Lardner-Burke.

I heard myself shouting, 'Are you all right?' – then knew immediately that he wasn't.

Pat's head was bowed and his shoulders slumped. He undid his mask, clumsily. 'They've got me in the back.' He was obviously in shock and pain.

I sought to comfort him. 'All right. Don't worry. Just hang on and we'll get you out.' I shouted to those beneath. 'Get the ambulance and a stretcher.' After which I began to consider how best to extricate him.

Whatever its virtues, the Hurricane was not designed to enable a damaged pilot to be evacuated easily. About ten feet in the air, the cockpit did not have a side-flap, as did the Spitfire, so that to dismount, the pilot was obliged to climb out backwards, using first the cockpit rim then one of the steps, before walking down the wing-root and jumping to the ground. Needless to say, such gymnastics were beyond anyone crippled by wounds.

Aware of the need to act quickly, I tried climbing on to the rim of the cockpit myself but found nowhere to put my feet. Then I thought about sitting on top of the open hood but saw immediately that I would not be able to reach down sufficiently to heave him up bodily. A pox on the man who designed this aircraft, I thought wildly, we would have to get a crane and winch him out. But there was no crane, or none that wouldn't take hours to find and fetch.

I said urgently, 'Pat, can you stand? Or climb out yourself? Otherwise we can't get at you.'

He said wearily, 'I'll try,' and painfully pulling himself to his feet whilst I grasped his shoulders, he croaked an entreaty which would remain with me always: 'Don't shake me, Ginger . . . for Christ's sake don't shake me.'

217

Somehow we all reached the ground, to be faced with two airmen with a collapsible canvas stretcher. Uncertain and a little shocked, they laid it down in the dust and we all stood looking at it.

I said tightly, 'Pick it up, for God's sake; he can't get down on his hands and knees.'

They did so but I sensed that as soon as he put his weight on it, they would drop him. Impatiently, I waved for several others to come forward and he eventually laid himself down and was lifted into the ambulance. It looked as though the bullet, or whatever, had gone clean through his left lung.

When the ambulance had moved off in the direction of Imtafa, I climbed back on to the aircraft. There was not much damage but what there was was frightening. Several bullets – point-fives from a Macchi 202 – had hit the side of the aircraft behind the cockpit and one had punched a hole in the armour-plate as though it had been nothing more than a sheet of aluminium. After that it had penetrated the back of the seat, gone completely through the pilot, before continuing through the dashboard and into the armour-plate and darkness beyond. I was shaken. I had seen German bullet and cannon-shell strikes on armour-plate before and they had never done more than raise small dimples in the rock-hard metal. But this one had ploughed ahead as though there had been no armour. Several other pilots joined me and breathed their horrified astonishment. Crikey! And we'd always thought—!

Pat Lardner-Burke never flew again in Malta and those of us who did discussed the possibility of fitting an extra thickness of armour behind our seats. But such a modification would be impossible, we were told; the stuff would weigh a ton, its installation would have to be a dockyard job, and it wasn't available anyway. No, the only solution was not to get hit!

For several days thereafter, I was to remember that hole – vividly! Who would have thought it?

*   *   *

There being masses of pilots and aircraft, I had a week off until 13 November, spending my time drawing, painting and mooching around Sliema and Valletta. Life was seldom dull, however, as scarcely a day passed without the whooping dirge of the air-raid sirens heralding the inevitable thumps and crumps of ack-ack, bursting shells, and bombs. Hulbert, Stuart, and several others had rented a splendid four-storey furnished house on the front in Sliema for the grand sum of £5 per month, and I was able to take advantage of their hospitality and lodge there occasionally. There was neither linen nor blankets on the beds but that didn't matter; the fleas were there in abundance, lining up for their ration of succulent English blood, and to me, a bed was less a place of repose than a handy refuge in the event of an adjacent bomb.

It was during that week in Sliema that an air-raid occurred one evening when I was escorting the delicious Patsy from a function we had attended together. As the bombs began to come unpleasantly close, she insisted on our taking shelter in the crypt of a nearby church, an area the size of a tennis court already accommodating a hundred or so local inhabitants whose rolling eyes and shivering fear verged on the comical. As we stood a little self-consciously among the crowd, I put on the special face I reserved for such occasions and was assuring Patsy that there was nothing whatever to worry about, when there was a thunderous explosion nearby and the building almost took off. Instantly, with a moan of horror and no doubt believing that the gates of heaven were rolling back to greet them, the entire congregation sank to their knees, crossing themselves meanwhile, so that in a moment I found myself the only person standing amid a sea of prostrate forms and wailing incantations. From a height of six feet three inches, I looked around in acute embarrassment; all I could see were foreheads against the floor – and bums! What did I do now, show the flag or join them? Then I began to giggle. Patsy looked up, more nervous than amused, then held out her hand. I took it and sank grudgingly to my knees. Ah, well! Not exactly British, I supposed, but when in Rome—!

It was during that week, too, that a Wing Commander Brown arrived to lead the Ta Kali wing, which was something of a joke as 249 had only recently been able to field more than nine aircraft. The newcomer, a Canadian, was a pleasant, rather stiff little man who wore a small military moustache. Known familiarly as 'Hilly', he had been in No. 1 Squadron in France at the outset of the war and had done very well. Earnest-faced, he appeared to be very serious about his new job.

On the night of the 11th, we all gathered in the ante-room of the mess around dinner-time to discuss an attack on Comiso airfield in Sicily to take place at dawn the following day. Both 249 and 126 would be involved but because I was still on leave, I was unable to include myself among the twelve members of the squadron taking part.

The new Wing Commander was full of quiet resolve. A strafing section would go in initially to divert the defending guns, then a dozen or so Hurricanes with bombs would follow, escorted by a further twelve acting as fighter escort. Tactics were discussed and precise targets identified. Surprise was a key factor – with so many enemy fighters based at Comiso and Gela, the possibility of a knock-down-drag-out fight if things went wrong was more than just remote. From my seat in the stalls, it all sounded very exciting and I began to feel quite enviously deprived.

The following morning, with lots of noise and fuss, all 24 Hurricanes took off in the half-light and disappeared towards the north. Shivering and in my bare feet, I watched them from the stone balcony beside my bedroom, still more than a little miserable at not being part of the show.

An hour or so later they were back – most of them, anyway. Some Eyetie aircraft had been caught on the ground, it appeared, and a few others attacked and dealt with in the air. But the first Hurricanes had run into trouble, our new Wing Commander being hit squarely by one of the defenders' first bursts, causing his aircraft to pull up steeply, stall, then dive straight into the ground. For several who had witnessed the incident, there was no question but that he had been killed instantly.

Poor old 'Hilly' Brown. Such an experienced and highly decorated officer, and on his very first operational sortie from the island, too. Although we had known him only a matter of hours, we were all shocked by his passing. It seemed so unfair.

Later, the Italians generously dropped a message on Malta with confirmation of 'Hilly's' death and his burial with full military honours, although I knew nothing of it at the time. There was news, too, of one of 126's sergeants who had been shot down into the sea and taken prisoner. In all, a rather confused and bitty operation which had hardly been a success. I was almost glad that I had been obliged to stay at home.

Later the same day but far away to the west, three more Hurricane squadrons were taking off from several aircraft carriers and flying towards the island. As occasionally happened with reinforcement flights, their journey was dogged by misfortune, one pilot landing in Sicily, two in North Africa, a fourth damaging his aircraft when taking off from the carrier *Argus*, and a fifth crash-landing at Hal Far. And it was on the following day, 13 November, that the *Ark Royal*, which had been part of the supply fleet and from which I myself had flown some six months earlier, was torpedoed on its return journey to Gibraltar.

We were all desperately sad to learn about the *Ark*, a German submarine finally putting paid to her after so many false claims. I recalled only too well her massive size and splendour, the courtesy of her officers and crew, the wardroom bright with lights and the mess kits, pink gins and wonderful food, my iron-hard bunk with the ridge down the middle, and that ghastly dawn when we had taken off into the endless void of hostile sea and cloud. And now she was sitting on the bottom somewhere, a silent rusting hulk. With most of her Fulmars and Swordfish, too, apparently. Well, perhaps *they* wouldn't be missed too much!

*   *   *

I was to be very busy until the end of November, although my hectic activity did not produce much in the way of results.

From 15 to 17 November, we were obliged to operate from Luqa as Ta Kali became flooded, a seemingly odd occurrence in a semi-desert country but understandable when it was explained that there were no drains in the area of our airfield and that it had at one time been a lake. Whatever the reasons, torrential rain forced us to do what the Germans and Italians had signally failed to accomplish – leave the place! However, although the Blenheims and Marylands remained fairly active, 249 was not called upon to operate. There was news that our forces in the Western Desert were on the move again, obliging everything in Malta – apart from ourselves – to search for and attack seaborne supplies en route for Axis forces in North Africa.

Back at Ta Kali on the 19th, we embarked on a series of scrambles and shortish trips, mainly in pursuit of Macchi 202s which either whipped across the top of the island beyond our reach or dived down to strafe Hal Far and Luqa. As they appeared to be ignoring us at Ta Kali, we concluded that the Blenheims, Swordfish and Albacores were doing rather more damage than the Huns and Eyeties were prepared to accept.

On the 22nd, when I was not on the state unfortunately, there was a major mix-up in the Gozo area when 126 and 249 encountered about twenty Eyetie 202s at heights varying between 25,000 and 35,000 feet. As the top elements of Macchis dived down to attack, a streaming fight ensued, the mass of aircraft descending upon 249, which happened to be the bottom squadron. Finally, with the Italians racing away to the north, there were many individual engagements, most of them inconclusive. Back on the ground there were widely conflicting stories regarding numbers of aircraft, types, who did what, and how things had developed. It was the same old business; those in the middle of a fight usually knew least about it.

In the calmer atmosphere of Monico's, Maxim's and the Phoenix Hotel in Valletta, and mightily fortified by John Collinses and hot pork sandwiches, the news was exchanged.

The Blenheims and Swordfish chaps had suffered terrible casualties, apparently; Force 'K' had played havoc with the Axis convoys, about three-quarters of which had been sunk; the Wellingtons were bombing everything within range into a pulp; and the Marylands, assisted by a few PRU Spits from Benson, had been combing the Med., north, south, east and west, in search of Rommel's seaborne supplies and reinforcements. The war had obviously started again in earnest; there were even dark rumours that the Huns were on their way back to Sicily.

In the convivial atmosphere of the Valletta bars, the prospect of once more being inundated with Ju 88s and Me 109s – not Es this time but Fs! – was little more than a grim joke, the general response being, so what? – we had clobbered them in England, so we could do so again. But could we? With the grog beginning to talk, my own confident assertions sounded suspiciously like bravado as more than most I was aware that our Hurricanes just did not have the performance to compete. Moreover, even with our newer aircraft, we were still having more than our share of engine failures; apart from others we didn't know about, Don Stones of MNFU had recently been forced to bale out when his engine had stopped and 'Polly' Sheddon had suffered a failure on take-off only a day or so earlier. Everyone had been bellyaching for Spitfires for months past, but to no effect; couldn't their Airships understand? Or even the AOC for that matter: Hugh Pughe kept stamping around breathing fire and brimstone but he didn't have to fly the wretched things, did he? I recalled only too well an incident some weeks before, when immediately following a particularly trying engagement, he had turned up at Ta Kali and loftily informed those of us present that 'it wasn't the aircraft, it was the man'. I recalled, too, the ugly silence that had followed, a silence in which, for one wildly absurd moment, I actually thought that someone might strike him. Even so, our problems were trifling compared with those of the Blenheims boys. How they kept going with casualties sometimes as high as 50 per cent, was beyond comprehension. Thank God I was on fighters – Hurricanes even!

It was towards the end of the month, too, that 'Butch' Barton and I heard that we would shortly be moving on. Though 'Butch' seemed glad to be leaving, rather to my surprise I found myself limply apathetic. Go or stay, I didn't give a damn; what did arouse my interest was the news that I would be returning to England and not travelling further east to the Desert and beyond. Hugh Pughe had confronted me in dispersal with his blue-eyed stare, then had winked and jerked his head towards the west. Home! I recall feeling profoundly relieved; another year in Khartoum, or wherever, would have just about finished me off. 'Butch' would be succeeded by a chap called Mortimer-Rose whilst my replacement was to be a Flight Lieutenant Sidney Brandt. The dates of their arrival were uncertain.

For the last five days of November I flew fairly hard and mostly over Sicily where, I observed in my letters and logbook, there seemed to be a dearth of enemy fighters on or around Comiso and Gela despite the recent flurries of excitement over Malta. Against the last entry for the month, I penned a note: 'searched 25 miles east Kalafrana Bay; one dinghy found.'

I have no recollection of the flight, the dinghy, or who it was I was instrumental in rescuing.

11 The End in Sight

December started quietly, the lull before the storm as it proved to be. The weather dull with rain and plenty of cloud, the Eyeties stayed away and only the Blenheims and Wellingtons from Luqa seemed active.

At Ta Kali, there was an atmosphere of uncertainty and change; 'Polly' Sheldon appeared with another half-stripe on his arm and became Station Commander and 'Butch' Barton slipped away one night to board a Sunderland in Kalafrana Bay bound for Gibraltar and home. There was no departing binge or palaver, he just went. Quietly. Without fuss. Disappearing as he had always fought, with unassuming distinction. I suspect he was glad to leave; he had been on the go since September 1939 and was beginning to believe that his luck would shortly run out. At about the same time, the new man, Mortimer-Rose, turned up, smallish, agreeable, a little younger than 'Butch', but with much the same background.

On 7 December, I took off for Sicily and, in and out of cloud most of the way, dropped my eight 40 lb bombs on Ragusa railway station. As my target was within spitting distance of the Eyetie fighter base at Comiso, I half expected to run into a clutch of hostile Macchis, or 109s even, but in the event I saw nothing, not even a burst of flak. Although I was not aware of it at the time, it was to be my last sortie over Sicily and with repatriation at least a subconscious thought, found myself thinking and acting a good deal more circumspectly than usual.

It was on that day, too, that the Japanese attacked Pearl Harbor with horrifying casualties to the United States Navy, although we did not hear of it until the following morning. Discussing the attack over dinner, apart from the general belief that America's entry into the war was a good thing, most of us felt that someone must have boobed. Surprise? The Americans ought to have known *something,* surely! And if not, why? We all recognized it as being a most significant event although more of a disaster than a turning point in the war. In fact, we were to be rather more concerned about the loss of our own battleships, *Repulse* and *Prince of Wales,* which occurred a few days later off the coast of Malaya. On that occasion, I found myself in a furious debate with several around the dinner table who were taking what I considered to be too pessimistic a view of events. After the Battle of Britain, *of course* we couldn't be beaten, I proclaimed passionately, and to suggest otherwise was pure defeatism. However, despite my vehemence, there were some gloomy faces around the table that night and it was clear that not everyone agreed with me.

Then, down at dispersal on 11 December, news that was both good and bad; my replacement, 'Butch' Brandt, was on his way from Gibraltar; however, at that very moment, the Wellington in which he was travelling was heavily under attack in the area of Pantelleria. With a horrifying vision of him being plucked from my grasp, I scrambled as quickly as ever I had done and, with Crossey and several others, fled out towards the west like an avenging angel.

I would like to think that it was our intervention that enabled the Wellington to escape, although I suspect that by the time we had raced the 100 or so miles, the die had already been cast. Whatever the reason, the Wellington survived although two of its several companions did not. When we arrived, swords bared and grimly prepared to murder every Macchi and CR 42 in sight, we encountered nothing other than wide open seas, scattered cloud at 4,000 feet, and the most brilliant and empty of autumn days. Still seething with hostility, we skirted the hump of Pantelleria looking for birds that had long since flown.

On the way back, we overtook the Wellington as it was approaching Malta and shepherded it into Luqa, returning ourselves to Ta Kali. Later, 'Butch' Brandt arrived at Ta Kali in a very sombre frame of mind. His Wellington had been attacked by a group of CR 42s, apparently, and although a passenger, he had manned an extra machine-gun from a makeshift position in the waist of the bomber, firing furiously in its defence. The Wellington had been hit, even so, and one or more of the crew wounded; a very close-run thing, in Brandt's opinion.

A small rather stocky man with dark hair, I found him amusingly matter-of-fact. I said that for four Wimpeys to fly past Pantelleria in broad daylight and at a few thousand feet, was simply asking for trouble, and he agreed. We both decided that bomber pilots were pretty odd people anyway, although on this occasion they were probably only acting on instructions. He then asked when he was likely to take over my flight, to which I replied that as far as I was concerned he had already done so. At that, his face fell so comically that I agreed to hang on for a time, and did so for the next four days, although nothing much happened during that period.

As we had all been warned that the Germans were back in Sicily, I was only too aware that sooner or later the axe would fall and that against Ju 88s and the new 109Fs, our Hurricanes were going to have a pretty thin time. Not only were the bombers themselves as tough as boots – as well I knew – but the initiative would always be with the enemy, our own aircraft doomed to be climbing into groups of fast-moving 109s, the Hun fighters being at least 50 miles per hour faster than the Hurricanes on the level and infinitely more nippy in the climb and dive. It was the Battle of Britain all over again, only more so. The Huns would have us on toast!

With these thoughts very much in mind, for several days I went to dispersal and watched my successor and his new command prepare themselves for the onslaught with mixed feelings of sympathy and regret, regret that for the first time in eighteen months I would not be taking part, and sympathy

227

for Brandt who, clearly an innocent abroad, was just about to learn what it was like fighting in an aircraft vastly inferior in performance to that of the enemy and with no immediate expectation of replacements or spares. Having already handed over, did I offer to help or let him get on with it? Rightly or wrongly, I chose the latter course of action and was to suffer sharp pangs of remorse as a result.

My worst fears were soon confirmed. On 19 December, the Luftwaffe made its first appearance in strength, although it was 126 Squadron which bore the brunt of the attack, one of its new Americans, Steele, being shot down into the sea. Although he was observed to be in, or near, his dinghy, when the rescue craft arrived he was nowhere to be seen. The Huns, too, suffered losses, but the significance of this their first attack was ominous. The remaining Americans took Steele's death very gloomily.

The following day, a mixed bag of Ju 88s, Macchis and 109s appeared in even greater strength and this time, 249 was heavily committed, claiming several 88s shot down or damaged but losing Sergeant Moran and the pleasant-faced Pilot Officer Cavan, both of whom were killed. I was especially unhappy about the youthful Cavan as he had been our guide and mentor on that first and memorable poodle-faking expedition, seven months earlier.

Then, for the next three days it was more of the same, with constant scrambles and breathless full-throttle climbs, the new 109Fs not only escorting their bombers with complete and obvious assurance but even sweeping down to sea level with the utmost disdain and attacking fishing boats off Grand Harbour. During this period a number of Hurricanes of 126 and 185 were lost in addition to two of 249, Graham Leggett being forced to bale out and the wry-smiling Robert Matthews being killed in dramatic circumstances when his aircraft, pursued by a 109, flew full-tilt into the sea wall in Valletta. With a number of other Hurricanes damaged in the various combats, 249 had lost more than half its complement of aircraft in three days, the Huns and

Italians combined having made twenty raids in less than a week.

Most of this I witnessed dolefully as I hung about dispersal, fretting over my enforced inactivity and saddened by the damage inflicted on my old flight and squadron. Beazley, Palliser, Crossey, Davis et al, continued in the thick of things and I was playfully encouraged to 'come back and have a go'. My successor, Brandt, clearly taken aback by the maelstrom into which he had been pitchforked and desperate to find serviceable aircraft, wore a funereal expression. Was this as it had always been? I tried to be encouraging, fearing the worst but keeping my apprehensions to myself; in my bones I knew it to be only the beginning.

Christmas Day came with no celebrations and an ominous silence; everyone waited on tenterhooks but there were no raids.[1]

That morning in our room in the mess, Crossey and I talked of the future. He was thinking of getting married, he confided. Married! My mouth fell open. To whom? The delectable Liliana di Georgio, apparently. I fell silent, amazed and suddenly sensing a new distance between us, between myself and someone I had known, lived with, and fought alongside for almost two years. Yes, the squadron was changing, disintegrating almost, the old faces moving slowly out of focus as though in a mist.

Later that day, I made up my logbook and added up the various columns and totals. Since arriving in Malta on 21 May, I had made 89 flights against the enemy and, in all, flown 320 operational hours since July 1940. Willing to admit to staleness, I did not feel spent exactly nor in any way unhappy about fighting; never having been badly mauled by enemy aircraft, I could honestly say they had never held any terrors for me; flak and those loathsome red balls, yes, but never aircraft. I was just less enthusiastic, without that

---

[1] Apparently the Germans made known their intention not to attack us on Christmas Day but we were never informed.

extra edge that made the difference between success and failure, between surviving and being killed. But more than that, I was fed up with engine failures, fed up with flying over endless miles of sea in lame-duck aircraft that sank like a stone as soon as they were forced to ditch, weary of the terrible sameness of scramble, climb, and the pursuit of an enemy who seemed always to be out of reach. Fed up, too, with sitting about for interminable hours at dispersal, limp and greasy with sweat, dust in my mouth and in my hair and in my indifferent food. And with the eternal mosquitos, the man-eating fleas, trotting off to the bogs once a month with a churning, liquid stomach, and the poisonous Flit! With Malta, in fact, although God knew, there were many worse places. Yes, I was probably due for a change. And another type of aircraft, please, *please* God? With any luck I would *never* have to fight in a Hurricane again.

There being nothing much doing in the mess, I went into Valletta on my own and eventually found myself mixed up in a party of pongos[1] who were celebrating riotously. An age and a Niagara of drink later, my head reeling and infinitely weary, I slept in my clothes on a strange bed in some Army barracks I never knew existed. Cold and restless throughout the night, I awoke at dawn, dry of mouth and with a splitting head, my memory weakly recalling the crescendo of enforced jollity the previous night and my own flagging, half-hearted contribution.

And now it was Boxing Day. Boxing Day! I recalled all too clearly Boxing Day, 1940. At North Weald. Waiting for that first flight over France, the one that was postponed. A thousand years ago now, or so it seemed. But I wasn't a member of 249 any more, was I? After almost twenty months of flying and fighting. No, things would never be the same. There was no-one left – or very few. It was time to go.

I was still in Valletta when the air-raid sirens began their whooping dirge and in the distance heard the first thudding

---

[1] One of the RAF's less objectionable names for the Army.

'tonk-tonk-tonks' of the ack-ack. But, gingerly treading some anonymous pavement, I was barely interested and did not even bother to look up. What the hell! If the Huns wanted to drop their bombs, let 'em get on with it; knock the whole place down for all I cared.

By degrees and by some means, I found my way back to Ta Kali and retired to bed. Crossey being on duty, our shared room was coldly empty. Hurricanes were racing off the ground again, the muted noise of their engines dying away into silence. Then more distant thuds and rumbles, but who cared? I closed my eyes. I wasn't part of it any more.

After a time – was it hours or minutes later? – I came to to the sound of my name being called. As I surfaced slowly, I recognized the voice of the very courteous Maltese youth with the khaki shorts and Rudolph Valentino moustache, who manned the telephone in a room the far side of the courtyard.

'Flight Lieutenant Neil?' His faintly Maltese accent. 'Mistair Neil? Sir? You're wanted on the telephone. Flight Lieutenant?'

I rose and, in my bare feet, padded sleepily to the half-open shutters. The little fellow was down below, shouting upwards in my direction.

'You're wanted on the telephone, sir. Air Headquarters. You must go to Valletta as soon as possible. Please come and speak to them. I think you are to go home, sir.'

Home! The little chap was smiling up at me. Home! As soon as possible! By *ship,* presumably! And on Boxing Day! It was all too much to take in.

When I arrived in Grand Harbour, the afternoon was well advanced and with a low and threatening overcast, the light was already beginning to fade. To my surprise, I found myself one of a small group, Harrington having accompanied me from Ta Kali, and Cassidy, late of 249 and now with MNFU, turning up with Peter Le Fevre of 126 Squadron. With our combined baggage in a sad and trivial heap among the

231

bollards, ropes and general impedimenta of a busy dockside, we stood surveying the scene with quiet interest.

There was much to see. The harbour was crowded; apart from several cruisers, at least six destroyers, and, in a far corner, a clutch of submarines nestling snugly together like vipers in a nest, there were some half a dozen merchantmen of various sizes. Everywhere a hive of industry, there was a vibrant air of tension and preparation, a new experience for me, as, although I had been to Valletta many times before, I had never been in the centre of the naval dockyard and so close to the business-end of Grand Harbour. All the vessels looked worn and tiredly travel-stained with peeling paintwork and rust streaks everywhere, their guns starkly in evidence and already elevated skywards like a thicket of grey sticks.

From several Service informants who had turned up to assist in our departure, we learned that four merchantmen, one of which would be our home for the immediate future, were refrigerator ships normally employed on the London-New Zealand run. These would form the nucleus of a convoy and, accompanied by at least the bulk of Force 'K', would be making a swift and desperate dash for Egypt, the passage likely to take three or four days. The omens were not good, however; the enemy, having sustained enormous shipping casualties of their own, were in a vicious mood and only the immediate crisis had forced this break-out on a reluctant navy and the even more reluctant merchantmen. If they did not get through, the consequences for Malta could be serious. Not get through! We exchanged doubtful glances. *Now* they tell us!

Within minutes we were being ushered aboard S.S. *Sydney Star* and I was taken below to the usual seven-by-seven cabin, furnished in the heaviest of mahogany, which set me speculating wryly that if the ship were torpedoed, my part of it, anyway, was likely to float! I noted with mild dismay, however, that not only was I situated in the middle of the ship and without either scuttle, fresh air or daylight, but, as in HMS *Furious,* I seemed to have more than my fair share of the hissings, suckings and blowings being manufactured in some devil's cauldron below. Even so, counting myself lucky to have a cabin to myself, I returned to the deck to see what was going on.

I had not long to wait. Within minutes, several of the destroyers[1] alongside us began to glide slowly towards the entrance of Grand Harbour and tremors beneath the deck indicated that we were about to follow. We were off. After seven months in Malta. Of my route and what lay ahead of me, I had not the slightest idea, nor did I care very much. I was going home. Home! Nothing else mattered.

My rose-tinged euphoria was to last barely a minute, however, as suddenly and without warning, the nearest of the destroyers fired several of its four-inch guns, as did other naval ships further afield, the violent reports coming so unexpectedly that I, and everyone near me, almost literally took off. Then, as we gave startled glances upwards to the ragged clouds above, strings of red balls began to climb away into the murk and a Ju 88, at not more than 800 feet, appeared as though by magic and flew directly overhead, tracer and ack-ack of every sort curving in its wake in a drifting veil of hate as though magnetically attracted by its presence. Weaving, banking and desperate to escape, the Hun aircraft lifted finally into the cloud and disappeared, the defending guns still barking furiously like maddened guard-dogs frustrated by their chains.

A voice sounded wearily in my ear. 'Christ! That's done it. Now we won't get a moment's peace 'til we reach Port Said.'

I looked around. The face of one of the ship's officers was a mask of dismay, his expression indicating all too clearly that he had seen it all before. Still, it was comforting to know that at least he expected us to get there!

---

[1] I remember the names of all of them: H.M. destroyers *Arrow*, *Lance*, *Lively*, *Gurkha*, *Foxhound* and *Nestor*.

12   Voyage to Egypt

That first evening at sea was uneventful, the weather overcast and damply miserable. I went on deck once and was greeted by a chilling wind and impenetrable darkness. Somewhere within yards of where I shivered was a cruiser, six destroyers and three other merchantmen. How on earth were they to avoid each other in the darkness? Mildly unsettled by the possibility of a collision, I left them to it and retired.

Nothing much happened that night nor even the following day, much to my surprise and, I suspect, the surprise of everyone else. There was the drab, wet greyness of an endless, white-flecked leaden sea; cloud, which sat above our heads in a solid layer, and ships everywhere, swaying and dipping in slow motion. To our left, about 400 yards away, sat the cruiser HMS *Dido,* its 5.25 inch dual-purpose guns pointing almost comically backwards and to the sky, whilst ahead, on either side and behind, the half-dozen destroyers sat placidly on station, at long intervals seeming to lose patience, at which times they would race about like grey whippets, leaning outwards on their curving turns with bow waves creaming majestically as they changed direction and position. Every-thing and everyone looked towards the north. In the direction of the enemy. Towards occupied Europe – and Crete!

Normally a good sailor, I found my tiny cabin oppressively claustrophobic, the lack of daylight and fresh air especially dispiriting. I tried reading, then drawing and painting, but could not settle to anything as the ship shuddered and pitched, the heavy mahogany furniture tilting, creaking and groaning in sympathy. Mealtimes were welcome breaks during which all four of us RAF officers dined at the Captain's table, the latter a worried little man who was only occasionally joined by the Chief Engineer and one or two others, their empty chairs serving to cast an additional shadow over our halting conversation. From time to time, the four of us would inject a little light-hearted banter into the proceedings but our witticisms fell mostly on deaf ears.

The following day, however, turned out to be somewhat different, by which time I judged we were somewhere south of Crete.

We had barely finished breakfast when the air-raid alarm sounded and we rushed on deck to find the guns barking away and the sky filled with bursting ack-ack. A Ju 88 was crossing overhead at about 4,000 feet and moving away westwards leaving a trail of ack-ack puffs in its wake as our guns strove unsuccessfully to keep pace with it. Within minutes it had vanished but the significance of its appearance was all too clear; we had been spotted and our course and speed estimated; from now on we could expect the worst.

Within the hour, there came a second alarm, at which we all raced on deck once more, this time to see another Ju 88, at about the same height, begin a shallow dive in our direction and, breasting a flurry of ack-ack bursts, drop a stick of bombs which curved swiftly downwards to explode in the sea within 100 yards of where we stood, slow-moving columns of white rising magnificently from the several muted eruptions. After which, the Hun aircraft scuttled away, weaving and banking, as the guns of the whole convoy went mad.

I was delighted. This was exciting stuff; and how lovely to see someone else being shot at for a change! It had not occurred to me for a moment that my life might be in jeopardy, the bombs had looked so innocuous, the incident simply adding spice to what had thus far been a fairly hum-drum voyage. Our good spirits restored, we retired for lunch talking animatedly about the attack and the uselessness of the ack-ack.

The Captain and several of his officers having joined us for the meal, it was obvious that the head-man was in a nervous and unsociable mood – as well he might be! Much less concerned, we joked about the attack, pointing out that the bombing had been about as effective as the gunfire, which seemed to us all bark and no bite. The gunners were hopeless, we opined; how could they expect to hit anything if they were ignorant of even the rudiments of deflection shooting? Being fighter pilots we knew all about such things, naturally; it was a pity the gun crews weren't similarly competent. We laid it on pretty thick, aware of our hosts' frowning and slightly injured silence.

Finally, the Captain stood up and blotted his lips. Did we think we could do any better? We all exchanged exaggerated glances of surprise. Of course we could; it was just a matter of know-how and practice, wasn't it? He nodded then turned away. In that case, when the next attack came, we could show him just how it was done. All right?

It was about 3 p.m., when, having retired to my cabin, I was jerked into wakefulness by a rap on the door. It was one of the ship's officers in a tense mood. The Captain's compliments and would I please report to the bridge; another air attack was imminent. A little taken aback, I followed the man with urgent steps, soon to be joined by Peter Le Fevre, Cassidy and Harrington. There we were told that radar plots suggested that a major attack was brewing. The Captain turned and pointed. There were two gun positions, one on each extremity of the bridge; perhaps we might like to get out there and man the machine-guns. We agreed, readily, and sorting ourselves out, Peter Le Fevre and I chose the one on the starboard wing and Cassidy and Harrington the other. We were fairly light-hearted about the whole business.

The small cupola to which Pete and I were introduced was on a projection high above the bridge itself and over the water. Climbing inside, where there was barely room even for one small person – and neither of us was small! – I looked down on the sea streaming beneath with a powerful feeling of insecurity. Thus far, our involvement had been a bit of a joke; now, for the first time, the ugly reality of what we had let ourselves in for was beginning to dawn. Besides ourselves in the cupola there was a mounting, a single American machine-gun called a Marlin, and yards of ammunition in a belt. Bullets! Real live bullets! And a man was showing us how it all worked.

Did we know anything about Marlins? We said that we didn't. All right then, this was the way it was loaded, and this was how it was fired. OK? We replied that we thought so and the man climbed down hastily and disappeared. I fingered the weapon a little uncertainly and caught sight of Cassidy and Harrington in the distance, grinning and waving like children on a Sunday-school outing. After which it was decided that I should do the firing and Pete should feed in and generally be in charge of the ammunition. I swung the gun around experimentally but not without difficulty as there was hardly space to breathe. Then, with nothing much else to do, we waited. For about ten minutes. Looking around to see what else was going on, and where.

From our eyrie, we were able to look down into the glazed bridge where the Captain was pacing up and down with all the anxiety of an expectant father in a maternity wing, and spaced at intervals along the main deck were several gun positions where small knots of men grouped themselves around long-barrelled 20 mm cannons. Immediately to our rear and almost within touching distance, was the funnel, a single dark column rising steeply upwards, and beyond that an abundance of lifeboats, railings and air vents, plus all the paraphernalia of an ocean-going vessel.

The four merchantmen in a rough line, I could not see much of the one ahead but the one following was about 300 yards away and a little off to our right. With more than casual interest I noted that if I fired my gun, it was likely that I would rake the decks of the next ship and, more to the point, that its guns would do exactly the same to us.

Deciding that this seemed to be a silly arrangement, I resolved to keep the matter in mind.

Alongside and some 400 yards to my left, ploughed the cruiser *Dido,* plunging and rearing magnificently, its guns all turned upwards and backwards towards the north, whilst further afield, the six destroyers – or was it now eight? – formed an inner and outer screen, some fairly close, others as far away as the near horizon, all of them radiating a vibrating awareness of impending battle.

Then without warning, a rapid series of sharp cracks, about eight of them. And smoke. The destroyers were firing. After which, and before I had time to sort out who was doing what, a salvo from the cruiser, which made me almost jump out of my skin, the guns themselves hurling out smoke and recoiling like snakes recovering from a strike. I then saw that the *Dido*'s main weapons had been dipped so that they were almost level and that the Captain just below me was jumping up and down, mouthing something in my direction, and pointing. I peered northwards and saw what he meant – aircraft low down and on the horizon. About a dozen of them. Not flying towards us but moving left and right, which I thought rather odd. Big ones, too! The guns now going mad and masses of ack-ack bursts in the far distance. It was the start of an attack all right, but of what I could not see. Torpedo bombers probably.

For some minutes there was something of a hiatus, the bigger guns banging away spasmodically and the aircraft still several miles away, wandering back and forth on the horizon. Peter Le Fevre and I, all keyed up by the prospects of action, exchanged slightly hysterical jokes in our tiny cupola. If the bombers were Eyeties, they were probably jugging up with Chianti to bolster their spirits; anyway, what did it matter if they *did* drop a few 'fish', they would only hit the other side of the ship, wouldn't they? – I was happy to harbour the quite ridiculous notion that only the port side of the vessel was then likely to sink! But as we continued in this lighter vein, things took a turn for the worse; the bombers all began to head west, then, skirting the rear of our convoy, made a wide circle towards the south. After which they began to deploy themselves – on *our* side of the ship!

With about half a dozen of them some 50 feet above the waves, the Italian Savoias – we had now identified them as such – began to approach with quite ominous method and discipline and for the first time I felt a chilling spasm of naked fear. It looked as though we were going to be torpedoed and there was nothing whatever we could do about it.

Then it started, three of the noisiest and most hair-raising minutes of my life, the engagement introduced by the crack of countless guns, the shriek of four- and five-inch shells as they ripped through the rigging above my head, the thud-thud-thud of the Bofors, the tearing rattle of cannon and machine-gun, the soaring curve of flaring incendiaries and the white streaks of smoking tracer as it whipped across the waves. But through it all, seemingly unscathed and with magnificent, even foolhardy, bravery, came the Savoias. Line abreast, a terrifying phalanx. Eight hundred yards – five hundred – three hundred.

Remembering the 'whites of their eyes' dictum, I began to fire, the Marlin gun juddering and rattling like a mad thing in my hands, the belt of bullets jerking then dissolving into nothing as the empty cases flew away beyond and into the cupola. One Savoia directly in front of me now, two hundred yards distant and coming my way: I could see the three engines and cockpit quite clearly, the pilot almost. Then Peter Le Fevre's voice, a single strangled cry: 'I'm off'. And in a flash he was gone, all fourteen stone of him over the side of the cupola like an eel, and away. Still everyone firing like madmen. Deafeningly. The sharp stink of cordite everywhere. My own gun shaking crazily, the belt jumping, heat and stench rising into my face. The Savoia almost within touching distance. And something falling, rearing up in slow motion, before finally splashing into the water. A torpedo! Aimed straight between my legs. It couldn't miss. I was going to die. *Die*! In five seconds, *I was going to die*!

*   *   *

There are very few occasions even in wartime when one *knows* that death is inevitable and that there is nothing whatever one can do to halt the process. Chaka's warriors ordered to march over the cliff must have experienced roughly the same feeling as I did when I watched that torpedo enter the water less than 100 yards away. I had five seconds, I estimated, before the explosion came that would take me into eternity, and with half my conscious thoughts – I was then otherwise engaged – I began to count, one, two, three . . . !

When I had reached five, I remember cringing. Then six – seven – eight. Eight? I was still alive! Nine – ten! Glorious, unbounded relief! What had happened? I had no idea, nor did I care. The gun still clamouring in my hands, I was following the Savoia closely as it careered towards me then roared, deafeningly, a mere 50 feet over the stern of the ship, everything visible, engines, cockpit, the insignia on the wings and side, the whirling propellers, even. Meanwhile, the whipping smoke-trail of my bullets streaming in pursuit, with a stab of dismay I realized I had just fired directly into the bridge of the following merchant ship. But my mind almost unhinged with excitement, I continued, following the Savoia across the rear of my own vessel, my bullets splashing through the funnel in a single perforating line, then out again amid the rigging and beyond. The din incredible, the sheer bloodlust unbelievable. Down below, half of one eye caught sight of the Captain racing madly from one side of the bridge to the other, shouting. On and on. Would it never end?

Then, two incredible incidents. A thin scream, a new noise. A small winged object streaked over my head and flew straight into the path of my stream of tracer. A Wildcat, coming to rescue us. A naval Wildcat, presumably from one of the Fleet Air Arm squadrons based in North Africa; one of several that were hurling themselves with incredible courage into the fray, through all the bullets, the cannon-shells and bursting ack-ack. And I had hit it! I had *hit it*! I heard myself screaming: 'Stop! Stop! Stop!' I released my own trigger, appalled by what had occurred. But to no avail. Every other gun, it seemed, kept firing, the clamour beyond the power of words to describe.

But the Savoia that I and a score of others had shot at and behind which the Wildcat was now racing into position, was staggering. Reeling sideways like a wounded animal, then falling. A brief picture of the aircraft in plan view as it cartwheeled downwards, followed by a huge eruption of spray, and flame, and smoke as it hit the water some 800 yards away. And the Wildcat . . . was it going in too? It couldn't be! But it was! It *was*! Oh Christ: No! No! *No*![1]

But there were other goings-on to claim my attention, aircraft everywhere, low on the water, streaking away north-wards – big ones, small ones, guns barking and kicking, smoke drifting, the cannons and machine-guns going mad, the sky pock-marked with puffs of ack-ack and criss-crossed with tracer and soaring red balls. On and on! Would it never end? How did one put an end to this inferno?

Finally the battle moved away and, limp with emotion, I was left surveying the globules of flame and the column of billowing black smoke that were the remains of the Savoia. Then, to my surprise, a destroyer with a flaring bow-wave, headed back towards it and stopped. Stopped! To search. I found myself protesting, incredulous but silent. Why there, for God's sake? Why not further afield for the remains of the Wildcat? I prayed that it would move on, but it didn't, after several minutes racing away to its former position in the screen. Why not, I felt like scream-ing. Our own man! Do something!

I felt stricken. How crazy was war, and more particularly war as waged by the British. Here we had been, hell-bent on destroying every vestige of the Italians and their wretched bombers; then when we had partially achieved our aim, the Navy rushes back and *stops* to pick up Italian survivors but not our own. Stops, jeopardising the safety of an entire ship

[1] The Wildcat was in fact shot down into the sea.

and its crew in submarine-infested waters when there were obviously no enemy survivors. In Malta we had been shooting down Italian rescue aircraft daubed with red crosses for the last seven months – under instruction, needless to say. And now this! War was crazy, all right!

By degrees the emotion ebbed away until finally the guns were silent, the sky clear and with every ship back in position, we were streaming ahead, rising and falling with the swell, seemingly as though nothing untoward had happened. By degrees, too, I regained my composure, tidied up the cupola and looked up at the line of holes in the funnel. Crikey! I supposed I ought to apologize about those!

That evening we talked a good deal about the attack and the fate of the Wildcat. Everyone seemed convinced that it had been shot down but with so much else falling in the water, no-one could say definitely that he had seen it crash. I felt very unhappy about the whole affair; it seemed that once the guns had started to fire it was almost impossible to get them to stop. The noise had come as a great surprise to me; how could any order be transmitted through all that din? Limp with so much discussion, I finally retired to my mahogany box in a depressed frame of mind.

The following day dawned bright and clear. Up on deck we welcomed our first sighting of the sun and were treated to a series of performances by the destroyers which kept racing about most spectacularly dropping depth charges; there were submarines in our area, it appeared, and the Navy was taking no chances. Then, after a time, a 'Granny'[1] turned up and wandered around for much of the day. suggesting to us all that we were pretty close to the North African coast and clear of Hun fighters. I had never seen a Sunderland flying boat in action before and was surprised by its lack of pace. I decided that flying around endlessly in circles at about the speed of a Tiger Moth would not have suited me, although it probably had an automatic pilot, enabling the crew to concentrate on

[1] Short Sunderland four-engined flying boat.

the important things – such as frying their eggs and bacon! Imagine, eighteen hours of that on the trot! Well, it took all sorts to make an Air Force, I supposed.

Now about twelve hours sailing from Port Said, much of the tension had disappeared; it looked as though we would make it after all and even the Captain's face was seen to crack into the occasional bleak smile. The weather was warmer, too, which was a joy.

Dinner was quite a chatty meal that night and we all retired to bed in a happier frame of mind – until I allowed myself to think of the Wildcat. What if I *had* shot it down?

Somewhere in the small hours, I awoke, aware that everything had stopped – no engine beat, no noise, no tremblings, no movement. I arose, slowly, and went up on deck.

There were few people about and it was dawn – the most beautiful, silent, heart-stirring dawn I had ever beheld. And the smelliest!

We were stationary, a mile or two from a low-lying jetty, the sea mirror-smooth, the early morning sky an endless expanse of pastel yellows, blues and greens, softened by the almost transparent milk of a dawn mist. It was cool but pleasant, without even a breath of wind. Egypt! For the first time in my life I could see it – and smell it! The scent of the east – plus the stench of 4,000 tons of rotting potatoes! The local peasantry were on strike, apparently; I recalled hearing it on the news.

Beside me on the bridge, the Captain had lost his smile and was pacing about irritably. What the hell were we doing hanging about out here? We could be torpedoed any minute. If they couldn't accommodate us in the Canal, why didn't they tell us to extend our voyage? Sheer bloody stupidity, that's what it was! On the horizon, two destroyers slunk about like grey wolves on the perimeter of a camp. I remember smiling. How nice to know that other people had their problems.

It was a Tuesday, 30 December 1941. We were to reach Cairo the following day, New Year's Eve.

Postscript

Although I was not to know it at the time, as I leaned over the rail of the ship that day, rejoicing in the still, silent beauty of a Middle Eastern morning, my successor in Malta, Flight Lieutenant Sidney 'Butch' Brandt, had already been dead some twelve hours.

Scrambled in the late afternoon of the 29th, he had rushed out to the north of the island where some 109s were attacking the Malta–Gozo ferry and, together with the youthful, fair-faced Sergeant Lawson, had been shot down and killed. Poor inexperienced 'Butch'! He hadn't lasted long, little more than a fortnight, in fact. And it could have been me. Anyone. It was to be the first of many.

By that time, too, 249's new commanding officer, Mortimer-Rose, had already been wounded, command passing to my old friend 'Beazle'[1], who himself would remain only several weeks before being posted away.

Among the others, the casualties mounted rapidly; the amiable 'Horse' (Pilot Officer Stuart) was killed when he suffered the almost inevitable engine failure on take-off; 'Jack' Hulbert was shot to death by 109s, together with Sergeant MacDowall, and there were others – all of them lambs to the slaughter. Palliser, Crossey, Davis and the rest were also soon to move on – a chapter had been completed, the remnants of the old squadron wiped away like chalk from a slate.

In those early months of 1942, it was to be a grossly unequal contest. The Hurricanes, totally out-performed, were soon reduced to impotence. Harried relentlessly in the air

[1] Flight Lieutenant John Beazley.

and attacked on the ground by a far superior fighter force, the Hun 109s eventually patrolling the Maltese airfields as though they were their own, they took to the air in reducing numbers, often being vectored away from the island for their own safety, until by March 1942, so few of them remained that some of the pilots of 249 were deployed on the rooftops in Valletta – to act as aircraft spotters!

Sadly, although this unhappy situation had been predicted, the warnings had been ignored by those who, earlier, might have strengthened the fighter force in Malta with Spitfires. Eventually, when driven to it, they did, the first Spits arriving in March of that year. By which time, alas, for some it was too late! Needlessly so, in the opinion of many.

Index

248

251